Ways to Poetry

WAYS
TO
POETRY

Stanley A. Clayes
John Gerrietts
Loyola University of Chicago

Harcourt Brace Jovanovich, Inc.

New York   Chicago   San Francisco   Atlanta

ISBN: 0-15-595137-8

Library of Congress Catalog Card Number: 74-15497

Printed in the United States of America

COPYRIGHTS AND ACKNOWLEDGMENTS

Pages 361–67 constitute a continuation of the copyright page.

Preface

Of the many ways to approach poetry we have focused on three: through the elements of poetry, through four poets read in depth, and through poems similar in subject and theme. Part One, dealing with the elements of poetry, begins with the voice and attitude of the speaker, because we have found that students are most quickly oriented by first identifying the voice they hear and considering its tone. Following that are treatments of the image, symbol, sound, and structure. Chapters 6, 7, and 8 are critically oriented, not to direct judgments, but to direct attention to differences among poets in diction (6) and style (7) and to the difference between poetry and prose—and between good poetry and great (8).

Part Two is unusual in books of this kind, even though students are often curious about the lives and personalities of poets as they become engaged by their poems. We hope that the biographical notes and the generous selection of poems will give students an opportunity to understand the interrelationship between the poet and the poems and to see the poems as giving shape to the poet's concerns and experience. In choosing poets, we have been directed by student interest and the importance of the poets. Time has tested the importance of Donne, Yeats, and Frost. For a more recent poet we have chosen Sylvia Plath, because of her great popularity with students. To show the poets' development we have arranged their poems in the order they were published.

Part Three is organized thematically. Comparing poems on similar themes brings into clearer focus not just ideas and attitudes but stylistic differences, both personal and historical. The thematic sections are organized historically to show these developments and contrasts. The section "Archetypal Cycles" continues the archetypal arrangement of Chapter 3.

There are more modern poems here than in most books of this kind, because modern styles are usually more accessible to students. The French of Valéry and the Spanish of Neruda are included for those who want to compare the original language with the translation, in order to examine the difficulties and achievements of the translator's art. Despite Frost's observation that the poetry is what evaporates from all translation, we think something can be learned about poetry by comparing translations.

Conventions of spelling, capitalization, and punctuation that have changed through the centuries present difficult decisions for anthologists. Sometimes, as with Blake and Emily Dickinson, the old convention of capitalizing certain words still serves its original purpose of giving emphasis. With other writers we have modernized capitalization, spelling, and punctuation, not to impose consistency on the text, but to make some poems easier to read.

Notes are provided only when they are clearly necessary; they often appear under the heading "Notes and Questions," so that the information given can be linked to questions suggesting its significance. The questions direct attention along certain lines, either to help students over difficulties or to show how a principle previously discussed applies to a particular poem.

We are especially grateful to Martin Stanford for his good counsel and to William Heilig, a rare kind of severe critic who was prepared with useful suggestions (and phrasing) to solve the problems he identified in several important chapters. Four colleagues were particularly helpful in advising us on the teachability of particular poems, many of which were discarded on their advice: Rita Clarkson, Peter Christensen, William Hiebel, and Robert Mann. We are also grateful to Dipti Shah for her care and efficiency in typing.

This book would not have existed in its present form without the support and guidance of William Pullin at Harcourt Brace Jovanovich. We appreciate also the editorial help of Dorothy Mott and Susan Tuttle of our publisher's staff, and the many suggestions, both severe and encouraging, of our readers, Walter K. Gordon of Rutgers University, Robert Pinsky of Wellesley College, and Linda Wagner of Michigan State University.

S. A. C.
J. G.

Summary of Contents

Table of Contents

PART ONE

1 The Speaker and His Attitude 3

3 *Symbol, Allusion, Myth, and Archetype* 41

4 Sound   71

Melody and Harmony in Poetry   72

Consonant Sounds   74

Vowel Sounds   76

Alliteration and Assonance   76

Rhyme   76

Rhythm in Poetry   79

The Metrical Line and Natural Speech   80

The Musical Phrase and Natural Speech   83

Onomatopoeia   85

Chronological Arrangement   87

5 Structure and Poetic Forms   97

6 Diction 123

7 *Style* 139

Varieties of Style 139

Translations Compared 153

8   *The Nature and Value of Poetry*   162

PART TWO

John Donne   181

William Butler Yeats   196

Robert Frost   214

Sylvia Plath   229

PART THREE

Love 243

The Family   256

Guilt and Responsibility   271

Personal   271

Social   279

Identity   294

Mutability   312

The Naturalistic Perspective   312

Archetypal Cycles 330

Death 345

Appendix
Writing about a Poem: Two Samples

Index

Elements of Poetry

1 The Speaker and His Attitude

The Speaker

To say that the following poem is about love is to say nothing important; what the poem is really about is the speaker's attitude toward being in love. Is the speaker really in love or sarcastic or playful? Is he sincere, or is he making fun of himself or of the other person? That is, to discover what a poem means the reader must focus on the attitude of the speaker. Whether he is speaking for himself or for someone else, what the poem is about can be determined only from his attitude toward his subject.

The Constant Lover

Out upon it! I have loved
  Three whole days together!
And am like to love three more
  If it prove fair weather.

This opening stanza of a four stanza poem makes clear an attitude of the speaker. That attitude seems to be arrogant until it is lightened by the playfulness of the last line, "If it prove fair weather." But this opening attitude is merely the poem's first stage. The poem moves from this attitude to a qualified reversal of it.

Time shall molt away his wings   5
Ere he shall discover
In the whole wide world again
Such a constant lover.

But the spite on't is, no praise
Is due at all to me: 10
Love with me had made no stays
Had it any been but she.

Had it any been but she,
And that very face
There had been at least ere this   15
A dozen dozen in her place.

Sir John Suckling (1609–1642)

The speaker states, with a clearly exaggerated frankness, that three days is indeed a long time for him to have been true because his previous habit had been to become interested in a "dozen dozen" in the space of three days. The attitude has remained playful, but the poem has progressed structurally from its initial attitude to the final one in which some sincerity is expressed. Surprising, frank, and ironic, this sincerity seems convincing because the speaker has so freely exaggerated his inconstant nature.

This poem has no moral or lesson. It communicates the speaker's attitude, directly and through implication, through the pose the speaker assumes to cover what may be very real feelings. Its subject is the surprising way that falling in love will solve the difficulty of being a constant lover and the need of the speaker to mask his feeling with playful wit. This might be the subject of a serious, philosophical poem or of a sincere, passionate one. The tone of another poem on the same subject might be wholly serious, without any of the playfulness that Suckling uses to mask his seriousness; it might be melancholy, self-righteous, or angry. The poem might have had other resolutions: the speaker might have decided to be better behaved or to reject the lady. But "The Constant Lover" is a poem in a tradition, the cavalier lyric, fashionable in the seventeenth century when writing poems of this kind was a social activity. The tradition developed from the love song of earlier centuries when the singer was not likely to declare so cavalier and careless an interest in his lady. The careless, passionate speaker here does not necessarily present the real feelings of the poet, nor does the poem recommend that young men in love should feel in any particular way.

In order to learn to distinguish and define the attitude of the speaker, it may be helpful to ask whether the speaker literally feels what he says or whether the attitude is a manner covering a somewhat different feeling. The speaker's feeling in "The Constant Lover" is somewhat ambiguous. The flippant insincerity he admits to in the first two stanzas establishes a tone which heavily qualifies his assertion in the last two stanzas that he is now in love. But this very shift in attitude is the essence of the poem's design and its wit. Does the speaker have a deeper feeling being masked by his attitude or does the attitude suggest that his attention will soon be diverted? This poet is not concerned with being clear about the depth of the speaker's real feeling. What is clear is the attitude he expresses, the pose he strikes, and the wit achieved. The poem's purpose is simply to depict the attitude it does with wit and style.

In the following poem the feeling of the poet and the attitude of the speaker are clearly the same.

When You Are Old

When you are old and grey and full of sleep,
And nodding by the fire, take down this book,
And slowly read, and dream of the soft look
Your eyes had once, and of their shadows deep;

How many loved your moments of glad grace,   5
And loved your beauty with love false or true,
But one man loved the pilgrim soul in you,
And loved the sorrows of your changing face;

And bending down beside the glowing bars,
Murmur, a little sadly, how Love fled   10
And paced upon the mountains overhead
And hid his face amid a crowd of stars.

William Butler Yeats (1865–1939)

Yeats and his speaker merge in our impression because the attitude expressed is so sincere that we feel it must be a part of the poet's own experience.

The Situation

Most poems present the reader with a dramatic situation: the speaker may, as in a play, be speaking to or about someone else, both of them fictional characters, but more often he is speaking about himself in a situation that is implied and must be inferred by the reader. The following poem indicates by its somewhat unusual use of quotation marks that it is a dialog between two persons.

Is My Team Ploughing

'Is my team ploughing,
    That I was used to drive
And hear the harness jingle
    When I was man alive?'

Ay, the horses trample,   5
    The harness jingles now;
No change though you lie under
    The land you used to plough.

'Is football playing
    Along the river shore,   10
With lads to chase the leather,
    Now I stand up no more?'

Ay, the ball is flying,
    The lads play heart and soul;
The goal stands up, the keeper   15
    Stands up to keep the goal.

'Is my girl happy,
    That I thought hard to leave,
And has she tired of weeping
    As she lies down at eve?'   20

Ay, she lies down lightly,
    She lies not down to weep:
Your girl is well contented.
    Be still, my lad, and sleep.

'Is my friend hearty,   25
    Now I am thin and pine,
And has he found to sleep in
    A better bed than mine?'

Yes, lad, I lie easy,
    I lie as lads would choose;   30
I cheer a dead man's sweetheart,
    Never ask me whose.

               A. E. Housman (1859–1936)

To understand this poem, the reader must recognize that there are two speakers (two attitudes) and that one of them who is dead is speaking to the other who is alive. The details of the poem depict the lives of farm boys and suggest that farm life for young men is easy-going, healthful, and natural. The details suggest that the facts of life, love, and death are to be accepted realistically, as the living speaker in "cheering" the dead man's sweetheart has accepted them, but the poem is structured by setting this attitude in contrast to that of the dead man. Life does go on much the same as it always has and the living turn their attention to the living, but the dead man, less real-istic in his outlook than his friend, reacts as though life had stood still, as though love were eternal, and as though without him the fields might not get ploughed. Does the poem mock his attitude? To some extent it does, but only to the extent that we are willing to mock our own unrealistic attitudes, because the attitudes of the two speakers are only the two sides of our own natures.

QUESTIONS

1. How does Housman make the situation clear?
2. How do you know that the intended effect of the poem is to be comic and not pathetic?
3. What effect would it have on the poem if you knew more about how the first speaker died and how his girl felt?
4. Explain the organization of the poem and its motion from initial attitude to final one. Could any stanzas be left out or interchanged?

A far more common pattern for poetry than an exchange between two speakers is the voice of a single speaker presenting his attitudes toward a particular place, situation, or relationship. The poet states and implies just enough of the facts of the situation to give the reader a sense of the dramatic relationship. Such poems usually work toward a statement, sometimes direct but often somewhat ironical. The fol-lowing poem illustrates an extensive presentation of a situation on which the speaker makes an ironic comment.

Faintheart in a Railway Train

At nine in the morning there passed a church,
At ten there passed me by the sea,
At twelve a town of smoke and smirch,
At two a forest of oak and birch,
    And then, on a platform she: 5

A radiant stranger, who saw not me.
I said, "Get out to her do I dare?"
But I kept my seat in search for a plea,
And the wheels moved on. O could it but be
   That I had alighted there!   10

Thomas Hardy (1840–1928)

A dramatic situation has been presented in words: it might have been filmed without words. The best filmmakers are able to achieve, without dialog, effects like those that Hardy has achieved here, because Hardy's images are visual and he presents them with much of the objectivity of the camera. But this poem is an extreme instance; the opposite extreme is the nondramatic, meditative lyric. In the meditative lyric, the speaker's voice merges with the poet's, the attitude is meditative, and a theme of universal experience is developed with very little photographable detail. An example of this is the following poem.

Ode on Solitude

Happy the man whose wish and care
   A few paternal acres bound,
Content to breathe his native air,
   In his own ground.

Whose herds with milk, whose fields with bread,   5
   Whose flocks supply him with attire,
Whose trees in summer yield him shade,
   In winter fire.

Blest, who can unconcern'dly find
   Hours, days, and years slide soft away,   10
In health of body, peace of mind,
   Quiet by day,

Sound sleep by night; study and ease,
   Together mixt; sweet recreation;
And Innocence, which most does please   15
   With meditation.

Thus let me live, unseen, unknown,
   Thus unlamented let me die,
Steal from the world, and not a stone
   Tell where I lie.   20

Alexander Pope (1688–1744)

Pope opens his poem where Hardy ended his, with a general state-
ment of the speaker's attitude. Pope then develops his poem with de-
tails less specific than Hardy's. "Health of body, peace of mind" can-
not be photographed as can Hardy's "At two a forest of oak and
birch." Even though both speakers speak of private feelings, Hardy's
method is factual, imagistic, and understated; Pope is not concerned
at all to present the facts of the speaker's situation, nor even to de-
velop a speaker's voice that can be distinguished from the poet's.
Pope's method is meditative; Hardy's is dramatic. Hardy presents a
little drama in which the speaker's situation is an essential part of
the poem's conception. Most poetry exists between these extremes.

Tone

The term "tone" in poetry designates the speaker's atti-
tude toward his situation or his subject or sometimes his audience.
The possibilities for variety in tone are as numerous as all the tones of
voice we have ever heard. The poet's effort is to create the voice we
hear in the poem so that he can present the speaker's attitude toward
his situation with all possible color, force, and precision. When it is
difficult to see the poem as a little drama in which the speaker is
involved, tone is the speaker's attitude toward a subject other than
his own situation, such as nature, politics, or the situation of another
person. The speaker's attitude toward his audience is of obvious im-
portance in the love poems in this chapter. "The Constant Lover" as-
sumes an audience or readers experienced with the tone of the cava-
lier lyric, and in "When You Are Old" it is interesting to know that
Yeats was addressing a particular person, Maud Gonne. But informa-
tion of this kind, though it increases our understanding of these
poems, is of relatively less importance with most poems than the
ability to hear the speaker's tone as it relates his attitude toward the
situation.

The tone of the poem might be solemn, bitter, sincere, sarcastic, or
playful, but it will often be difficult to describe accurately until it is
approached analytically. Who is speaking? What is his situation or his
subject? What is his attitude toward that situation or subject? What
words or strategies in the poem reveal his attitude most clearly? Is
his attitude the poet's attitude? If not, how far apart are their atti-
tudes? Is the poet merely describing objectively the attitude of an-
other or does he judge that attitude?

All the poems that follow in this chapter provide opportunities for
examining tone. The first two present interesting problems of subtlety
and sophistication.

A Street in Bronzeville: Southeast Corner

The School of Beauty's a tavern now.
The Madam is underground.
Out at Lincoln, among the graves
Her own is early found.
Where the thickest, tallest monument   5
Cuts grandly into the air
The Madam lies, contentedly.
Her fortune, too, lies there,
Converted into cool hard steel
And right red velvet lining;   10
While over her tan impassivity
Shot silk is shining.

Gwendolyn Brooks (b. 1917)

Janet Waking

Beautifully Janet slept
Till it was deeply morning. She woke then
And thought about her dainty-feathered hen,
To see how it had kept.

One kiss she gave her mother.   5
Only a small one gave she to her daddy
Who would have kissed each curl of his shining baby;
No kiss at all for her brother.

"Old Chucky, old Chucky!" she cried,
Running across the world upon the grass   10
To Chucky's house, and listening. But alas,
Her Chucky had died.

It was a transmogrifying bee
Came droning down on Chucky's old bald head
And sat and put the poison. It scarcely bled,   15
But how exceedingly

And purply did the knot
Swell with the venom and communicate
Its rigor! Now the poor comb stood up straight
But Chucky did not.   20

So there was Janet
Kneeling on the wet grass, crying her brown hen
(Translated far beyond the daughters of men)
To rise and walk upon it.

And weeping fast as she had breath   25
Janet implored us, "Wake her from her sleep!"
And would not be instructed in how deep
Was the forgetful kingdom of death.

John Crowe Ransom (1888–1974)

QUESTIONS

1. "Janet Waking" may at first seem to deal insincerely with what for Janet was a real loss. Explain the speaker's tone in relation to his audience. What words seem most condescending, which most comical?
2. The meaning of "transmogrifying" is to change into a different shape, usually a bizarre or fantastic shape. Why has Ransom used this strange (insincere?) word? In the next stanza how many meanings of "rigor" apply? Dictionaries give the following meanings: (1) severity of action, (2) trying circumstance, (3) a severe or cruel act, (4) a state of rigidity in living tissues that prevents response to stimuli, (5) obsolete: stiffness.
3. What effects are achieved by the words "instructed" and "translated"?
4. Show how the poem mixes language of the child's innocence and the speaker's experience. Where are the shifts in tone most comic?
5. The last two stanzas contain phrasing formal in tone that we usually encounter in connection with the death of humans. Which phrases are these? Why has Ransom introduced this formality of tone here?

Persona

Another term used loosely instead of the "speaker" is the term *persona*. The term derives from the mask worn by actors in classical Greek drama. Just as the mask hid the face of the real actor, the *persona*, the voice of a character, hides the voice of the poet. Whether the voice we hear is a *persona* or merely an attitude of the poet is theoretically a difficult distinction, but in practice the term *persona* is used interchangeably with "speaker" or *persona* is used in preference to "speaker" when a character has been created whose attributes and situation are clearly not the poet's.

The Ruined Maid

"O 'Melia, my dear, this does everything crown!
Who could have supposed I should meet you in Town?
And whence such fair garments, such prosperi-ty?"—
"O didn't you know I'd been ruined?" said she.

—"You left us in tatters, without shoes or socks,   5
Tired of digging potatoes, and spudding up docks;
And now you've gay bracelets and bright feathers three!"—
"Yes: that's how we dress when we're ruined," said she.

—"At home in the barton you said 'thee' and 'thou,'
And 'thik oon,' and 'theas oon,' and 't'other'; but now   10
Your talking quite fits 'ee for high compa-ny!"—
"Some polish is gained with one's ruin," said she.

—"Your hands were like paws then, your face blue and bleak
But now I'm bewitched by your delicate cheek,
And your little gloves fit as on any la-dy!"—   15
"We never do work when we're ruined," said she.

—"You used to call home-life a hag-ridden dream.
And you'd sigh, and you'd sock; but at present you seem
To know not of megrims or melancho-ly!"—
"True. One's pretty lively when ruined," said she.   20

—"I wish I had feathers, a fine sweeping gown,
And a delicate face, and could strut about Town!"—
"My dear—a raw country girl, such as you be,
Cannot quite expect that. You ain't ruined," said she.

                                        Thomas Hardy (1840–1928)

QUESTIONS

1. Explain the condescending tone of the ruined maid as a comic reversal of what we expect in her tone. What is the parallel reversal in the respectable maid?

2. Explain how Hardy has maintained a comic distance from both of his *personae*.
3. Where is the poem's language most successfully comic? How does the stanzaic structure contribute to the comedy?
4. What social criticism is implied in the poem's title and certain of its details?

Ringing the Bells

And this is the way they ring
the bells in Bedlam
and this is the bell-lady
who comes each Tuesday morning
to give us a music lesson   5
and because the attendants make you go
and because we mind by instinct,
like bees caught in the wrong hive,
we are the circle of the crazy ladies
who sit in the lounge of the mental house   10
and smile at the smiling woman
who passes us each a bell,
who points at my hand
that holds my bell, E flat,
and this is the gray dress next to me   15
who grumbles as if it were special
to be old, to be old,
and this is the small hunched squirrel girl
on the other side of me
who picks at the hairs over her lip,   20
who picks at the hairs over her lip all day,
and this is how the bells really sound,
as untroubled and clean
as a workable kitchen,
and this is always my bell responding   25
to my hand that responds to the lady
who points at me, E flat;
and although we are no better for it,
they tell you to go. And you do.

Anne Sexton (1928–1974)

Subject Pair

A *narrow* Fellow *in the* Grass

A narrow Fellow in the Grass
Occasionally rides—
You may have met Him—did you not
His notice sudden is—

The Grass divides as with a Comb—   5
A spotted shaft is seen—
And then it closes at your feet
And opens further on—

He likes a Boggy Acre
A Floor too cool for Corn—   10
Yet when a Boy, and Barefoot—
I more than once at Noon

Have passed, I thought, a Whip lash
Unbraiding in the Sun
When stooping to secure it   15
It wrinkled, and was gone—

Several of Nature's People
I know, and they know me—
I feel for them a transport
Of cordiality—   20

But never met this Fellow
Attended, or alone
Without a tighter breathing
And Zero at the Bone—

Emily Dickinson (1830–1886)

To the Snake

Green Snake, when I hung you round my neck
and stroked your cold, pulsing throat
        as you hissed to me, glinting
arrowy gold scales, and I felt
        the weight of you on my shoulders,   5
and the whispering silver of your dryness
        sounded close at my ears—

Green Snake—I swore to my companions that certainly
  you were harmless! But truly
I had no certainty, and no hope, only desiring 10
  to hold you, for that joy,
       which left
a long wake of pleasure, as the leaves moved
and you faded into the pattern
of grass and shadows, and I returned 15
smiling and haunted, to a dark morning.

         Denise Levertov (b. 1923)

QUESTIONS

1. Insofar as their attitudes toward snakes reveal them, characterize the two speakers of Dickinson's and Levertov's poems.
2. Why is the subject not named in the first poem while the second poem is dedicated "To the Snake"?
3. Dickinson develops a conventional attitude. Find the observations and the phrases that give the poem its wit and freshness.
4. Levertov develops an unconventional attitude and assumes that the reader has the conventional attitude. What observations and particular words mock the conventional attitude?
5. To define their attitudes, why does each speaker refer to the past? What defense of present attitudes do these references present?

Chronological Arrangement

Deor's Lament

Weland knew full well the meaning of exile;
That strong man suffered much;
Sorrow and longing stood him company,
And wintry exile; when *Nithhad*
Had fettered him, put supple bonds of sinew 5
Upon a better man, misfortunes beset him.
  That passed away, this also may!

To *Beadohild,* her brothers' death was not
So great a cause for grief as her own state
When she realized she was 10
With child; she sank into despair
Whenever she thought what would come of it.
  That passed away, this also may!

Many of us have learned that *Geat's* love
For *Mæthhild* grew too great for human frame,   15
So that their grievous passion prevented them from sleeping.
   That passed away, this also may!

For thirty years *Theodric* ruled
The stronghold of the Mærings; that was known to many.
   That passed away, this also may!   20

We have heard of the wolfish mind
Of *Ermanarich*; a savage man,
He held wide sway in the kingdom of the Goths.
Many a warrior sat, full of sorrow
And expecting adversity, often wishing   25
That some foe would conquer his country.
   That passed away, this also may!

If a man sits in despair, deprived of all pleasure,
His mind moves upon sorrow; it seems to him
That there is no end to his share of hardship.   30
Then he should remember that the wise Lord
Often moves about this middle-earth:
To many he grants glory,
Certain fame, to some a sorrowful lot.
I will say this about myself,   35
That once I was a minstrel of the Heodeningas,
Dear to my lord. *Deor* was my name.
For many years I had an excellent office
And a gracious lord, until now *Heorrenda*,
A man skilled in song, has inherited the land   40
Once given to me by the guardian of men.
   That passed away, this also may!

> Deor: an Old English scop
> translated by Kevin Crossley-Holland

Fragment from Petronius Arbiter

Doing a filthy pleasure is and short;
And done we straight repent us of the sport:

NOTE

Petronius Arbiter (title): a Roman of the first century whom Jonson believed
to be the author of the poem in Latin translated here.

Let us not then rush blindly on unto it,
Like lustful beasts, that only know to do it,
For lust will languish and that heat decay;   5
But thus, thus, keeping endless holiday,
Let us together closely lie and kiss;
There is no labor, nor no shame in this.
This hath pleased, doth please,
   and long will please; never   10
Can this decay, but is beginning ever.

Ben Jonson (1573?–1637)

A Satirical Elegy on the Death of a Late Famous General, 1722

His Grace! impossible! what, dead!
Of old age too, and in his bed!

And could that Mighty Warrior fall?
And so inglorious, after all!
Well, since he's gone, no matter how,   5
The last loud trump must wake him now:
And, trust me, as the noise grows stronger,
He'd wish to sleep a little longer.
And could he be indeed so old
As by the news-papers we're told?   10
Threescore, I think, is pretty high;
'Twas time in conscience he should die.
This world he cumbered long enough;
He burnt his candle to the snuff;
And that's the reason, some folks think,   15
He left behind so great a stink.

Behold his funeral appears,
Nor widow's sighs, nor orphan's tears,
Wont at such times each heart to pierce,
Attend the progress of his hearse.   20

But what of that, his friends may say,
He had those honors in his day.
True to his profit and his pride,
He made them weep before he died.

Come hither, all ye empty things,   25
Ye bubbles raised by breath of Kings;
Who float upon the tide of state,
Come hither, and behold your fate.
Let pride be taught by this rebuke,
How very mean a thing's a Duke;   30
From all his ill-got honors flung,
Turned to that dirt from whence he sprung.

                 Jonathan Swift (1667–1745)

Soliloquy of the Spanish Cloister

Gr-r-r—there go, my heart's abhorrence!
    Water your damned flower-pots, do!
If hate killed men, Brother Lawrence,
    God's blood, would not mine kill you!
What? your myrtle-bush wants trimming?   5
    Oh, that rose has prior claims—
Needs its leaden vase filled brimming?
    Hell dry you up with its flames!

At the meal we sit together:
    Salve tibi! I must hear   10
Wise talk of the kind of weather,
    Sort of season, time of year:
Not a plenteous cork-crop: scarcely
    Dare we hope oak-galls, I doubt:
What's the Latin name for "parsley"?   15
    What's the Greek name for Swine's Snout?

NOTE

Salve tibi (10): "God save you!"

Whew! We'll have our platter burnished,
    Laid with care on our own shelf!
With a fire-new spoon we're furnished,
    And a goblet for ourself,   20
Rinsed like something sacrificial
    Ere 'tis fit to touch our chaps—
Marked with L for our initial!
    (He-he! There his lily snaps!)

Saint, forsooth! While brown Dolores   25
    Squats outside the Convent bank
With Sanchicha, telling stories,
    Steeping tresses in the tank,
Blue-black, lustrous, thick like horsehairs,
    —Can't I see his dead eye glow,   30
Bright as 'twere a Barbary corsair's?
    (That is, if he'd let it show!)

When he finishes refection,
    Knife and fork he never lays
Cross-wise, to my recollection,   35
    As do I, in Jesu's praise.
I the Trinity illustrate,
    Drinking watered orange-pulp—
In three sips the Arian frustrate;
    While he drains his at one gulp.   40

Oh, those melons? If he's able
    We're to have a feast! so nice!
One goes to the Abbot's table,
    All of us get each a slice.
How go on your flowers: None double?   45
    Not one fruit-sort can you spy?
Strange!—And I, too, at such trouble,
    Keep them close-nipped on the sly!

There's a great text in Galatians,
    Once you trip on it, entails   50
Twenty-nine distinct damnations,
    One sure, if another fails:

NOTES

corsair (31): pirate. *Arian* (39): one who denied the Trinity and the divinity of Christ.

If I trip him just a-dying,
    Sure of heaven as sure can be,
Spin him round and send him flying   55
    Off to hell, a Manichee?

Or, my scrofulous French novel
    On grey paper with blunt type!
Simply glance at it, you grovel
    Hand and foot in Belial's gripe: 60
If I double down its pages
    At the woeful sixteenth print,
When he gathers his greengages,
    Ope a sieve and slip it in't?

Or, there's Satan—one might venture   65
    Pledge one's soul to him, yet leave
Such a flaw in the endenture
    As he'd miss till, past retrieve,
Blasted lay that rose-acacia
    We're so proud of! *Hy, Zy Hine* . . .   70
'St, there's Vespers! *Plena gratiâ*
    Ave, Virgo! Gr-r-r—you swine!

                   Robert Browning (1812–1889)

NOTES

Manichee (56): a believer in the Manichean heresy that good can never triumph in the eternal struggle between good and evil. *Belial* (60): the Devil. *Hy, Zy, Hine* (70): mimicry of the sound of bells calling him to Vespers. *Plena . . . Virgo* (71–72): Full of Grace, Hail, Virgin. The speaker reverses the normal word order in these words opening Vespers.

2 The Image: Literal and Figurative

The Literal Image

An image is a mental representation of something perceived or perceivable by one or more of the senses. We should rid ourselves of any misapprehension that an image is only a picture or is related only to what can be seen. An image may be a perception of any one or more of the five senses: (1) of sight (visual), (2) of hearing (auditory), (3) of smell (olfactory), (4) of taste (gustatory), (5) of touch (tactile).

The word "dog" creates in our mind a picture of a certain kind of animal which produces a certain category of sounds and odors and is usually furry to touch. We respond with four of the senses. Different people will think of different dogs and have different responses to the word "dog." To some people a dog is a friendly companion, while to others a dog is either a protector or a threat. Whether the image the reader gets is threatening or loving must depend on the context in which the writer uses the word. "Dog" occurs in many common phrases in which context and common usage make the sense only relatively clear. When we use the phrase "a dog's life," we suggest to the reader images of a life with little freedom and few rewards, images of dogs being left out in the rain or confined or chained, of dogs hungry and begging, of dogs having to be obedient or punished, or of dogs lonely and howling. We do not think of dogs content, sleeping beside a loving master. But because so many images are possible we cannot call the imagery precise. The effect of the image is far more precise when Shakespeare in *Julius Caesar* has Antony threaten to "let slip the dogs of war." Here the image is of dogs, teeth bared, ready to spring to the kill. Both the image and its implications are more specific. In a poem the concrete details are used to stimulate the reader to create images in his own mind.

We can have a mental image in any of four ways: (1) by direct sense perception, (2) through memory, (3) through imagination, or (4) through the medium of language. Thus, as you sit in a classroom, you may *see* the blackboard or a classmate's hair, *hear* the teacher's voice or the siren of a fire engine, smell a classmate's perfume or another's unwashed feet, *taste* your chewing gum or the tip of your pencil, or *touch* (or *feel*) the fabric of your jacket or the texture of your skin. These would all be *direct* apprehensions of images. Later after you have left the classroom you might recall any or all of these images through *memory*. Or, at another time, you may perhaps conjure up through your *imagination* images of things that are either nonexistent or at least not directly and presently perceivable, such as the sight of a purple cow or of a blue elephant, the sound of a jet engine whispering, the smell of a desert flower, the taste of baby octopi, or the feel of Martian dust.

But in trying to understand how a poem works on its readers, we are most interested in the images that we get through the language of the poem. These images are the basis for the thought and feeling that the poem creates in us.

The problem for the writer is how to present, rather than just talk about, an emotion that is to be his poem's subject. One way to make this presentation is to evoke an equivalent emotion in the reader by causing him to call up images of events, people, objects, sounds, odors, and so forth—the facts of experience in general—so that the reader will have an equivalent emotion in his own response. This method of working with imagery is the method of many ancient writers. Chinese and Japanese poetry provide particularly good examples because of their heavy reliance upon literal imagery. A poem by Li Po of the eighth century in China, adapted by Ezra Pound (who gave Li Po the Japanese name Rihaku), illustrates how literal concrete details depict not just the speaker's attitude and situation but also the emotion beneath them.

The River-Merchant's Wife: A Letter

While my hair was still cut straight across my forehead
I played about the front gate, pulling flowers.
You came by on bamboo stilts, playing horse,
You walked about my seat, playing with blue plums.
And we went on living in the village of Chokan: 5
Two small people, without dislike or suspicion.

At fourteen I married My Lord you.
I never laughed, being bashful.
Lowering my head, I looked at the wall.
Called to, a thousand times, I never looked back.   10

At fifteen I stopped scowling,
I desired my dust to be mingled with yours
Forever and forever and forever.
Why should I climb the look out?

At sixteen you departed,   15
You went into far Ku-to-yen, by the river of swirling eddies,
And you have been gone five months.
The monkeys make sorrowful noise overhead.

You dragged your feet when you went out.
By the gate now, the moss is grown, the different mosses,   20
Too deep to clear them away!
The leaves fall early this autumn, in wind.
The paired butterflies are already yellow with August
Over the grass in the West garden;
They hurt me. I grow older.   25
If you are coming down through the narrows of the river Kiang,
Please let me know beforehand,
And I will come out to meet you
                    As far as Cho-fu-Sa.

> Ezra Pound, an adaption of a Chinese poem by Li Po
> (Rihaku) (701–762 A.D.)

Though the emotions of the wife are not discussed, they are presented
to the reader in the cumulative effect of the images of her situation.

QUESTIONS

1. Is there a difference between the wife's real emotions and her attitude as speaker in the poem? How can you tell?
2. What does "Why should I climb the look out?" (14) mean?
3. What vivid images do you find, and how do you explain their effectiveness?
4. How does the poet create the voice we hear?
5. Which details overstate and which understate the wife's feelings?

Images either interact objectively with other images or interact with the speaker's subjective statement. Two Japanese haiku illustrate these alternatives. Haiku is a rigid poetic form centuries old and still practiced in Japan. The form requires seventeen syllables in three lines, five each in the first and third, and seven in the second. But the essence of the haiku technique is the image and its interaction with something else, either another image or the poet's statement; the interaction usually involves something unexpected. The initial image is most often an observation of nature that always suggests the season. The interaction usually suggests a parallel between the change in nature and change in man's life.

Bell Tones

As bell tones fade,
    blossom scents take up the ringing—
evening shade!

                    Basho (1644–1694)

Summer Voices

So soon to die,
    and no sign of its showing—
locust cry.

                    Basho

Both these poems contain something to be imaged by the reader—the fading bell tones and the shrill sound of the locust—but they work somewhat differently. Against the fading bell tones, the first poem places new details, the scent of the blossoms and the evening shade. In all the five senses but one (taste), we feel the passing of something transitory and beautiful. The sound of the bell is succeeded by the scent of the blossoms, but the scent and the blossoms too will fade and the evening will darken to night. As the cool of the evening turns colder in the night, the briefness of our own lives is suggested, and to the Japanese there are religious suggestions. Not only is the bell a temple bell but also the oneness of all things is suggested (imaged?) by the phrasing of the second line; the scents "take up" the ringing. Night will be succeeded by day, the blossom will bear fruit, and one generation will succeed another.

The method of the second haiku, closer to the way most poets writing in English use literal imagery, is to juxtapose the image to a comment by the speaker. The abstract observation is somewhat unexpectedly applied to the cry of the locust. "So soon to die" seems regretful and not the attitude usually associated with the shrill, incessant cry of the locust. The reference is probably to the type of locust (cicada) that spends thirteen to seventeen years of its life underground so that on this summer night it is in the last stage of its life. But the focus is on the more human observation that there is no sign in the noise, the song, to suggest that the locust will ever die.

Good poetry works toward this kind of human (and universal) observation. Though most poets writing in English have found the rigid crystalization of the haiku form too restrictive, they still develop images, both literal and figurative, to engage the reader's senses in the situation. We vary greatly in our imaging abilities. Some of us are prone to respond to a given passage with many and rich images; others respond to the idea associated with the image without being clear about the image itself. Virtually everyone responds emotionally, but reading poetry well means first being clear about the image and the speaker's attitude and only then thinking about what the image implies in terms of that attitude.

A poetry of ideas, a poetry made up of words that stand for abstract concepts (love, freedom, death) rather than a poetry of images (objects, odors, gestures, actions, sounds, and so forth) may also produce thought and feeling in us, but the basis for our reaction will differ. Usually the poetry will be less precise, less vivid, less sensual, and less particularized.

The Author's Epitaph

Even such is time, which takes in trust
Our youth, our joys, and all we have,
And pays us but with age and dust,
Who in the dark and silent grave,
When we have wandered all our ways,   5

Shuts up the story of our days:
And from which earth, and grave, and dust,
The Lord shall raise me up I trust.

Sir Walter Ralegh (1552?–1618)

Ralegh's subject is an attitude—brave, trusting, and steadfast—toward all of life and death. Much of our admiration for the poem comes from our automatic respect for the courage and confidence that the poet affirms. The experience is not presented; the general language, although dignified and graceful in its phrasing, merely invites us to fill in our own experience.

Dolor

I have known the inexorable sadness of pencils,
Neat in their boxes, dolor of pad and paper-weight,
All the misery of manilla folders and mucilage,
Desolation in immaculate public places,
Lonely reception room, lavatory, switchboard,   5
The unalterable pathos of basin and pitcher,
Ritual of multigraph, paper-clip, comma,
Endless duplication of lives and objects.
And I have seen dust from the walls of institutions,
Finer than flour, alive, more dangerous than silica,   10
Sift, almost invisible, through long afternoons of tedium,
Dropping a fine film on nails and delicate eyebrows,
Glazing the pale hair, the duplicate grey standard faces.

Theodore Roethke (1908–1963)

A Time to Talk

When a friend calls to me from the road
And slows his horse to a meaning walk,
I don't stand still and look around
On all the hills I haven't hoed,
And shout from where I am, "What is it?"   5
No, not as there is a time to talk.
I thrust my hoe in the mellow ground,
Blade-end up and five feet tall,
And plod: I go up to the stone wall
For a friendly visit.   10

Robert Frost (1874–1963)

The Unknown Citizen

(To JS/07/M/378
This Marble Monument
Is Erected by the State)

He was found by the Bureau of Statistics to be
One against whom there was no official complaint,
And all the reports on his conduct agree
That, in the modern sense of an old-fashioned word, he was a saint,
For in everything he did he served the Greater Community.   5
Except for the War till the day he retired
He worked in a factory and never got fired,
But satisfied his employers, Fudge Motors Inc.
Yet he wasn't a scab or odd in his views,
For his Union reports that he paid his dues,   10
(Our report on his Union shows it was sound)
And our Social Psychology workers found
That he was popular with his mates and liked a drink.
The Press are convinced that he bought a paper every day
And that his reactions to advertisements were normal in every
   way.   15
Policies taken out in his name prove that he was fully insured,
And his Health-card shows he was once in hospital but left it cured.
Both Producers Research and High-Grade Living declare
He was fully sensible to the advantages of the Instalment Plan
And had everything necessary to the Modern Man,   20
A phonograph, a radio, a car and a frigidaire.
Our researchers into Public Opinion are content
That he held the proper opinions for the time of year;
When there was peace, he was for peace; when there was war, he
   went.
He was married and added five children to the population,   25
Which our Eugenist says was the right number for a parent of
   his generation,
And our teachers report that he never interfered with their
   education.
Was he free? Was he happy? The question is absurd:
Had anything been wrong, we should certainly have heard.

W. H. Auden (1907–1973)

The Figurative Image

Almost every image to which we have called attention in this chapter thus far has been a *literal* image—an image that is to be taken for what it is (rather than one that stands for something other than what it is): the contented dog is a contented dog; the threatening dog is a threatening dog. When the river-merchant's wife in her childhood pulled flowers at the front gate, that is exactly what the poet wants us to visualize.

But one image we discussed was not literal: the one in the phrase "let slip the dogs of war." If "the dogs of war" were to be taken literally, it would mean a war in which actual dogs were utilized as a force against the enemy. That is certainly not what Shakespeare's Antony meant. To say what he meant literally he would have had to get rid of the image of "dogs" and say something abstract like "let loose the terrorizing forces of war."

A figure of speech (in the sense in which the term is used in this book[1]) is the means by which a writer communicates an abstract or relatively abstract idea ("forces of war") by comparing it imaginatively to something relatively more concrete ("dogs of war"). Not all comparisons are figurative: to compare the breadth of the Mississippi and that of the Amazon is to make a literal comparison, because they are both rivers. In a figurative comparison the two items are in essence different (forces, dogs), but resemble one another in some respect (ferocity); the imaginative comparison provides or heightens the concreteness, the vividness, the whole appeal to the reader. To call a river a wall between two countries or two armies is to use a figurative comparison.

T. S. Eliot in the third of his *Four Quartets* compares a god and a river:

I do not know much about gods; but I think that the river
Is a strong brown god—sullen, untamed and intractable. . . .

The larger context of the poem deals with the speaker's sense of the presence of divine power in the world. He makes his sense of that abstract power concrete by saying that he thinks of that power as a river—"sullen, untamed and intractable."

---

[1] Some writers use the term in a broader sense, to include matters that are treated elsewhere in this book, such as "onomatopoeia" (see Chapter 4) and "irony," "hyperbole," "understatement," and "paradox" (see Chapter 6).

Simile

Of the two main kinds of figure of speech, simile and metaphor, simile is a figure in which the comparison is explicitly stated, usually by means of "like," "as," or "as if."

For Sale

Poor sheepish plaything,
organized with prodigal animosity,
lived in just a year—
my Father's cottage at Beverly Farms
was on the market the month he died.   5
Empty, open, intimate,
its town-house furniture
had an on tiptoe air
of waiting for the mover
on the heels of the undertaker.   10
Ready, afraid
of living alone till eighty,
Mother mooned in a window,
as if she had stayed on a train
one stop past her destination.   15

Robert Lowell (b. 1917)

Robert Lowell's "For Sale" is organized in three five-line sentences, with the final one, lines 11–15, conveying the melancholy most profoundly. Of the final five lines the first two are literal. Whether line 13 is literal or figurative depends on the word "mooned"; originally probably a figure signifying "to act is if moonstruck," the meaning of this verb has evolved (through a process that is common in the development of language) to the point where the original figure has been lost and "to moon" now quite literally means to pass time, act, or move in a languid, listless, aimless, abstracted manner. But it is through the simile in the last two lines that Lowell conveys most specifically, most concretely, most tellingly just what the speaker's feeling for his mother was.

Metaphor

When the figurative comparison is not explicitly stated, but instead is simply equated with what it stands for, the figure is called a metaphor. The "Father's cottage" is not said to be *like* a poor sheepish plaything; it *is* a "poor sheepish plaything." The function of a simile and metaphor is elaboration and focus in terms of the speaker's attitude. The speaker's attitude in "For Sale" moves from criticism of his father to pity for his mother—from the focus given by the image of a "sheepish plaything" organized with "prodigal animosity" to the final image, elaborated by the closing simile, of the mother who mooned in a window. Of all the ambivalent attitudes the speaker might actually have had, particular ones have been selected and elaborated by these opening and closing images. Between them is the image of the elegant town-house furniture with a metaphorically "on tiptoe air," an image, in the exact center of the poem, elaborating the silent inactivity of the present as the balance point between past and future.

The following figures of speech can be classified as other forms of the metaphor:

Metonymy. In metonymy, instead of naming something, the poet substitutes something associated with it. When Edward Bulwer-Lytton wrote "The pen is mightier than the sword," the statement was striking, and it has endured largely because of the vivid substitution of "the sword" for the physical force and even more notably of "the pen" for the influence of writing and speech.

Synecdoche. Closely related to metonymy, synecdoche is the figure in which the part is substituted for the whole or the whole for the part. If "bread" is construed to mean "sustenance," the plea in the Lord's Prayer "give us this day our daily bread," is a substitution of the part for the whole. When Milton speaks of a table on which "all Autumn" is piled, meaning all the autumn harvest, he is substituting the whole for the part.

Personification. Personification consists in attributing human characteristics to something nonhuman or sometimes the characteristics of other living things to something inanimate. William Butler Yeats uses personification in the conclusion of "When You are Old" (page 5) with the lines ". . . Love fled / And paced upon the mountains overhead / And hid his face amid the crowd of stars." The inanimate fog becomes a cat in "The yellow fog that rubs its back upon the window-pane" (page 299, T. S. Eliot's "The Love Song of J. Alfred Prufrock").

Apostrophe. Related to personification, apostrophe is the figure in which an abstraction or an inanimate object is addressed as if it were human or a human who is not present is addressed as if he were. John Keats' "To Autumn" (page 332) is both a personification of and an address to autumn. John Donne's "At the Round Earth's Imagined Corners" (page 194) begins as an address to angels and to the souls of the dead.

Habana

Soldiers fuzz the city in khaki confusion
Pincushioned with weapons
Seedy orange venders squeeze among the pulpy masses
Camera pregnant tourists click down the Prado
Loteria salesmen tear along the dotted line   5
Guitars pluck loafers into corner bars
Uniformed schoolgirls genuflect languorously
Climactic roaming rainbow dresses cling slowly
Punctuating neon orgasms in the mambo night
and above Fidel's sandpaper voice,   10
"You want a girl, maybe?"

Julian Bond (b. 1940)

I taste a liquor never brewed

I taste a liquor never brewed—
From Tankards scooped in Pearl—
Not all the Vats upon the Rhine
Yield such an Alcohol!

Inebriate of Air—am I—   5
And Debauchee of Dew—
Reeling—thro endless summer days—
From inns of Molten Blue—

When "Landlords" turn the drunken Bee
Out of the Foxglove's door—   10
When Butterflies—renounce their "drams"—
I shall but drink the more!

Till Seraphs swing their snowy Hats—
And Saints—to windows run—
To see the little Tippler   15
Leaning against the—Sun—

Emily Dickinson (1830–1886)

NOTES AND QUESTIONS

1. "I taste a liquor never brewed" is a sustained metaphor. The literal subject is an experience expressed most explicitly in the second stanza. What is it? Is the literal subject in itself concrete? If so, why does Dickinson compare it to something else? Trace through the poem all of the words and phrases related to intoxication, a word that Dickinson does *not* use.
2. The poem also contains subsidiary figures. Identify them. What is the particular effectiveness of "little tippler / Leaning against the —sun—"?

The Bustle in a House

The Bustle in a House
The Morning after Death
Is solemnest of industries
Enacted upon Earth—

The Sweeping up the Heart   5
And putting Love away
We shall not want to use again
Until Eternity.

Emily Dickinson (1830–1886)

Liu Ch'e

The rustling of the silk is discontinued,
Dust drifts over the court-yard,
There is no sound of foot-fall, and the leaves
Scurry into heaps and lie still,
And she the rejoicer of the heart is beneath them: 5

A wet leaf that clings to the threshold.

Ezra Pound (1885–1972)

NOTE

Liu Ch'e (title): the original author from whom Ezra Pound translated this poem, a Chinese poet who in 140 B.C. became the sixth emperor of the Han dynasty.

The Death of the Ball Turret Gunner

From my mother's sleep I fell into the State,
And I hunched in its belly till my wet fur froze.
Six miles from earth, loosed from its dream of life,
I woke to black flak and the nightmare fighters.
When I died they washed me out of the turret with a hose.   5

Randall Jarrell (1914–1965)

NOTE

Ball turret (title): a plexiglass bulb on the body of a World War II fighter
plane, from which machine gunners fired at the enemy.

A Hillside Thaw

To think to know the country and not know
The hillside on the day the sun lets go
Ten million silver lizards out of snow!
As often as I've seen it done before
I can't pretend to tell the way it's done.   5
It looks as if some magic of the sun
Lifted the rug that bred them on the floor
And the light breaking on them made them run.
But if I thought to stop the wet stampede,
And caught one silver lizard by the tail,   10
And put my foot on one without avail,
And threw myself wet-elbowed and wet-kneed
In front of twenty others' wriggling speed—
In the confusion of them all aglitter,
And birds that joined in the excited fun   15
By doubling and redoubling song and twitter—
I have no doubt I'd end by holding none.

It takes the moon for this. The sun's a wizard
By all I tell; but so's the moon a witch.
From the high west she makes a gentle cast   20
And suddenly, without a jerk or twitch,
She has her spell on every single lizard.
I fancied when I looked at six o'clock
The swarm still ran and scuttled just as fast.
The moon was waiting for her chill effect.   25
I looked at nine: the swarm was turned to rock
In every lifelike posture of the swarm,
Transfixed on mountain slopes almost erect.

Across each other and side by side they lay.
The spell that so could hold them as they were   30
Was wrought through trees without a breath of storm
To make a leaf, if there has been one, stir.
It was the moon's: she held them until day,
One lizard at the end of every ray.
The thought of my attempting such a stay!   35

Robert Frost (1874–1963)

QUESTIONS

1. The title of the poem is not directly mentioned in the poem. How
   is it related to the poem and to the poem's division into two parts?
2. What metaphor is sustained throughout the poem? Is this a kind
   of personification?
3. Frost uses the word "magic" in line 6. Identify each word in the
   second part that pursues the idea of magic.
4. Identify the personifications in the second part.
5. The first and the last lines of the poem are related to one another
   and reveal that the subject of the poem is not so much the hillside
   thaw as the speaker's attitude toward it. What is that attitude?

Subject Pair

To an Athlete Dying Young

The time you won your town the race
We chaired you through the market-place;
Man and boy stood cheering by,
And home we brought you shoulder-high.

To-day, the road all runners come,   5
Shoulder-high we bring you home,
And set you at your threshold down,
Townsman of a stiller town.

Smart lad, to slip betimes away
From fields where glory does not stay   10
And early though the laurel grows
It withers quicker than the rose.

Eyes the shady night has shut
Cannot see the record cut,
And silence sounds no worse than cheers   15
After earth has stopped the ears:

Now you will not swell the rout
Of lads that wore their honours out,
Runners whom renown outran
And the name died before the man.   20

So set, before its echoes fade,
The fleet foot on the sill of shade,
And hold to the low lintel up
The still-defended challenge-cup.

And round that early-laurelled head   25
Will flock to gaze the strengthless dead
And find unwithered on its curls
The garland briefer than a girl's.

                    A. E. Housman (1859–1936)

Ex-Basketball Player

Pearl Avenue runs past the high-school lot,
Bends with the trolley tracks, and stops, cut off
Before it has a chance to go two blocks,
At Colonel McComsky Plaza. Berth's Garage
Is on the corner facing west, and there,   5
Most days, you'll find Flick Webb, who helps Berth out.

Flick stands tall among the idiot pumps—
Five on a side, the old bubble-head style,
Their rubber elbows hanging loose and low.
One's nostrils are two S's, and his eyes   10
An E and O. And one is squat, without
A head at all—more of a football type.

Once Flick played for the high-school team, the Wizards.
He was good: in fact, the best. In '46
He bucketed three hundred ninety points,   15
A county record still. The ball loved Flick.
I saw him rack up thirty-eight or forty
In one home game. His hands were like wild birds.

He never learned a trade, he just sells gas,
Checks oil, and changes flats. Once in a while,   20
As a gag, he dribbles an inner tube.
But most of us remember anyway.
His hands are fine and nervous on the lug wrench.
It makes no difference to the lug wrench, though.

Off work, he hangs around Mae's Luncheonette.   25
Grease-grey and kind of coiled, he plays pinball,
Sips lemon cokes, and smokes those thin cigars;
Flick seldom speaks to Mae, just sits and nods
Beyond her face towards bright applauding tiers
Of Necco Wafers, Nibs, and Juju Beads.   30

John Updike (b. 1932)

QUESTIONS

1. How do the attitudes of Housman's and Updike's speakers differ?
2. How does their use of imagery differ?
3. Despite the discipline to largely literal imagery, a discipline that gives the impression of a simple report of the facts, Updike's speaker is characterized. In what phrasing is his character shown? At such places how is the reader's attitude different from the speaker's?
4. Explain how the two poems, specifically about athletes, are really about other aspects of experience as well.
5. Is the portrait of Flick realistic and fair or exaggerated and satirical? Do we see a pathetic victim of his society?

Chronological Arrangement

Love Is a Sickness

Love is a sickness full of woes,
    All remedies refusing;
A plant that with most cutting grows,
    Most barren with best using.
        Why so?   5
More we enjoy it, more it dies;
If not enjoyed, it sighing cries—
        Heigh ho!

Love is a torment of the mind,
   A tempest everlasting;   10
And Jove hath made it of a kind
Not well, nor full nor fasting.
   Why so?
More we enjoy it, more it dies;
If not enjoyed, it sighing cries—   15
   Heigh ho!
           Samuel Daniel (1562–1619)

Ozymandias

I met a traveller from an antique land
Who said: Two vast and trunkless legs of stone
Stand in the desert. Near them, on the sand,
Half sunk, a shatter'd visage lies, whose frown,
And wrinkled lip, and sneer of cold command,   5
Tell that its sculptor well those passions read
Which yet survive, stamp'd on these lifeless things,
The hand that mock'd them and the heart that fed:
And on the pedestal these words appear:
"My name is Ozymandias, king of kings: 10
Look on my works, ye Mighty, and despair!"
Nothing beside remains. Round the decay
Of that colossal wreck, boundless and bare
The lone and level sands stretch far away.
           Percy Bysshe Shelley (1792–1822)

NOTES AND QUESTIONS

1. *Ozymandias* (title): the Egyptian king Rameses II (thirteenth century B.C.), who presumably erected a mighty statue of himself.
2. From the middle of line 3 to the end of line 8 the literal meaning and the grammar are complex enough to make a close paraphrase useful. What specific word in the preceding lines does the word *them* in line 8 stand for? In line 8 whose hand is being referred to? Whose heart? Is "hand" literal? A metaphor? A metonymy? A synecdoche? Apply the same questions to "heart."

The Eagle

He clasps the crag with crooked hands;
Close to the sun in lonely lands,
Ring'd with the azure world, he stands.

The wrinkled sea beneath him crawls;
He watches from his mountain walls,   5
And like a thunderbolt he falls.

Alfred, Lord Tennyson (1809–1892)

The Return

See, they return; ah, see the tentative
Movements, and the slow feet,
The trouble in the pace and the uncertain
Wavering!

See, they return, one, and by one,   5
With fear, as half-awakened;
As if the snow should hesitate
And murmur in the wind,
                    and half turn back;
These were the "Wing'd-with-Awe,"   10
            Inviolable.

Gods of the wingèd shoe!
With them the silver hounds,
            sniffing the trace of air!

Haie!   Haie!   15
            These were the swift to harry;
These the keen-scented;
These were the souls of blood.

Slow on the leash,
                    pallid the leash-men!   20

Ezra Pound (1885–1972)

Thirteen Ways of Looking
at a Blackbird

I

Among twenty snowy mountains,
The only moving thing
Was the eye of the blackbird.

II

I was of three minds,
Like a tree   5
In which there are three blackbirds.

III

The blackbird whirled in the autumn winds.
It was a small part of the pantomime.

IV

A man and a woman
Are one.   10
A man and a woman and a blackbird
Are one.

V

I do not know which to prefer,
The beauty of inflections
Or the beauty of innuendoes,   15
The blackbird whistling
Or just after.

VI

Icicles filled the long window
With barbaric glass.
The shadow of the blackbird   20
Crossed it, to and fro.
The mood
Traced in the shadow
An indecipherable cause.

VII

O thin men of Haddam,   25
Why do you imagine golden birds?
Do you not see how the blackbird
Walks around the feet
Of the women about you?

VIII

I know noble accents   30
And lucid, inescapable rhythms;
But I know, too,
That the blackbird is involved
In what I know.

IX

When the blackbird flew out of sight,   35
It marked the edge
Of one of many circles.

X

At the sight of blackbirds
Flying in a green light,
Even the bawds of euphony   40
Would cry out sharply.

XI

He rode over Connecticut
In a glass coach.
Once, a fear pierced him,
In that he mistook   45
The shadow of his equipage
For blackbirds.

XII

The river is moving.
The blackbird must be flying.

XIII

It was evening all afternoon.   50
It was snowing
And it was going to snow.
The blackbird sat
In the cedar-limbs.

                    Wallace Stevens (1879–1955)

3 Symbol
Allusion
Myth and
Archetype

Symbol

We do not think dreams but experience them in a series of images that arouse emotion and perhaps thought in us. The images may be of objects, of actions (often a journey or a search), or of people, either people we know or mysterious strangers. Primitive man's conviction that his dreams meant something is now confirmed by psychoanalysis, which has made a science of the interpretation of symbols. Although there are many kinds of symbols, there are basically only two literary ones, the conventional (or the mythic) and the personal, that is, those that have generally the same meaning in everyone's experience and those that accumulate meaning largely in our own personal anxieties. Mythic literature is full of journeys and searches (usually in quest of something lost—innocence, love, hope) that have resulted in a number of conventional symbols, now trite— the beaten path, the crossroads, paths that cross, the rocky road, smooth sailing, the long journey, and people who go downhill when the way to virtue is up.

In literature the conventional mythic symbol is at first sight full of associations. What does a cross symbolize? Each person in any classroom would answer somewhat differently—truth, suffering, grace, death, eternal life, a way of life, hope, charity—all would be right. Even those who had chosen to say that the cross represents some kind of a false promise or way of life would have got the symbolism right, but they would have imposed a judgment upon what the symbol represents. They like the others would have understood that the symbol represents many things and would have had the same understanding of its meaning. A poet using the cross as a symbol may want to include all possible associations or he may want to restrict them with a context that focuses on only certain aspects of the conventional meaning.

What does the "Cross" symbolize in the following lines?

from *Choruses from "The Rock," VIII*

Remember the faith that took men from home
At the call of a wandering preacher.
Our age is an age of moderate virtue
And of moderate vice
When men will not lay down the Cross   5
Because they will never assume it.
Yet nothing is impossible, nothing,
To men of faith and conviction.
Let us therefore make perfect our will.
O GOD, help us.   10

T. S. Eliot (1888–1965)

Among the other symbols rooted in our human and cultural heritage are the rose and the worm. The following poem is a good example of an entirely symbolic poem in which a great many associations are possible.

The Sick Rose

O rose, thou art sick!
The invisible worm
That flies in the night,
In the howling storm,

Has found out thy bed   5
Of crimson joy,
And his dark secret love
Does thy life destroy.

William Blake (1757–1827)

Blake works from a traditional set of symbolic literary associations—even though knowledge of the literary tradition is not necessary for an understanding of the sense of the poem. Any reader can get the proper sense of the central conflict between something invisible that flies in night and storm and the rose with its traditional associations of beauty. Even melodrama has instructed us in how to respond to beauty and virtue threatened in bed by the "dark secret love" of a worm that destroys. In the literary tradition the worm suggests the snake of the garden of Eden, and since it flies in the night it seems to have been transmitted like a disease to which all, not just the rose, are vulnerable. The tradition of the rose as symbol suggests ideal femininity, love, and nature in its ideal form. We can easily enough develop the image of a rose bed with worms invisible either because they are hidden by the rose or are not to be apprehended visually. But the image must be reinforced by the context of sexual assault, secrecy and storm, and that context gives important definition to the symbol. All that is ideal, beautiful, and naturally to be desired and loved is under assault, secretly in the night. The symbol of the rose secretly blighted in a world of darkness and storm has as many applications in our own world as in Blake's. In both worlds what is open, natural, and beautiful is threatened by motives that are secret and unknown.

The Yachts

contend in a sea which the land partly encloses
shielding them from the too-heavy blows
of an ungoverned ocean which when it chooses

tortures the biggest hulls, the best man knows
to pit against its beatings, and sinks them pitilessly.   5
Mothlike in mists, scintillant in the minute

brilliance of cloudless days, with broad bellying sails
they glide to the wind tossing green water
from their sharp prows while over them the crew crawls

ant-like, solicitously grooming them, releasing,   10
making fast as they turn, lean far over and having
caught the wind again, side by side, head for the mark.

In a well guarded arena of open water surrounded by
lesser and greater craft which, sycophant, lumbering
and flittering follow them, they appear youthful, rare   15

as the light of a happy eye, live with the grace
of all that in the mind is fleckless, free and
naturally to be desired. Now the sea which holds them

is moody, lapping their glossy sides, as if feeling
for some slightest flaw but fails completely.   20
Today no race. Then the wind comes again. The yachts

move, jockeying for a start, the signal is set and they
are off. Now the waves strike at them but they are too
well made, they slip through, though they take in canvas.

Arms with hands grasping seek to clutch at the prows.   25
Bodies thrown recklessly in the way are cut aside.
It is a sea of faces about them in agony, in despair

until the horror of the race dawns staggering the mind;
the whole sea become an entanglement of watery bodies
lost to the world bearing what they cannot hold. Broken,   30

beaten, desolate, reaching from the dead to be taken up
they cry out, failing, failing! their cries rising
in waves still as the skillful yachts pass over.

William Carlos Williams (1883–1963)

Allusion

Allusion is a reference in a literary work to something else
in the cultural tradition—literary, religious, historical, artistic, mytho-
logical, philosophical. Because allusion introduces many resonances
from the traditional knowledge alluded to, its function is enrichment,
but the enrichment of one work by allusion to another depends upon
knowledgeable readers. Only the best known works are therefore al-
luded to by poets who expect a wide audience. In English poetry
certain classical myths, the Bible, and Shakespeare's plays are the
most frequent sources of allusion.

Certain historical events also develop a popular mythology that is
evoked when certain names are mentioned—for example, Plato, Bru-
tus, Cleopatra, Washington, Waterloo, Lincoln, Marx, Victoria, Freud,
Hitler, Gandhi, and Churchill.

The Oxen

Christmas Eve and twelve of the clock.
  "Now they are all on their knees,"
An elder said as we sat in a flock
  By the embers in hearthside ease.

We pictured the meek mild creatures where   5
  They dwelt in their strawy pen,
Nor did it occur to one of us there
  To doubt they were kneeling then.

So fair a fancy few would weave
  In these years! Yet, I feel,   10
If someone said on Christmas Eve,
  "Come; see the oxen kneel,

"In the lonely barton by yonder coomb
  Our childhood used to know,"
I should go with him in the gloom,   15
  Hoping it might be so.

Thomas Hardy (1840–1928)

The Magi

Now as at all times I can see in the mind's eye,
In their stiff, painted clothes, the pale unsatisfied ones
Appear and disappear in the blue depth of the sky
With all their ancient faces like rain-beaten stones,
And all their helms of silver hovering side by side,   5
And all their eyes still fixed, hoping to find once more,
Being by Calvary's turbulence unsatisfied,
The uncontrollable mystery on the bestial floor.

William Butler Yeats (1865–1939)

Past Ruined Ilion Helen Lives

Past ruined Ilion Helen lives,
  Alcestis rises from the shades;
Verse calls them forth; 'tis verse that gives
  Immortal youth to mortal maids.

Soon shall Oblivion's deepening veil   5
  Hide all the peopled hills you see,
The gay, the proud, while lovers hail
  In distant ages you and me.

The tear for fading beauty check,
  For passing glory cease to sigh;   10
One form shall rise above the wreck,
  One name, Ianthe, shall not die.

                    Walter Savage Landor (1775–1864)

NOTE

Alcestis (2): promised by Apollo that she might save her husband's life by
sacrificing her own, Alcestis gave her life but was brought back from the
underworld by Hercules.

No Second Troy

Why should I blame her that she filled my days
With misery, or that she would of late
Have taught to ignorant men most violent ways,
Or hurled the little streets upon the great,
Had they but courage equal to desire?   5
What could have made her peaceful with a mind
That nobleness made simple as a fire,
With beauty like a tightened bow, a kind
That is not natural in an age like this,
Being high and solitary and most stern?   10
Why, what could she have done, being what she is?
Was there another Troy for her to burn?

                    William Butler Yeats (1865–1939)

NOTE

her (1): Maud Gonne, an Irish revolutionary, whom Yeats loved in vain.

When I Came from Colchis

When I came from Colchis
Where the spring fields lay green,
A land famed for fine linen,
Bounded northerly
By the glistering Caucasus,   5
By the Euxine westerly,

Most I spoke of fine linen
But did, in truth, tell something
Of Jason who had come sailing
And poised upon that shore   10
His fabulous excursion.
All turned the incredulous ear.

From Troy, over the water
Returning, I recounted
The tale of wrecked walls, but said   15
That gray waves lap and surround
That shore as any other.
With a shrewd smile they listened.

Now if, amazed, I come
From the deep bourn of your hand,   20
A stranger up from the sunned
Sea of your eyes, lady,
What fable should I tell them,
That they should believe me?

W. S. Merwin (b. 1927)

NOTES

Colchis (1): in ancient geography, a country in Asia south of the Caucasus
on the Black Sea, here called Euxine (ūk′ sīn). Colchis was the destination
of the long voyage of the Argonauts, led by Jason, to obtain the Golden
Fleece. It was a voyage full of bloody adventures and tests to be passed
by Jason, aided by Medea, who later in revenge for his betraying her
killed their children. *Troy* (13): an ancient city on the coast of Asia Minor
near the Hellespont and the destination of another voyage, c. 1200 B.C.
This voyage by the Greeks to defeat Troy and return Helen to Greece
left Troy in ruins.

Myth and Archetype

The literature of all religions and the epic literature of all cultures tell stories that imply answers to man's most frustrating questions: why must he suffer, why is he tempted and caught in the process of the loss of innocence, why does life seem meaningless, what comes after death? Because they deal with such basic concerns, these stories have affected, even regulated, men's lives more than most people have been conscious of. The earliest myths, those of agricultural people living at the mercy of nature and in awe of the changing seasons, saw agricultural and sexual fertility as the essential factors for their survival under easily angered gods who controlled the seasons. The sun was the most natural image of god for such people. In their time rivers also became sacred (the Ganges, the Nile). The need that inspired the mythic imagination was for order and stability, good crops and children who survived; and the motive of the myth maker was to give concrete form to a power that could be petitioned and praised. The issues were life against death: fertility in plant, animal, and man against all the power of darkness that threatened the survival of the race. All cultures, having begun in awe of the power of nature, evolved a religious and poetic imagery with certain elements in common.

The cycle of the seasons, the cycle of the rising and the setting sun, of darkness and light, of sleeping and dreaming and waking, all were associated with the idea of birth, rebirth and a life after death. If we awaken from sleep, which looks like death, there must be some awakening after death. In myth as in experience, both waking and dreaming, winter is associated with death and spring with birth and rebirth. Fertility in man, animal, and crops, along with phallic symbols to represent it, was celebrated. To explain the facts of winter and death, stories developed of dying gods reborn in spring as man might be reborn after death. In ancient Greece two myths were developed to explain the cycle of the vegetative year. Persephone, abducted by Hades to be his bride in the underworld, was allowed to spend two-thirds of the year on earth, spring to early autumn, and when she returned to Hades (called Pluto by the Romans) winter returned to earth. The coming of spring was celebrated by the Festival of Dionysus (called Bacchus by the Romans), who represented the surge and excitement of life and growth. Dionysus (Bacchus) is the god of wine and sexual impulse, while Persephone is the more orderly goddess of grain. The myth of Dionysus, like that of Isis in Egypt, is a story of death, dismemberment, and rebirth. His body, having been scattered among the people, is reborn in the spring, the rebirth celebrated in gratitude and joy. With the idea of human imperfection came the need for explanations—the scapegoat, the temptress, the devil, and fallen man—and the need for a method to regain innocence—the initiation, the task, the journey, the quest. Whether the story involves the sons of gods (Krishna, Jesus) or mortals (Adam, Percival, Siegfried) is of less importance than the ability myth has or once had to satisfy the human need to see life in a meaningful pattern.

These elements which have a common significance in the religious and epic literature of many cultures are called "archetypes." The temptress of our dreams and fantasies has the same archetypal significance as the temptress of religious and epic literature. In dreams and in reality, floods and storms still awaken in us an awe and fear similar to that felt by primitive man, and they have the same archetypal significance in our literature as they had in his. The archetype is a category of meaning, an idea common in many myths and cultures. The category may be a season of the year, a time of day, a character (God, the hero, the devil), an action (dancing, bathing), symbolic objects (fruit, flowers, phallic symbols), or an event (thunder, flood, death).

Epic and narrative poetry deal with the larger mythic pattern. A lyric poem deals with only one moment of it. The lyric presents the speaker's personal response to experience. It works for an imaginative and unified effect, and the imagination of the poet may or may not work with archetypal elements. Although archetype theory has been developed by learned scholars who have studied the world's religions and epic literature and discovered the similar meaningful incidents called archetypes, what is most impressively archetypal in poetic imagery is a primitive spirituality that perceives all of life as a part of a single process. The process from death to rebirth of the vegetative season was but an intimation of the survival of the human spirit, a force that survived calamity and had its source in a divine power. That power was symbolized in the death and rebirth of Isis in Egypt, of Dionysus in Greece, and is still symbolized for Christians today in the rebirth of Christ.

Archetypal Characters

The Divine Image

The Divine Image

To Mercy, Pity, Peace, and Love
All pray in their distress:
And to these virtues of delight
Return their thankfulness.

For Mercy, Pity, Peace, and Love   5
Is God, our father dear:
And Mercy, Pity, Peace, and Love
Is Man, his child and care.

For Mercy has a human heart,
Pity, a human face,   10
And Love, the human form divine,
And Peace, the human dress.

Then every man of every clime,
That prays in his distress,
Prays to the human form divine,   15
Love, Mercy, Pity, Peace.

And all must love the human form,
In heathen, turk, or jew;
Where Mercy, Love, and Pity dwell
There God is dwelling too.   20

William Blake (1757–1827)

God's Grandeur

The world is charged with the grandeur of God.
    It will flame out, like shining from shook foil;
    It gathers to a greatness, like the ooze of oil
Crushed. Why do men then now not reck his rod?
Generations have trod, have trod, have trod;   5
    And all is seared with trade; bleared, smeared with toil;
    And wears man's smudge and shares man's smell: the soil
Is bare now, nor can foot feel, being shod.

And for all this, nature is never spent;
   There lives the dearest freshness deep down things;   10
And though the last lights off the black West went
   Oh, morning, at the brown brink eastward, springs—
Because the Holy Ghost over the bent
   World broods with warm breast and with ah! bright wings.

Gerard Manley Hopkins (1844–1889)

Divinities

Having crowded once onto the threshold of mortality
And not been chosen
There is no freedom such as theirs
That have no beginning

The air itself is their memory   5
A domain they cannot inhabit
But from which they are never absent

What are you they say *that simply exist*
And the heavens and the earth bow to them
Looking up from their choices   10
Perishing

All day and all night
Everything that is mistaken worships them
Even the dead sing them an unending hymn

W. S. Merwin (b. 1927)

NOTES AND QUESTIONS

1. What characteristics of the divine image appear in Blake, Hopkins, and Merwin?
2. Hopkins explained in a letter (January 4, 1883) that *shook foil* (2) refers to goldfoil shaken, which gives off flashing light, "like lightning." How is "oil crushed" related to this image? How is the "shook foil" image related to *rod* (4), a symbol of law and authority?
3. Identify the definitive idea of each divine image.
4. Why does Blake, who sees the divine in the human, change the order in stanza three of Mercy, Pity, Peace and Love? In stanza four resolve the paradox of "the human form divine."
5. Find the paradoxes in Merwin's "Divinities" and show how the idea that informs them is the opposite of Blake's idea.

The Heroic Image

The Windhover

To Christ our Lord

I caught this morning morning's minion, king-
   dom of daylight's dauphin, dapple-dawn-drawn Falcon, in
      his riding
Of the rolling level underneath him steady air, and striding
High there, how he rung upon the rein of a wimpling wing
In his ecstasy! then off, off forth on swing,   5
   As a skate's heel sweeps smooth on a bow-bend: the hurl and
      gliding
Rebuffed the big wind. My heart in hiding
Stirred for a bird,—the achieve of, the mastery of the thing!

Brute beauty and valour and act, oh, air, pride, plume, here
   Buckle! AND the fire that breaks from thee then, a billion   10
Times told lovelier, more dangerous, O my chevalier!

No wonder of it: shéer plód makes plough down sillion
Shine, and blue-bleak embers, ah my dear,
   Fall, gall themselves, and gash gold-vermilion.

Gerard Manley Hopkins (1844–1889)

Ulysses

It little profits that an idle king,
By this still hearth, among these barren crags,
Matched with an aged wife, I mete and dole
Unequal laws unto a savage race,
That hoard, and sleep, and feed, and know not me.   5
I cannot rest from travel; I will drink
Life to the lees. All times I have enjoyed
Greatly, have suffered greatly, both with those
That loved me, and alone; on shore, and when
Through scudding drifts the rainy Hyades   10
Vexed the dim sea. I am become a name;
For always roaming with a hungry heart

NOTE

Hyades (10): seven stars in the constellation Taurus.

Much have I seen and known—cities of men,
And manners, climates, councils, governments,
Myself not least, but honored of them all—   15
And drunk delight of battle with my peers,
Far on the ringing plains of windy Troy.
I am a part of all that I have met;
Yet all experience is an arch wherethrough
Gleams that untraveled world whose margin fades   20
Forever and forever when I move.
How dull it is to pause, to make an end,
To rust unburnished, not to shine in use!
As though to breathe were life! Life piled on life
Were all too little, and of one to me   25
Little remains; but every hour is saved
From that eternal silence, something more,
A bringer of new things; and vile it were
For some three suns to store and hoard myself,
And this gray spirit yearning in desire   30
To follow knowledge like a sinking star,
Beyond the utmost bound of human thought.

This is my son, mine own Telemachus,
To whom I leave the scepter and the isle—
Well-loved of me, discerning to fulfill   35
This labour, by slow prudence to make mild
A rugged people, and through soft degrees
Subdue them to the useful and the good.
Most blameless is he, centered in the sphere
Of common duties, decent not to fail   40
In offices of tenderness, and pay
Meet adoration to my household gods,
When I am gone. He works his work, I mine.

There lies the port; the vessel puffs her sail;
There gloom the dark, broad seas. My mariners,   45
Souls that have toiled, and wrought, and thought with me—
That ever with a frolic welcome took
The thunder and the sunshine, and opposed
Free hearts, free foreheads—you and I are old;
Old age hath yet his honour and his toil.   50
Death closes all; but something ere the end,
Some work of noble note, may yet be done,
Not unbecoming men that strove with gods.
The lights begin to twinkle from the rocks;
The long day wanes; the slow moon climbs; the deep   55

Moans round with many voices. Come, my friends,
'Tis not too late to seek a newer world.
Push off, and sitting well in order smite
The sounding furrows; for my purpose holds
To sail beyond the sunset, and the baths   60
Of all the western stars, until I die.
It may be that the gulfs will wash us down;
It may be we shall touch the Happy Isles,
And see the great Achilles, whom we knew.
Though much is taken, much abides; and though   65
We are not now that strength which in old days
Moved earth and heaven, that which we are, we are—
One equal temper of heroic hearts,
Made weak by time and fate, but strong in will
To strive, to seek, to find, and not to yield.   70

                    Alfred, Lord Tennyson (1809–1892)

NOTE

Happy Isles (63): the earthly paradise of the Greeks.

The Devil

The Demon Lover

"O where have you been, my long, long love,
    This long seven years and mair?"
"O I'm come to seek my former vows
    Ye granted me before."

"O hold your tongue of your former vows,   5
    For they will breed sad strife;
O hold your tongue of your former vows,
    For I am become a wife."

He turned him right and round about,
    And the tear blinded his ee:°   10   eye
"I wad never have trodden on Irish ground,
    If it had not been for thee.

"I might have had a king's daughtèr,
    Far, far beyond the sea;
I might have had a king's daughtèr,   15
    Had it not been for love o' thee."

"If ye might have had a king's daughtèr,
   Yer sel' ye had to blame;
Ye might have taken the king's daughtèr,
   For ye kend° that I was nane.   20   knew

"If I was to leave my husband dear,
   And my two babes also,
O what have you to take me to,
   If with you I should go?"

"I have seven ships upon the sea—   25
   The eighth brought me to land—
With four-and-twenty bold mariners,
   And music on every hand."

She has taken up her two little babes,
   Kissed them baith° cheek and chin: 30   both
"O fair ye weel, my ain two babes,
   For I'll never see you again."

She set her foot upon the ship,
   No mariners could she behold;
But the sails were o' the taffetie,°   35   taffeta
   And the masts o' the beaten gold.

She had not sailed a league, a league,
   A league but barely three,
When dismal grew his countenance,
   And drumlie° grew his ee.   40   dangerous

They had not sailed a league, a league,
   A league but barely three,
Until she espied his cloven foot,
   And she wept right bitterly.

"O hold your tongue of your weeping," says he,   45
   "Of your weeping now let me be;
I will show you how the lilies grow
   On the banks of Italy."

"O what hills are yon, yon pleasant hills,
   That the sun shines sweetly on?"   50
"O yon are the hills of heaven," he said,
   "Where you will never win."

"O whaten a mountain is yon," she said,
   "All so dreary wi' frost and snow?"
"O yon is the mountain of hell," he cried,   55
   "Where you and I will go."

He strack the tap-mast wi' his hand,
  The fore-mast wi' his knee,
And he brake that gallant ship in twain,
  And sank her in the sea.   60

Anonymous

Lucifer in Starlight

On a starred night Prince Lucifer uprose.
Tired of his dark dominion swung the fiend
Above the rolling ball in cloud part screened,
Where sinners hugged their specter of repose.
Poor prey to his hot fit of pride were those.   5
And now upon his western wing he leaned,
Now his huge bulk o'er Afric's sands careened,
Now the black planet shadowed Arctic snows.
Soaring through wider zones that pricked his scars
With memory of the old revolt from Awe,   10
He reached a middle height, and at the stars,
Which are the brain of heaven, he looked, and sank.
Around the ancient track marched, rank on rank
The army of unalterable law.

George Meredith (1828–1909)

The Temptress

La Belle Dame Sans Merci

O what can ail thee, knight-at-arms,
  Alone and palely loitering?
The sedge has withered from the lake,
  And no birds sing.

O what can ail thee, knight-at-arms,   5
  So haggard and so woe-begone?
The squirrel's granary is full,
  And the harvest's done.

I see a lily on thy brow
  With anguish moist and fever dew,   10
And on thy cheek a fading rose
  Fast withereth too.

I met a lady in the meads,
   Full beautiful—a faery's child;
Her hair was long, her foot was light,   15
   And her eyes were wild.

I made a garland for her head,
   And bracelets too, and fragrant zone;
She looked at me as she did love,
   And made sweet moan.   20

I set her on my pacing steed,
   And nothing else saw all day long,
For sidelong would she bend, and sing
   A faery's song.

She found me roots of relish sweet,   25
   And honey wild, and manna dew,
And sure in language strange she said—
   "I love thee true!"

She took me to her elfin grot,
   And there she wept and sighed full sore,   30
And there I shut her wild, wild eyes
   With kisses four.

And there she lullèd me asleep,
   And there I dreamed—ah! woe betide!
The latest dream I ever dreamed   35
   On the cold hill's side.

I saw pale kings and princes too,
   Pale warriors, death-pale were they all;
They cried—"La Belle Dame sans Merci
   Hath thee in thrall!"   40

I saw their starved lips in the gloam,
   With horrid warning gapèd wide,
And I awoke and found me here,
   On the cold hill's side.

And this is why I sojourn here,   45
   Alone and palely loitering,
Though the sedge is withered from the lake
   And no birds sing.

                John Keats (1795–1821)

Thomas Rymer

True Thomas lay on Huntlie bank;
   A ferlie° he spied wi' his e'e;   a wonder
And there he saw a ladye bright
   Come riding doun by Eildon Tree.

Her skirt was o' the grass-green silk,   5
   Her mantle o' the velvet fyne;
At ilka°tett°o' her horse's mane   each lock
   Hung fifty siller bells and nine.

True Thomas he pu'd aff his cap,
   And louted° low doun on his knee: 10   bowed
"Hail to thee, Mary, Queen of Heaven!
   For thy peer on earth could never be."

"O no, O no, Thomas," she said,
   "That name does not belang to me;
I'm but the Queen o' fair Elfland,   15
   That am hither come to visit thee.

"Harp and carp,° Thomas," she said;   sing
   "Harp and carp along wi' me;
And if ye dare to kiss my lips,
   Sure of your bodie I will be."   20

"Betide me weal, betide me woe,
   That weird° shall never daunten me."   fate
Syne° he has kissed her rosy lips,   soon
   All underneath the Eildon Tree.

"Now ye maun° go wi' me," she said,   25   must
   "True Thomas, ye maun go wi' me;
And ye maun serve me seven years,
   Thro' weal or woe as may chance to be."

She's mounted on her milk-white steed,
   She's ta'en true Thomas up behind;   30
And aye, whene'er her bridle rang,
   The steed gaed° swifter than the wind.   went

O they rade on, and farther on,
   The steed gaed swifter than the wind;
Until they reached a desert wide,   35
   And living land was left behind.

"Light down, light down now, true Thomas,
    And lean your head upon my knee;
Abide ye here a little space,
    And I will show you ferlies three.   40

"O see ye not yon narrow road,
    So thick beset wi' thorns and briars?
That is the Path of Righteousness,
    Though after it but few inquires.

"And see ye not yon braid, braid° road,   45   *broad*
    That lies across the lily leven?°   *light*
That is the Path of Wickedness,
    Though some call it the Road to Heaven.

"And see ye not yon bonny road
    That winds about the fernie brae?°   50   *hill*
That is the road to fair Elfland,
    Where thou and I this night maun gae.

"But, Thomas, ye sall haud° your tongue,   *hold*
    Whatever ye may hear or see;
For speak ye word in Elfyn-land,   55
    Ye'll ne'er win back to your ain countrie."

O they rade on, and farther on,
    And they waded rivers abune° the knee;   *above*
And they saw neither sun nor moon,
    But they heard the roaring of the sea.   60

It was mirk, mirk night, there was nae starlight,
    They waded thro' red blude to the knee;
For a' the blude that's shed on the earth
    Rins° through the springs o' that countrie.   *runs*

Syne° they came to a garden green,   65   *soon*
    And she pu'd an apple frae a tree:
"Take this for thy wages, true Thomas;
    It will give thee the tongue that can never lee."°   *lie*

"My tongue is my ain,"° true Thomas he said;   *own*
    "A gudely gift ye wad gie° to me!   70   *would give*
I neither dought° to buy or sell   *am able*
    At fair or tryst° where I might be.   *market*

"I dought neither speak to prince or peer,
  Nor ask of grace from fair ladye!"
"Now haud° thy peace, Thomas," she said,   75   hold
  "For as I say, so must it be."

He has gotten a coat of the even cloth,
  And a pair o' shoon° of the velvet green;   shoes
And till seven years were gane and past,
  True Thomas on earth was never seen.   80

                                        Anonymous

The Outcast

Saint Judas

When I went out to kill myself, I caught
A pack of hoodlums beating up a man.
Running to spare his suffering, I forgot
My name, my number, how my day began,
How soldiers milled around the garden stone   5
And sang amusing songs; how all that day
Their javelins measured crowds; how I alone
Bargained the proper coins, and slipped away.

Banished from heaven, I found this victim beaten,
Stripped, kneed, and left to cry. Dropping my rope   10
Aside, I ran, ignored the uniforms:
Then I remembered bread my flesh had eaten,
The kiss that ate my flesh. Flayed without hope,
I held the man for nothing in my arms.

                                James Wright (b. 1927)

Miniver Cheevy

Miniver Cheevy, child of scorn,
  Grew lean while he assailed the seasons;
He wept that he was ever born,
  And he had reasons.

Miniver loved the days of old   5
  When swords were bright and steeds were prancing;
The vision of a warrior bold
  Would set him dancing.

Miniver sighed for what was not,
   And dreamed, and rested from his labors;   10
He dreamed of Thebes and Camelot,
   And Priam's neighbors.

Miniver mourned the ripe renown
   That made so many a name so fragrant;
He mourned Romance, now on the town,   15
   And Art, a vagrant.

Miniver loved the Medici,
   Albeit he had never seen one;
He would have sinned incessantly
   Could he have been one.   20

Miniver cursed the commonplace
   And eyed a khaki suit with loathing;
He missed the mediæval grace
   Of iron clothing.

Miniver scorned the gold he sought,   25
   But sore annoyed was he without it;
Miniver thought, and thought, and thought,
   And thought about it.

Miniver Cheevy, born too late,
   Scratched his head and kept on thinking;   30
Miniver coughed, and called it fate,
   And kept on drinking.

             Edwin Arlington Robinson (1869–1935)

The Wise Fool

Tom o' Bedlam's Song

From the hag and hungry goblin
   That into rags would rend ye,
And the spirit that stands by the naked man
   In the book of moons, defend ye,

NOTE

o' Bedlam (title): a shortening of "of Bethlehem," which refers to The
Hospital of Saint Mary in Bethlehem, a hospital for the mad in London,
from which the inmates were released in chains and permitted to beg.
The refrain song is the song Tom sang to attract attention begging.

That of your five sound senses   5
    You never be forsaken,
Nor wander from yourselves with Tom,
    Abroad to beg your bacon.
        While I do sing: Any food,
            Any feeding, drink, or clothing?   10
        Come, dame or maid, be not afraid,
            Poor Tom will injure nothing.

Of thirty bare years have I
    Twice twenty been enragèd,
And of forty been three times fifteen   15
    In durance soundly cagèd
On the lordly lofts of Bedlam,
    With stubble soft and dainty,
Brave bracelets strong, sweet whips, ding-dong,
    With wholesome hunger plenty.   20
        And now I sing: Any food,
            Any feeding, drink, or clothing?
        Come, dame or maid, be not afraid,
            Poor Tom will injure nothing.

With a thought I took for Maudlin,   25
    And a cruse of cockle pottage,
With a thing thus tall, sky bless you all,
    I befell into this dotage.
I slept not since the Conquest,
    Till then I never wakèd,   30
Till the roguish boy of love° where I lay   Cupid
    Me found and stripped me naked.
        And now I sing: Any food,
            Any feeding, drink, or clothing?
        Come, dame or maid, be not afraid,   35
            Poor Tom will injure nothing.

When I short have shorn my sour-face,
    And swigged my horny barrel,
In an oaken inn I pound my skin,
    As a suit of gilt apparel.   40
The moon's my constant mistress,
    And the lowly owl my morrow;
The flaming drake and the night-crow make
    Me music to my sorrow.

While I do sing: Any food,   45
Any feeding, drink, or clothing?
Come, dame or maid, be not afraid,
Poor Tom will injure nothing.

The palsy plagues my pulses,
When I prig° your pigs or pullen,°   50   steal, poultry
Your culvers° take, or matchless make   pigeons
Your chanticleer or sullen.
When I want provant,° with Humphrey   food
I sup, and when benighted,
I repose in Powles with waking souls,   55
Yet never am affrighted.
But I do sing: Any food,
Any feeding, drink, or clothing?
Come, dame or maid, be not afraid,
Poor Tom will injure nothing.   60

I know more than Apollo,
For oft when he lies sleeping,
I see the stars at bloody wars
In the wounded welkin° weeping,   sky
The moon embrace her shepherd,°   65   Endymion
And the queen of love° her warrior,°   Venus, Mars
While the first doth horn° the star of morn,°   cuckold, Jupiter
And the next the heavenly Farrier.°   Vulcan
While I do sing: Any food,
Any feeding, drink, or clothing?   70
Come, dame or maid, be not afraid,
Poor Tom will injure nothing.

The gipsy Snap and Pedro
Are none of Tom's comradoes.
The punk° I scorn, and the cutpurse sworn,   75   prostitute
And the roaring boys'° bravadoes.   gangs
The meek, the white, the gentle,
Me handle, touch, and spare not;
But those that cross Tom Rhinoceros
Do what the panther dare not.   80

NOTES

with Humphrey I sup (53–54): to go hungry. *Powles* (55): St. Paul's Church-yard. *The moon . . . Farrier* (65–68): Tom refers to the most bawdy versions of these myths in which Diana (the moon) has many children by Endymion and Venus is unfaithful to Vulcan with Mars.

Although I sing: Any food,
    Any feeding, drink, or clothing?
Come, dame or maid, be not afraid,
    Poor Tom will injure nothing.

With an host of furious fancies   85
    Whereof I am commander,
With a burning spear and a horse of air
    To the wilderness I wander.
By a knight of ghosts and shadows
    I summoned am to tourney   90
Ten leagues beyond the wide world's end,
    Methinks it is no journey.
Yet will I sing: Any food,
    Any feeding, drink, or clothing?
Come, dame or maid, be not afraid,   95
    Poor Tom will injure nothing.

                    Anonymous (17th century)

Crazy Jane Talks with the Bishop

I met the Bishop on the road
And much said he and I.
'Those breasts are flat and fallen now,
Those veins must soon be dry;
Live in a heavenly mansion,   5
Not in some foul sty.'

'Fair and foul are near of kin,
And fair needs foul,' I cried.
'My friends are gone, but that's a truth
Nor grave nor bed denied,   10
Learned in bodily lowliness
And in the heart's pride.

'A woman can be proud and stiff
When on love intent;
But Love has pitched his mansion in   15
The place of excrement;
For nothing can be sole or whole
That has not been rent.'

                    William Butler Yeats (1865–1939)

Poems with Archetypal Imagery

To Spring

O thou with dewy locks, who lookest down
Thro' the clear windows of the morning, turn
Thine angel eyes upon our western isle,
Which in full choir hails thy approach, O Spring!

The hills tell each other, and the list'ning   5
Valleys hear; all our longing eyes are turned
Up to thy bright pavilions: issue forth,
And let thy holy feet visit our clime.

Come o'er the eastern hills, and let our winds
Kiss thy perfumed garments; let us taste   10
Thy morn and evening breath; scatter thy pearls
Upon our love-sick land that mourns for thee.

O deck her forth with thy fair fingers; pour
Thy soft kisses on her bosom; and put
Thy golden crown upon her languish'd head,   15
Whose modest tresses were bound up for thee!

William Blake (1757–1827)

Sonnet: The world is too much with us

The world is too much with us; late and soon,
Getting and spending, we lay waste our powers:
Little we see in Nature that is ours;
We have given our hearts away, a sordid boon!
The Sea that bares her bosom to the moon;   5
The winds that will be howling at all hours,
And are up-gathered now like sleeping flowers;
For this, for everything, we are out of tune;
It moved us not.—Great God! I'd rather be
A Pagan suckled in a creed outworn;   10
So might I, standing on this pleasant lea,
Have glimpses that would make me less forlorn;
Have sight of Proteus rising from the sea;
Or hear old Triton blow his wreathèd horn.

William Wordsworth (1770–1850)

Snake

A snake came to my water-trough
On a hot, hot day, and I in pyjamas for the heat,
To drink there.

In the deep, strange-scented shade of the great dark carob-
    tree
I came down the steps with my pitcher   5
And must wait, must stand and wait, for there he was at
    the trough before me.

He reached down from a fissure in the earth-wall in the
    gloom
And trailed his yellow-brown slackness soft-bellied down,
    over the edge of the stone trough
And rested his throat upon the stone bottom,
And where the water had dripped from the tap, in a small
    clearness,   10
He sipped with his straight mouth,
Softly drank through his straight gums, into his slack long
    body,
Silently.

Someone was before me at my water-trough,
And I, like a second comer, waiting.   15

He lifted his head from his drinking, as cattle do,
And looked at me vaguely, as drinking cattle do,
And flickered his two-forked tongue from his lips, and
    mused a moment,
And stooped and drank a little more,
Being earth-brown, earth-golden from the burning bowels
    of the earth   20
On the day of Sicilian July, with Etna smoking.

The voice of my education said to me
He must be killed,
For in Sicily the black, black snakes are innocent, the gold
    are venomous.

And voices in me said, If you were a man   25
You would take a stick and break him now, and finish
    him off.

But must I confess how I liked him,
How glad I was he had come like a guest in quiet, to drink
    at my water-trough
And depart peaceful, pacified, and thankless,
Into the burning bowels of this earth?   30

Was it cowardice, that I dared not kill him?
Was it perversity, that I longed to talk to him?
Was it humility, to feel so honoured?
I felt so honoured.

And yet those voices: 35
If you were not afraid, you would kill him!

And truly I was afraid, I was most afraid,
But even so, honoured still more
That he should seek my hospitality
From out the dark door of the secret earth.   40

He drank enough
And lifted his head, dreamily, as one who has drunken,
And flickered his tongue like a forked night on the air, so
    black;
Seeming to lick his lips,
And looked around like a god, unseeing, into the air,   45
And slowly turned his head,
And slowly, very slowly, as if thrice adream,
Proceeded to draw his slow length curving round
And climb again the broken bank of my wall-face.

And as he put his head into that dreadful hole,   50
And as he slowly drew up, snake-easing his shoulders, and
    entered farther,
A sort of horror, a sort of protest against his withdrawing
    into that horrid black hole,
Deliberately going into the blackness, and slowly drawing
    himself after,
Overcame me now his back was turned.

I looked round, I put down my pitcher,   55
I picked up a clumsy log
And threw it at the water-trough with a clatter.

I think it did not hit him,
But suddenly that part of him that was left behind con-
    vulsed in undignified haste,

Writhed like lightning, and was gone   60
Into the black hole, the earth-lipped fissure in the wall-
    front,
At which, in the intense still noon, I stared with fascination.

And immediately I regretted it.
I thought how paltry, how vulgar, what a mean act!
I despised myself and the voices of my accursed human
    education.   65

And I thought of the albatross,
And I wished he would come back, my snake.

For he seemed to me again like a king,
Like a king in exile, uncrowned in the underworld,
Now due to be crowned again.   70

And so, I missed my chance with one of the lords
Of life.
And I have something to expiate;
A pettiness.

D. H. Lawrence (1885–1930)

Charges

I have begged the bin of wheat
keep the flour sweet,
and the wines that, when he drinks,
not catch sharply at his throat.
And wheat and wine that heard me   5
moved, as he that moving swears . . .

I have shouted to the black bear from the rock,
he that we have named the fortune-less,
that, if he climb up on the crag,
not any beast may rend, not any.   10
And the black bear promised me
with his back no sun nor moon has borne . . .

I have left word to the crispèd ear
of the thorn, which is a poisoner,
that if she sting, she may not kill him,   15
even if her blossom be full-blown.
And the thorn, all understanding,
moved, swearing my oath, swearing . . .

And I have made this charge upon the river,
which is bad water, as for conjuring,   20
that it know and never drown him,
should he cross the very river-mouth.
And in a gesture live with spume
the bad river swears it to me . . .

I'm all entranced in showing him   25
to the beings, one by one,
and I'm laughed at by the women
when I take the babe out of his cradle,
even though they live by wind and rainstorm,
the pomegranate and the olive.   30

When we're safely back again
in our darkling nutshell house,
I begin my prayer to the world,
as one that nags and hastens it,
that the world, like a mother,   35
may be maddened with my madness,
and take him in its arms and lift him,
this little child my waist has carried!

Gabriela Mistral (1889–1957)
translated by James Graham-Luján

Hail, Dionysos

Hail, Dionysos,
god of frenzy and release, of trance and visions,
hail to the manifestations of your might,
thanks for admittting me to your ritual.

Inspirer of divine speech: 5
    da da da da da da da da da;
releaser of subterranean energies;
    a man lies snoring on the sofa;
giver of fierce grace:
    a girl staggers among chairs, reels against the wall;   10
endower with new sensations and powers:
    a man vomits on the rug—an aromatic painting,
    and a girl, a lovely creature,
    wets her panties.

Hail, Dionysos,   15
god of frenzy and release, of trance and visions.
I see them recede,
handsome men, beautiful women,
brains clever and bright, spirits gay and daring,
see eyes turned glassy, tongues grow thick,   20
limbs tremble and shake,
caught in your divine power,
carried away on the stream of your might,
Dionysos.

Dudley Randall (b. 1914)

The Force That Through the Green Fuse Drives the Flower

The force that through the green fuse drives the flower
Drives my green age; that blasts the roots of trees
Is my destroyer.
And I am dumb to tell the crooked rose
My youth is bent by the same wintry fever.   5

The force that drives the water through the rocks
Drives my red blood; that dries the mouthing streams
Turns mine to wax.
And I am dumb to mouth unto my veins
How at the mountain spring the same mouth sucks.   10

The hand that whirls the water in the pool
Stirs the quicksand; that ropes the blowing wind
Hauls my shroud sail.
And I am dumb to tell the hanging man
How of my clay is made the hangman's lime.   15

The lips of time leech to the fountain head;
Love drips and gathers, but the fallen blood
Shall calm her sores.
And I am dumb to tell a weather's wind
How time has ticked a heaven round the stars.   20

And I am dumb to tell the lover's tomb
How at my sheet goes the same crooked worm.

Dylan Thomas (1914–1953)

4 Sound

Both the nursery rhyme "Mary had a little lamb . . ." and the mnemonic device "Thirty days have September . . ." have certain pleasing qualities of sound, but neither of them is in any sense poetry. So too, a radio or television commercial may have fascinating sound, but we would rarely or never be tempted to call one a poem: all are merely attractive sound. It is clear that the sound quality alone is not the element that makes a poem a poem. In a few exceptional instances, such as some of the poems of Edgar Allan Poe, the sound may be the most important poetic element, but in most poems sound is simply one of several important elements.

Although far back in history, in the time of the scops and bards, poetry was probably most commonly read or recited aloud, today it is most often read silently. But even when the sound is not heard by the sensory ear, it is being heard by the "mind's ear." All forms of literature utilize to greater or lesser degrees many of the features of poetry, such as imagery, figures, rhetorical devices, tone, and feeling; but poetry is unique among them in its concern for the sound of a word, of a phrase, of a line, of a stanza, of a whole poem. In prose we are ordinarily concerned with what the words, sentences, paragraphs are saying to us; in poetry it is this and more—both what is being said and the very sound of the saying of it.

Because the medium of poetry is language, we get from a poem not only images, ideas, feelings, experiences, but also auditory perception of its sound. Since sound is wholly the medium of music and partially the medium of poetry, there are resemblances. Analogous to the control of tones, singularly or in combination, in the melody and harmony in music, is the poet's control of consonant and vowel sounds; both the musical composer and the poet deal also in rhythms.

71

Melody and Harmony in Poetry

Analyzing how we react to the sounds of our native language is difficult because we cannot react to sounds in isolation from meaning, though we may think we can. In one study, people who did not know English selected "cellar door" as the most attractive sound from a list that included the word "beautiful." English-speaking people, however, cannot dissociate the image of a cellar door from the sound. We do find some sounds intrinsically harsh and ugly and others attractive, and poets do use these responses but only to reinforce ideas and the effect of imagery.

Listen to the first two lines of Wilfred Owen's "Dulce et Decorum Est" (p. 290):

Bent double, like old beggars under sacks,
Knock-kneed, coughing like hags, we cursed through sludge . . .

The experience of hearing these lines consists not only in receiving the ugly and uncomfortable images, but also in hearing the harsh sound. The harshness is due largely to the dominance of a certain class of consonant sounds frequently in prominent positions: the *b*'s at the beginning of "bent" and "beggar," reinforced by the less obvious *b* in "double"; the *k* sounds at the beginning of "coughing" and "cursed," anticipated and reinforced by the same sound in "sacks," at the end of "knock," and in "like"; and others as well.

· Just as the person who claims that he does not know one musical note may nevertheless enjoy music, so the reader of poetry who knows nothing about the phonetic elements of language may nevertheless enjoy the sounds of poetry; but the music listener who has some knowledge of music will derive a deeper enjoyment from it, and the poetry reader who knows at least something of phonetics will enjoy more fully the poems he reads.

"Kubla Khan" is not a whole poem but only a fragment of one never completed. According to the poet himself, Samuel Taylor Coleridge, he set it down without effort upon awaking from a drug-induced sleep but could not recapture the rest of it after he was interrupted. He spoke of it rather as "a psychological curiosity" than as something to be considered as "of any supposed *poetic* merits"; but scholars and other readers, sometimes incredulous of his own account of its composition, have consistently recognized the high poetic merit of its imagery, its tone, and particularly its musical quality.

Kubla Khan

In Xanadu did Kubla Khan
A stately pleasure-dome decree:
Where Alph, the sacred river, ran
Through caverns measureless to man
   Down to a sunless sea.   5

So twice five miles of fertile ground
With walls and towers were girdled round:
And there were gardens bright with sinuous rills,
Where blossomed many an incense-bearing tree;
And here were forests ancient as the hills,   10
Enfolding sunny spots of greenery.

But oh! that deep romantic chasm which slanted
Down the green hill athwart a cedarn cover!
A savage place! as holy and enchanted
As e'er beneath a waning moon was haunted   15
By woman wailing for her demon-lover!
And from this chasm, with ceaseless turmoil seething,
As if this earth in fast thick pants were breathing,
A mighty fountain momently was forced:
Amid whose swift half-intermitted burst   20
Huge fragments vaulted like rebounding hail,
Or chaffy grain beneath the thresher's flail:
And 'mid these dancing rocks at once and ever
It flung up momently the sacred river.
Five miles meandering with a mazy motion   25
Through wood and dale the sacred river ran,
Then reached the caverns measureless to man,
And sank in tumult to a lifeless ocean:
And 'mid this tumult Kubla heard from far
Ancestral voices prophesying war!   30
   The shadow of the dome of pleasure
   Floated midway on the waves;
   Where was heard the mingled measure
   From the fountain and the caves.
It was a miracle of rare device,   35
A sunny pleasure-dome with caves of ice!

A damsel with a dulcimer
In a vision once I saw:
It was an Abyssinian maid,
And on her dulcimer she played,   40
Singing of Mount Abora.
Could I revive within me
Her symphony and song,
To such a deep delight 'twould win me,
That with music loud and long,   45
I would build that dome in air,
That sunny dome! those caves of ice!
And all who heard should see them there,
And all should cry, Beware! Beware!
His flashing eyes, his floating hair!   50
Weave a circle round him thrice,
And close your eyes with holy dread,
For he on honey-dew hath fed,
And drunk the milk of Paradise.

Samuel Taylor Coleridge (1772–1834)

Consonant Sounds

Plosive Consonants. Of the various complicated classifications to which consonant sounds may be subjected, two, at opposite extremes, are particularly notable to the ear. The first of these is "plosives" (or "stops"): *p, b, t, d, k, g.* These six sounds are called plosives because the sound comes forth literally as an explosion: to pronounce any one of them, we put our vocal apparatus into the right position while holding our breath, and the sound explodes when we release our breath.

The plosives are the shortest of all the consonant sounds: they are sudden, abrupt, staccato. Listen to the old tongue-twister: "Peter Piper picked a peck of pickled peppers." The staccato effect is due not only to the obvious *p*'s but to the fact that almost all of the consonant sounds are plosives—PeTer PiPer PiKKeD a PeKK of PiKKleD PePPers—and is enhanced by the shortness of the vowels in "pIcked," "pEck," "pIckled," and "pEppers."

Listen once more to the opening lines of "Dulce et Decorum Est," and to the other plosive sounds that reinforce those that we have already mentioned:

BenT DouBle, liKe olD BeGGars unDer saKKs,
knoKK-kneeD, Koughing liKe haGs, we KurseD through sluDge.

The effect of the numerous plosives, which was comic in "Peter Piper," is harsh and ugly here.

Liquid Consonants. The opposite extreme among the classes of consonant sound is what are popularly called "liquids": *l, m, n,* and *r.* Of these the middle two are really nasal sounds, but for the purposes of the music of poetry all four of them are considered liquid, smooth-flowing. Think of the many feminine names that are notably liquid: Mary, Marie, Laura, Lillian, Nora, Norma, etc. Consider masculine nicknames in relation to the names: Bob for Robert, Chuck for Charles, Jack for John, Hank for Henry, Bill for William, Tony for Anthony—each one exhibiting a plosive replacing a liquid or other soft sound.

The slow-moving, soft, smooth effect of liquids is heard in lines 25–26 of "Kubla Khan":

five miLes MeaNdeRiNg with a Mazy MotioN
thRough wood aNd daLe the sacRed RiveR RaN.

Nor is it just the prominence of the liquids (which outnumber the plosives three to one) that creates the effect; most of the other consonant sounds are also soft, and except for the few *d* and *k* sounds, there are no plosives. The muted sensation of the languid river is conveyed by both the sense and the sound of the lines.

Other Consonant Sounds. Between the extremes of the plosives and the liquids are a number of other consonant sounds that poets also utilize in their creation of the music of poetry. None of these has as much distinctive power to catch the listener's ear as the plosives, which are uniquely abrupt, and the liquids, which create soft, mellifluous effects. Yet each of these intermediate classes of consonant sounds can produce striking effects. Note, for example, the numerous initial *w* and *h* sounds in lines 14–16 of "Kubla Khan":

A savage place! as holy and enchanted
As e'er beneath a waning moon was haunted
By woman wailing for her demon-lover!

Vowel Sounds

Just as important to the poet in his quest for musical phrasing as consonant sounds is his management of the vowel sounds. Although the language has only five vowel letters (or six, if *y* is included), it has many, many vowel sounds; analysis of these sounds for our purposes must therefore be greatly oversimplified.

The five words *big, beg, bag, bog, bug* illustrate the five so-called short vowels, arranged in a certain progression. It is unnatural to try to give any duration to short *i*, which is inherently a very short, high-pitched sound; we have already noted how the short *i* and *e* sounds enhance the staccato effect in ". . . picked a peck of pickled peppers." The so-called long vowels are illustrated in the five words *mite, meet, mate, moat, mute.* In addition to all of these, there are many other vowel sounds in English, including what is probably the lowest, longest, most reverberating and melodious of them all, the *u* or *oo* sound in "tune": thus the frequent rhymes of *tune, croon, June, moon* in the moody lyrics of the songwriters of the Bing Crosby era and earlier.

Alliteration and Assonance

Alliteration is the occurrence of the same initial consonant sound in two or more words or, more significantly, two or more accented syllables, as in "in xanaDu Did kubla khan / a stately pleasure-Dome Decree," or in "in xanadu did Kubla Khan / a stately pleasure-dome deKree."[1]

Assonance is the correspondence or similarity of vowel sounds, as in the long *i* sounds of line 6 of "Kubla Khan": "So twIce fIve mIles of fertile ground."

Rhyme

Rhyme is the repetition of the end sounds of lines ("end rhyme") or, less commonly, of the end sound of the first half of a line with the end sound of the line ("internal rhyme"). In a normal rhyme the repetition of sound extends from the last accented vowel to the end

---

[1] The term "consonance," less commonly used, means to some writers any correspondence of consonant sounds, and to others it means the correspondence of terminal consonant sounds.

(with the implication that the sound preceding the last accented vowel is different): def*end,* compreh*end.*

In masculine rhyme, which is the more common, the vowel of the last syllable is accented, so that the rhyme is confined to that vowel and the consonant sounds, if any, that follow it. In feminine rhyme, which is less common, the vowel of the last syllable is not accented, so that the rhyme begins in a preceding syllable and includes the last accented vowel and all sounds that follow. Because feminine rhyme consists of larger units and occurs less frequently, it is usually more noticeable.

Any scheme of end rhymes is conventionally designated by letters of the alphabet. We say that a quatrain (a four-line stanza) is rhymed *xaxa* (*x* designating an unrhymed line) to indicate that the second and fourth lines rhyme; or we say that another quatrain is rhymed *abab* to indicate that the first and third lines also rhyme with one another.

Song: The splendor falls

The splendor falls on castle walls
   And snowy summits old in story;
The long light shakes across the lakes,
   And the wild cataract leaps in glory.
Blow, bugle, blow, set the wild echoes flying,   5
Blow, bugle; answer, echoes, dying, dying, dying.

O, hark, O, hear! how thin and clear,
   And thinner, clearer, farther going!
O, sweet and far from cliff and scar
   The horns of Elfland faintly blowing!   10
Blow, let us hear the purple glens replying,
Blow, bugle; answer, echoes, dying, dying, dying.

O love, they die in yon rich sky,
   They faint on hill or field or river;
Our echoes roll from soul to soul,   15
   And grow for ever and for ever.
Blow, bugle, blow, set the wild echoes flying,
And answer, echoes, answer, dying, dying, dying.

      Alfred, Lord Tennyson (1809–1892)

The rhyme scheme of each of the three stanzas of "The Splendor Falls" is *xaxabb*, and all of the end rhymes are feminine (in lines 14–16 the rhyme of "river" and "ever" is imperfect); in each of the lines that lack end rhyme, the first and third lines of each stanza, there is masculine internal rhyme.

We cannot know just how much of poets' musical effects are due to conscious, deliberate effort, with or without systematic knowledge of phonetics, and how much of the music is simply the result of their instinctive ear for sound. For example, lines 6–7 of "Kubla Khan" display an extraordinary rhyming effect:

| So twice five miles of | f/er/ t/ile/ g/ r/ound |
| With walls and towers were | g/ ir/d/l /ed/ r/ound |

Since the last syllable in each of these lines is accented, the "normal" masculine rhyme would call for the correspondence of sound to extend back only to the last vowel sound, *-ound*. But the correspondence of sound—similar although not identical—begins with the *-er* and *-ir*, followed by the closely related dental sounds *t* and *d*, then the *l* sound, then plosives, then the *r* sound, and finally the normal rhyme. Whether or not Coleridge created this effect consciously and whether or not the listener recognizes it for what it is, it is undoubtedly an element in the music that the listener hears, even if subconsciously.

Since the mid-nineteenth century, various poets have experimented with many kinds of approximate rhyme or off-rhyme—deliberate alterations in the expected exact repetition of end sounds. One of the earliest of these was Emily Dickinson, who had a general disdain for convention and whose off-rhymes sometimes seem more careless than deliberate. But in her "If I shouldn't be alive," off-rhyme is essential to the total effect of the poem.

If I shouldn't be alive
When the Robins come,
Give the one in Red Cravat,
A Memorial crumb.

If I couldn't thank you,   5
Being fast asleep,
You will know I'm trying
With my Granite lip!

Emily Dickinson (1830–1886)

The normal rhyme of "come" and "crumb" in the second and fourth lines of the first stanza produces the expectation of normal rhyme in the second and fourth lines of the second stanza; but our expectation that the last sound of the poem will repeat the "-eep" of "asleep" is only disappointingly fulfilled when the poem concludes with ". . . Granite lip!"—a wry, flat note that seems appropriate to the wryness of the idea.

Rhythm in Poetry

Rhythm is everywhere about us. Only in a silent, motionless existence would it be absent. We speak of the rhythm of the stars, of the seasons, of a machine, of a person's gait, of a swimmer, of a dog's snoring, of a dance, of music.

The resemblance between poetry and music, as sound, exists not only in the melody and harmony derived from the skillful interweaving of the consonant and vowel sounds (like the individual notes and harmonies of music), but in the rhythm as well. Rhythm is a recurrence of stress that creates a pattern of expectation and satisfaction. This recurrence, or beat, heightens our response both emotionally and intellectually.

A beat may occur in some prose as well as in poetry. Although an evident rhythm may be a distraction in most prose, rhythm of some kind is necessary in poetry. What draws attention to the rhythm is the *line*. Arranging a piece of prose into poetic lines will focus attention on any rhythm there may be in the prose.

No man is an island, entire of itself;
every man is a piece of the continent,
a part of the main.
If a clod be washed away by the sea,
Europe is the less,
as well as if a promontory were,
as well as if a manor of thy friend's
or of thine own were.
Any man's death diminishes me
because I am involved in mankind,
and therefore never send to know for whom the bell tolls;
it tolls for thee.

John Donne, *Meditation XVII*

> The sailors were all in amazement,
> and asked me a thousand questions,
> which I had no inclination to answer.
>
> Jonathan Swift, *Gulliver's Travels*

The great rhythmic quality of Donne's prose becomes evident in the arrangement into poetic lines. The line-breaks increase our awareness of the rhythmic units and that awareness of the proper stress increases the impact of the sense. In the Swift passage, even though the grammatical and line units are of more nearly equal length, the arrangement discloses little that it interesting rhythmically and nothing that enhances the sense. This function of rhythm to enhance sense is an essential quality of poetry.

The Metrical Line and Natural Speech

From the late Middle Ages until at least the middle of the nineteenth century, rhythm in English poetry was based on traditional "metrical" patterns of accented and unaccented syllables in the line, and frequently still is. In poetry as in music accents may be of varying intensity, and other factors in the rhythm include pitch, duration of syllables, and pause. The chief kinds of meter are four: two of them called "rising" meters because they move toward accents and two of them called "falling" meters because they fall from accents.[2] A "foot," or single unit, of each of these four meters is as follows:

		Rising		Falling	
Two-syllable foot	Iamb	(àt hóme)	Trochee	(hómelỳ)	
Three-syllable foot	Anapest	(ìn thĕ hóme)	Dactyl	(hómelìnèss)	

The number of feet or units in a line is designated as follows:

Monometer	One foot
Dimeter	Two feet
Trimeter	Three feet
Tetrameter	Four feet
Pentameter	Five feet
Hexameter	Six feet
Heptameter	Seven feet

---

[2] Numerous other kinds of feet can be identified, such as the amphibrach (x ⁄ x), the spondee (⁄ ⁄), and the pyrrhic (x x), but these are used chiefly as isolated substitutions in the dominant meter of a poem.

Iambic meter is by far the most common in English. Our normal English speech cadences tend to move toward accents: notice, for example, our very common use of unaccented articles before nouns, of the unaccented "to" to begin infinitives, of our unaccented monosyllabic prepositions to begin prepositional phrases. Although poets have sometimes made the dominant meter of a poem something other than iambic,[3] they more commonly utilize other metrical feet as substitutions for iambs in basically iambic poems—to provide the variations that are intrinsic to the natural rhythm of the language.

Variety is obtained both through the use of these substituted feet and more importantly through the interplay of the stress of normal speech with the accent of the meter. Spoken without attention to the iambic meter, two stresses dominate the four accents of "The splendor fálls on castle wálls," and this is the right way to read the line. To read the four accents evenly would be to level out the variety that is part of its conception.

The most common line lengths are pentameters and tetrameters, and in metrical poetry attention is focused on the line where, although the number of accents is regular, the degree of accent is relative to the stress imposed by natural speech. Reading a pentameter line as natural speech will increase the stress on accents that coincide with natural speech stresses and decrease the force of the remaining accents. But no matter how much one may ignore the pentameter, reducing the five accents to three or four stresses to produce a natural reading, the pentameter is still there regulating the pace of the line. To prove how strong our sense of the line is, one need only try to move the final syllable of a pentameter line to the next line. This sense of the line exists even though not all readers agree on how to mark the accents, the sense stresses, and the pauses.

For discussion, the following two lines by Wordsworth have been marked to show the accented and the unaccented syllables and the feet divisions:

$$\overset{x}{T}\text{he w\'orld} \mid \overset{x}{\text{is}} \text{t\'oo} \mid \overset{x}{\text{much}} \text{w\'ith} \mid \overset{x}{\text{us; l\'ate}} \mid \overset{x}{\text{and s\'oon,}}$$

$$\text{G\'etting} \mid \overset{x}{\text{and}} \text{sp\'end} \mid \overset{x}{\text{ing, we}} \mid \text{l\'ay w\'aste} \mid \overset{x}{\text{our p\'owers.}}$$

[3] The dominant meter of George Gordon, Lord Byron's "The Destruction of Sennacherib" (see end of chapter) is anapestic; the dominant meter of Edgar Allan Poe's "The Raven" (not in this book) is trochaic; the dominant meter of Henry Wadsworth Longfellow's "Evangeline" (not in this book) is dactylic—dactylic hexameters in imitation of the Roman poet Virgil's epic *Aeneid*.

The first line establishes the basic iambic pentameter, which is varied in the second line by three substituted feet: a trochee, a pyrrhic, and a spondee. The natural speech stresses will appear if we rearrange the lines as prose:

The wórld is too much wíth us; láte and soón, gétting and spénd-

ing, we lay wáste our pówers.

A natural reading of the prose version of the first line results in only four stresses, which break the monotonous effect of the regular iambic pentameter, even though our sense of it is not lost. The second line, not likely to seem monotonous because of the frequency of substituted feet, retains the sense of the iambic pentameter both because an expectation of it has been established and because the end of the line fulfils that expectation.

Pauses, both within the line and at the end, are our means of getting the sense right. Read any lines of poetry or prose aloud and you will discover that the sign of your getting the sense right will be that you paused at the right places. These pauses will come at the end of sense units and, as illustrated by the lines from John Donne, mark the natural rhythmic units as well. When the sense units coincide with the line units, the lines are called "end-stopped." When the sense runs on, without punctuation or the completion of a grammatical unit, to the next line, the line is called "run-on." The run-on line keeps the rhythm and sense in motion, varying the pace when the general pattern is end-stopped. Varied with run-on lines, the end-stopped line provides emphasis and closes one unit of a poem's development and thought. Sense pauses within lines are called *caesuras*.

The discipline of the iambic pentameter line has been employed to enhance the memorable quality of many frequently quoted end-stopped lines.

To err is human; to forgive divine.

Alexander Pope

Uneasy lies the head that wears a crown.

William Shakespeare

Its flexibility, less often observed than its discipline, is better illustrated in a longer passage of blank verse where the flow of the rhythm is regulated by the speech pauses occurring variously within and at the end of some lines.

Blank Verse. The metrical line is the basis for blank verse, which consists of an indefinite succession of unrhymed iambic pentameters. Blank verse is called "blank" because it does not employ rhymes; the term is to be distinguished from free verse, which is called "free" because it is free of meter. Blank verse is intrinsically dignified and natural and can be extended indefinitely without monotony. The great variety of characters in Shakespeare's plays who speak in blank verse attests to its adaptability to natural and dramatic speech rhythms.

The following excerpt from Wordsworth's "Lines Composed a Few Miles Above Tintern Abbey" illustrates the natural, unforced effect of the metrical line in blank verse. The speaker meditates on the effect that a country scene near Tintern Abbey has on him.

> These beauteous forms,
> Through a long absence, have not been to me
> As is a landscape to a blind man's eye:
> But oft, in lonely rooms, and 'mid the din
> Of towns and cities, I have owed to them,   5
> In hours of weariness, sensations sweet,
> Felt in the blood, and felt along the heart;
> And passing even into my purer mind,
> With tranquil restoration:—feelings too
> Of unremembered pleasure: such, perhaps,   10
> As have no slight or trivial influence
> On that best portion of a good man's life,
> His little, nameless, unremembered, acts
> Of kindness and of love.

Observe how natural phrasing dominates the meter, how naturally the pauses occur, sometimes at the end of lines and sometimes internally, and how even though we lose the sense of di DUM, di DUM, di DUM, the iambic pentameter is still effective in controlling the pace of the meditative tone.

The Musical Phrase and Natural Speech

A phrase, quite apart from its grammatical definition, is an auditory experience of a series of sounds that take a certain time, tone, and accent to pronounce and hear. A phrase can be musical, can be an engaging auditory experience without being merely pretty sound. It can catch our attention with the sound values of stress, duration, and pause, and the interplay of vowel and consonant sounds. Heard, as music is heard, a phrase can seem monotonous, be pleasantly melodious or harsh, seem restful or exciting, dignified, dull, playful, strident, or blue. What matters to poets is that they catch the appropriate sound so that they can work with the contrast and interplay between the musical phrase and the sound of natural speech. Natural speech sounds that seem realistic to the reader are not necessarily musical at all, but they are the basis for the dramatic quality of the speaker's tone.

Tennyson's line "The splendor falls on castle walls" conveys its image in a rhythm that to some may seem excessively metrical, with internal rhyme and vowel and liquid sounds that may seem to qualify as too musical, but it is nonetheless as musical sound that we are first attracted to it. The opening of Suckling's "The Constant Lover"—"Out upon it! I have loved/ Three whole days together!"—is in striking contrast. The iambic is lost, the melody is gone, and the sound is engaging entirely as dramatic natural speech. In "The Constant Lover" this sound, apart from the sense, engages us for the variety, the harsh energy of the first phrase, and the slow length of "Three whole days." But the sense cannot be left out; the reason for the effectiveness of the sound is its appropriateness to the speaker and his attitude.

Free Verse. The examples in the previous paragraph are from the metrical tradition. The free verse tradition, only about a century old, freed the sound of the poem from metrical restraint so that the interplay of the musical phrase with natural speech could control the rhythm. This interplay is illustrated in these lines from Wallace Stevens' "Thirteen Ways of Looking at a Blackbird" (page 39).

> The blackbird whirled in the autumn winds.
> It was a small part of the pantomime.

Free verse is a rhythmic technique, not a declaration of freedom from rhythm. It characteristically employs a great variety of cadences and the interplay of variable measures no longer defined as the foot is in terms of fixed numbers of accented and unaccented syllables. When prose rhythm is highly organized as it is in the prose passage by John Donne (put into poetic lines to show its organization), we can see the basis of free verse in measure and cadence.

E. E. Cummings used the very appearance of the poem—the typography—to show visually the auditory measures he had in his ear—and to suggest the cadence at which they should be read. Most free verse poets use the line and the caesura to indicate visually the measure and cadence built into their phrasing. "Rhythm is form cut into time," Ezra Pound said, and the rhythm must be in the language of the poem before the line will aid the reader visually to hear it.

Buffalo Bill's

Buffalo Bill's
defunct
    who used to
    ride a watersmooth-silver
                stallion   5
and break onetwothreefourfive pigeonsjustlikethat
                             Jesus

he was a handsome man
                and what i want to know is
how do you like your blueeyed boy   10
Mister Death

                      e. e cummings (1894–1962)

It is not easier for a poet to compose good free verse than metrical verse, for lacking the discipline of meter, he must certainly have an ear for measure and cadence. Nor is the poet who writes metrical verse assured that his work will be rhythmically successful, for all of our most successful metrists have also had an ear for natural and musical phrasing.

Onomatopoeia

Onomatopoeia is the use of words whose sounds resemble their meanings. In the strictest sense, therefore, only those words which designate certain sounds could be considered onomatopoetic, such as "bark," "hiss," "murmur," "shriek." But in a larger sense onomatopoeia exists not just in individual words, but in larger units, even as large as a whole poem, and not just in words that designate sounds, but in the more intangible support that sound gives to sense and mood.

Onomatopoeia, wedding sense and sound, exists in many passages already referred to: the harshness, ugliness, and discomfort of the

opening lines of Owen's "Dulce et Decorum Est"; the exotic quality
in Coleridge's "Kubla Khan"; and the wryness of the concluding
off-rhymed "Granite lip" in Dickinson's "If I shouldn't be alive."

The Dance

In Breughel's great picture, The Kermess,
the dancers go round, they go round and
around, the squeal and the blare and the
tweedle of bagpipes, a bugle and fiddles
tipping their bellies (round as the thick-   5
sided glasses whose wash they impound)
their hips and their bellies off balance
to turn them. Kicking and rolling about
the Fair Grounds, swinging their butts, those
shanks must be sound to bear up under such   10
rollicking measures, prance as they dance
in Breughel's great picture, The Kermess.

William Carlos Williams (1883–1963)

NOTES AND QUESTIONS

1. *Breughel* (1): sixteenth century Flemish painter. *The Kermess* (1):
   an annual festival in the Low Countries; the dancing of the folk
   at the festival. Even if you have never seen Breughel's painting,
   what kind of dancing do you think is portrayed in it? Is your
   impression of the dancing due solely to the images that Williams
   evokes or is it conveyed also by the very sound of the poem?
2. "The Dance," a modern poem, does not have a regular metrical
   line; yet its rhythm depends upon the dominance of a meter.
   Whether that meter is anapestic or dactylic may be argued, but
   most of the feet consist clearly of three syllables. How does this
   rhythm enhance the onomatopoeia?
3. Find instances of alliteration; of assonance; of internal rhyme.
   What effect is created by the lack of sense pauses at the ends of
   lines? By the lack of end-rhyme? How are all of these related to
   the onomatopoeia?

Chronological Arrangement

Sonnet: Since there's no help

Since there's no help, come let us kiss and part;
Nay, I have done, you get no more of me,
And I am glad, yea glad with all my heart
That thus so cleanly I myself can free;
Shake hands forever, cancel all our vows,   5
And when we meet at any time again,
Be it not seen in either of our brows
That we one jot of former love retain.
Now at the last gasp of love's latest breath,
When, his pulse failing, passion speechless lies,   10
When faith is kneeling by his bed of death,
And innocence is closing up his eyes,
Now if thou wouldst, when all have given him over,
From death to life thou mightst him yet recover.

Michael Drayton (1563–1631)

QUESTIONS

1. What is the dominant meter of the poem? Identify the feet in the poem in which stress occurs differently from what the dominant meter leads you to expect.
2. Taking into account that pronunciations change through the years, that sometimes a rhyme may be more evident to the eye than to the ear, and that a poet may knowingly use off-rhyme (although seldom at so early a date as this), determine the rhyme scheme.
3. Most of the rhymes are masculine. Which are feminine? Why are the feminine rhymes particularly effective at the point where they occur?

Song: Drink to me only

Drink to me only with thine eyes,
   And I will pledge with mine;
Or leave a kiss but in the cup
   And I'll not ask for wine.
The thirst that from the soul doth rise   5
   Doth ask a drink divine;
But might I of Jove's nectar sup,
   I would not change for thine.

I sent thee late a rosy wreath,
   Not so much honoring thee   10
As giving it a hope that there
   It could not withered be.
But thou thereon didst only breathe,
   And sent'st it back to me;
Since when it grows, and smells, I swear,   15
   Not of itself, but thee.

Ben Jonson (1573?–1637)

A Song for Saint Cecilia's Day

November 22, 1687

I

From harmony, from heavenly harmony
   This universal frame began:
   When Nature underneath a heap
     Of jarring atoms lay
   And could not heave her head,   5
The tuneful voice was heard from high:
   "Arise, ye more than dead."
Then cold and hot and moist and dry
   In order to their stations leap,
    And Music's power obey.   10
From harmony, from heavenly harmony
   This universal frame began:
   From harmony to harmony
Through all the compass of the notes it ran,
The diapason closing full in man.   15

II

What passion cannot Music raise and quell?
   When Jubal struck the corded shell
   His listening brethren stood around,
    And, wondering, on their faces fell
   To worship that celestial sound.   20
Less than a god they thought there could not dwell
   Within the hollow of that shell,
   That spoke so sweetly, and so well.
What passion cannot Music raise and quell?

III

The Trumpet's loud clangor   25
Excites us to arms,
   With shrill notes of anger,
      And mortal alarms.
The double double double beat
      Of the thund'ring Drum   30
      Cries, "Hark! the foes come;
      Charge, charge, 'tis too late to retreat!"

IV

The soft complaining Flute
In dying notes discovers
The woes of hopeless lovers;   35
Whose dirge is whisper'd by the warbling Lute.

V

Sharp Violins proclaim
Their jealous pangs and desperation,
Fury, frantic indignation,
Depth of pains, and height of passion,   40
   For the fair, disdainful dame.

VI

But oh! what art can teach,
What human voice can reach
   The sacred Organ's praise?
Notes inspiring holy love,   45
Notes that wing their heavenly ways
   To mend the choirs above.

VII

Orpheus could lead the savage race
And trees uprooted left their place,
Sequacious of the Lyre.   50
But bright Cecilia raised the wonder higher:
When to her Organ vocal breath was given,
An angel heard, and straight appeared
   Mistaking earth for heaven.

Grand Chorus

As from the power of sacred lays   55
  The spheres began to move,
And sung the great Creator's praise
  To all the blest above;
So when the last and dreadful hour
This crumbling pageant shall devour,   60
  The trumpet shall be heard on high,
  The dead shall live, the living die,
And music shall untune the sky.

John Dryden (1631–1700)

NOTE

Saint Cecilia (title): the patron saint of music, traditionally identified with the organ.

The Destruction of Sennacherib

The Assyrian came down like the wolf on the fold,
And his cohorts were gleaming in purple and gold;
And the sheen of their spears was like stars on the sea,
When the blue wave rolls nightly on deep Galilee.

Like the leaves of the forest when summer is green,   5
That host with their banners at sunset were seen:
Like the leaves of the forest when autumn hath blown,
That host on the morrow lay wither'd and strown.

For the Angel of Death spread his wings on the blast,
And breathed in the face of the foe as he pass'd;   10
And the eyes of the sleepers wax'd deadly and chill,
And their hearts but once heaved, and forever grew still!

And there lay the steed with his nostril all wide,
But through it there roll'd not the breath of his pride;
And the foam of his gasping lay white on the turf,   15
And cold as the spray of the rock-beating surf.

And there lay the rider distorted and pale,
With the dew on his brow, and the rust on his mail:
And the tents were all silent, the banners alone,
The lances unlifted, the trumpet unblown.   20

And the widows of Ashur are loud in their wail,
And the idols are broke in the temple of Baal;
And the might of the Gentile, unsmote by the sword,
Hath melted like snow in the glance of the Lord!

George Gordon, Lord Byron (1788–1824)

NOTES

Sennacherib (title): king of Assyria (701 B.C.) whose armies were attacked by a plague while besieging Jerusalem. *Ashur* (21): Assyria.

The City in the Sea

Lo! Death has reared himself a throne
In a strange city lying alone
Far down within the dim West,
Where the good and the bad and the worst and the best
Have gone to their eternal rest.   5
There shrines and palaces and towers
(Time-eaten towers that tremble not!)
Resemble nothing that is ours.
Around, by lifting winds forgot,
Resignedly beneath the sky   10
The melancholy waters lie.

No rays from the holy heaven come down
On the long night-time of that town;
But light from out the lurid sea
Streams up the turrets silently—   15
Gleams up the pinnacles far and free—
Up domes—up spires—up kingly halls—
Up fanes—up Babylon-like walls—
Up shadowy long-forgotten bowers
Of sculptured ivy and stone flowers—   20
Up many and many a marvellous shrine
Whose wreathèd friezes intertwine
The viol, the violet, and the vine.

Resignedly beneath the sky
The melancholy waters lie.   25
So blend the turrets and shadows there
That all seem pendulous in air,
While from a proud tower in the town
Death looks gigantically down.

There open fanes and gaping graves   30
Yawn level with the luminous waves;
But not the riches there that lie
In each idol's diamond eye—
Not the gaily-jewelled dead
Tempt the waters from their bed;   35
For no ripples curl, alas!
Along that wilderness of glass—
No swellings tell that winds may be
Upon some far-off happier sea—
No heavings hint that winds have been   40
On seas less hideously serene.

But lo, a stir is in the air!
The wave—there is a movement there!
As if the towers had thrust aside,
In slightly sinking, the dull tide—   45
As if their tops had feebly given
A void within the filmy Heaven.
The waves have now a redder glow—
The hours are breathing faint and low—
And when, amid no earthly moans,   50
Down, down that town shall settle hence,
Hell, rising from a thousand thrones,
Shall do it reverence.

                    Edgar Allan Poe (1809–1849)

I like to see it lap the Miles

I like to see it lap the Miles—
And lick the Valleys up—
And stop to feed itself at Tanks—
And then—prodigious step

Around a Pile of Mountains—   5
And supercilious peer
In Shanties—by the sides of Roads—
And then a Quarry pare

To fit its sides and crawl between
Complaining all the while   10
In horrid—hooting stanza—
Then chase itself down Hill—

And neigh like Boanerges—
Then—punctual as a Star
Stop—docile and omnipotent   15
At its own stable door—
Emily Dickinson (1830–1886)

NOTE

Boanerges (13): sons of thunder.

The Caged Skylark

As a dare-gale skylark scanted in a dull cage
    Man's mounting spirit in his bone-house, mean house,
        dwells—
    That bird beyond the remembering his free fells;
This in drudgery, day-labouring-out life's age.

Though aloft on turf or perch or poor low stage,   5
    Both sing sometímes the sweetest, sweetest spells,
    Yet both droop deadly sómetimes in their cells
Or wring their barriers in bursts of fear or rage.

Not that the sweet-fowl, song-fowl, needs no rest—
Why hear him, hear him babble and drop down to his nest,   10
    But his own nest, wild nest, no prison.

Man's spirit will be flesh-bound when found at best,
But uncumberèd: meadow-down is not distressed
    For a rainbow footing it nor he for his bónes rísen.
Gerard Manley Hopkins (1844–1889)

Peter Quince at the Clavier

I

Just as my fingers on these keys
Make music, so the selfsame sounds
On my spirit make a music, too.

Music is feeling, then, not sound;
And thus it is that what I feel,   5
Here in this room, desiring you,

Thinking of your blue-shadowed silk,
Is music. It is like the strain
Waked in the elders by Susanna.

Of a green evening, clear and warm,   10
She bathed in her still garden, while
The red-eyed elders watching, felt

The basses of their beings throb
In witching chords, and their thin blood
Pulse pizzicati of Hosanna.   15

II

In the green water, clear and warm,
Susanna lay.
She searched
The touch of springs,
And found   20
Concealed imaginings.
She sighed,
For so much melody.

Upon the bank, she stood
In the cool   25
Of spent emotions.
She felt, among the leaves,
The dew
Of old devotions.

She walked upon the grass,   30
Still quavering.
The winds were like her maids,
On timid feet,
Fetching her woven scarves,
Yet wavering.   35

A breath upon her hand
Muted the night.
She turned—
A cymbal crashed,
And roaring horns.   40

III

Soon, with a noise like tambourines,
Came her attendant Byzantines.

They wondered why Susanna cried
Against the elders by her side;

And as they whispered, the refrain   45
Was like a willow swept by rain.

Anon, their lamps' uplifted flame
Revealed Susanna and her shame.

And then, the simpering Byzantines
Fled, with a noise like tambourines.   50

IV

Beauty is momentary in the mind—
The fitful tracing of a portal;
But in the flesh it is immortal.
The body dies; the body's beauty lives.
So evenings die, in their green going,   55
A wave, interminably flowing.
So gardens die, their meek breath scenting
The cowl of winter, done repenting.
So maidens die, to the auroral
Celebration of a maiden's choral.   60

Susanna's music touched the bawdy strings
Of those white elders; but, escaping,
Left only Death's ironic scraping.
Now, in its immortality, it plays
On the clear viol of her memory,   65
And makes a constant sacrament of praise.

Wallace Stevens (1879–1955)

NOTES AND QUESTIONS

1. *Peter Quince at the Clavier* (title): Peter Quince is a clownish carpenter in Shakespeare's *A Midsummer Night's Dream*. A clavier is a keyboard or any keyboard stringed instrument, such as a harpsichord or piano. The tone established by the notion of Peter Quince at the clavier is contradicted by the elegant fluency of the poem's style, a music made as Peter Quince says (3) by his spirit, not his awkward hands. In what sense is music "feeling, then, not sound"? (4)

2. *elders by Susanna* (9): an allusion to the story of Susanna in *The Apocrypha*. The beautiful Susanna, while bathing languorously in her garden, is shocked to discover that she is being spied upon lustfully by "ancients of the people." They give her a choice between satisfying their lust or being accused of having been caught in the act of sex with a younger man. Finally Susanna is cleared of the false accusation and the elders put to death. What is Stevens' attitude toward the old men of the story? How much of that attitude can be attributed to Stevens and how much to the imagination of Peter Quince?

3. *pizzicati of Hosanna* (15): a plucking of strings in expression of praise to God or the Messiah. *Hosanna* is derived from the Hebrew meaning "save us."

4. The four parts of the poem suggest the four parts of the sonata form in music: the first part presents contrasting themes to be resolved in the final part; part II is slow in contrast to the fast or comic scherzo tempo of part III. Show how Stevens has achieved effects similar to those of the sonata.

5. Part IV, the resolution, opens with a paradox, that beauty in the flesh is immortal. Show how that paradox is resolved in the three metaphors that follow.

5 Structure and Poetic Forms

Structure

The term "structure" refers to the way a poem moves from one thing (event, idea, image) to another. The term is used to refer to the movement between parts and to the organization of the whole.

Structure as organization of a poem over its total length may be controlled by logic or may quite illogically follow the free association of ideas and images in the mind of the speaker. A poem may tell a story, describe a feeling or a place, or explain an idea. It may be organized in the form of question and answer, comparison and contrast, or it may simply repeat variations on an idea in different images. Whatever we see its total organization to be will be the basis on which we can see smaller parts of its structure operating. The first half of this chapter begins with three structural devices, then shows them operating in poems arranged under three common organizational headings: the chronological, the logical, and organization through imagery. Most poems in one category will exhibit characteristics of poems in other categories; a poem developing a single image as the basis of its organization may as a structural whole contain time elements and logical relationships among its parts. In addition, it may contain any or all of three common structural devices structuring smaller units.

Three Structural Devices

The Turn of Thought.   When the reader is presented with two details in chronological order, he expects a poem organized chronologically. When he finds pleasant images, he expects a development of them. But such expectations are often created to be reversed. The turn of thought, whether it is a subtle change in image or tone or a dramatic reversal of the whole thrust of what preceded, is a common structural device of poetry. One part of the poem sets up an expectation to be developed or reversed in the next part.

Epigram from the French

Sir, I admit your gen'ral rule
That every poet is a fool.
But you yourself may serve to show it,
That every fool is not a poet.

Alexander Pope (1688–1744)

The turn of thought in this quatrain is between the third and fourth lines and is strongly supported by the form of the quatrain, which in the regularity of its iambic tetrameter and rhyme scheme creates a pattern of expectation in sound which is ironically fulfilled even though the sense is reversed. A similar turn in the thought occurs in the following "couplet" by Pope where there is also a fulfillment of expectation in meter and rhyme.

We think our fathers fools, so wise we grow;
Our wiser sons, no doubt, will think us so.

Recurrence and Contrast.   Basic to our sense of structure and design is our perception of recurrence—of color in the pattern of a dress, of a theme with variations in music, and in poetry of complex recurrences not just of sound, but of tone, theme, words, images, symbols, situations, and so forth. A predictable pattern occurs in meter, in the refrain, and in a poem organized by question and answer. But much more common and more basic to the structure of all poetry are sets of recurring contrasts which function in any poem's structure, and in its style as well—contrasts between present and past time, never and now, between here and over there, above and below, or between loss and something salvaged or learned, between youth and age, assent and denial, matter and spirit, heart and mind. In theme and image these balanced contrasts may be stated or implied, but the tension between them is an essential part of the poem's structure and style.

With Rue My Heart Is Laden

With rue my heart is laden
For golden friends I had,
For many a rose-lipt maiden
And many a lightfoot lad.
By brooks too broad for leaping   5
The lightfoot boys are laid;
The rose-lipt girls are sleeping
In fields where roses fade.

A. E. Housman (1859–1936)

The Movement between Statement and Image. Some poems are entirely structured upon a single shift from abstract statement to an image (see Ezra Pound's "Liu Ch'e," page 32) or the reverse, a concrete and imagistic presentation followed by the speaker's abstract statement. The latter is a frequent practice of Robert Frost and is exemplified in condensed form in the poem below.

The Span of Life

The old dog barks backward without getting up.
I can remember when he was a pup.

Robert Frost (1874–1963)

Most poetry moves from image to statement and back more frequently and less noticeably, but to see how the poem is structured, it is helpful to become aware of the interplay of image and statement.

Chronological Organization

Stories, novels, and plays are usually organized chronologically. Fiction and actual events are easiest to follow when told in chronological order, even though it may suit the purpose of a novelist or a filmmaker to report some incidents in flashbacks or in the time sequence of the stream of consciousness. The briefer length of most poems makes those which are chronologically organized closer to the structure of a personal anecdote, in which we have a sense of one incident leading to another toward a conclusion involving a surprising, a pathetic, or an absurd turn of thought.

A poem chronologically organized, whether narrative or lyric, begins at one point in time and ends at another. A narrative poem has a plot and often contains events from the speaker's memory reported out of chronological order; but the lyric, though it may imply a plot, will usually lack any quality of story and focus instead on the speaker's feelings. Most lyrics contain only an incidental time element (placing two events in chronological order, or contrasting present and past or present and future time); but there are some lyrics in which the basis for the whole structure is the arrangement of image and thought in a time sequence.

I Was the Midmost

I was the midmost of my world
  When first I frisked me free,
For though within its circuit gleamed
  But a small company,
And I was immature, they seemed   5
  To bend their looks on me.

She was the midmost of my world
  When I went further forth,
And hence it was that, whether I turned
  To south, east, west, or north,   10
Beams of an all-day Polestar burned
  From that new axe of earth.

Where now is midmost in my world?
  I trace it not at all:
No midmost shows it here, or there,   15
  When wistful voices call
"We are fain! We are fain!" from everywhere
  On Earth's bewildering ball!

Thomas Hardy (1840–1928)

NOTES AND QUESTIONS

1. Although the stanzas are organized chronologically, how does each stanza develop an image related to the word "midmost"?
2. *Polestar* (11): a guiding principle, but also the star Polaris, the North Star. How do both meanings apply? Why an "all-day" Polestar?

3. *axe* (12): axis. Relate the chronological organization to all the imagery of light and celestial bodies.
4. *fain* (17): glad, joyful. Why are the voices wistful? Explain the tone of the whole poem. Is it bitter, playful, wistful?

The Convergence of the Twain

(*Lines on the loss of the "Titanic"*)

I

In a solitude of the sea
Deep from human vanity,
And the Pride of Life that planned her, stilly couches she.

II

Steel chambers, late the pyres
Of her salamandrine fires,   5
Cold currents thrid, and turn to rhythmic tidal lyres.

III

Over the mirrors meant
To glass the opulent
The sea-worm crawls—grotesque, slimed, dumb, indifferent.

IV

Jewels in joy designed   10
To ravish the sensuous mind
Lie lightless, all their sparkles bleared and black and blind.

V

Dim moon-eyed fishes near
Gaze at the gilded gear
And query: "What does this vaingloriousness down here?" . . .   15

VI

Well: while was fashioning
This creature of cleaving wing,
The Immanent Will that stirs and urges everything

VII

Prepared a sinister mate
For her—so gaily great—   20
A Shape of Ice, for the time far and dissociate.

VIII

And as the smart ship grew
In stature, grace, and hue,
In shadowy silent distance grew the Iceberg too.

IX

Alien they seemed to be: 25
No mortal eye could see
The intimate welding of their later history,

X

Or sign that they were bent
By paths coincident
On being anon twin halves of one august event,   30

XI

Till the Spinner of the Years
Said "Now!" And each one hears,
And consummation comes, and jars two hemispheres.

Thomas Hardy (1840–1928)

The Thing

Suddenly they came flying, like a long scarf of smoke,
Trailing a thing—what was it?—small as a lark
Above the blue air, in the slight haze beyond,
A thing in and out of sight,
Flashing between gold levels of the late sun,   5
Then throwing itself up and away from the implacable swift pursuers,
Confusing them once flying straight into the sun
So they circled aimlessly for almost a minute,
Only to find, with their long terrible eyes
The small thing diving down toward a hill,   10
Where they dropped again
In one streak of pursuit.

Then the first bird
Struck;
Then another, another,   15
Until there was nothing left,
Not even feathers from so far away.

And we turned to our picnic
Of veal soaked in marsala and little larks arranged on a long platter,
And we drank the dry harsh wine   20
While I poked with a stick at a stone near a four-pronged flower,
And a black bull nudged at a wall in the valley below,
And the blue air darkened.

Theodore Roethke (1908–1963)

At the Slackening of the Tide

Today I saw a woman wrapped in rags
Leaping along the beach to curse the sea.
Her child lay floating in the oil, away
From oarlock, gunwale, and the blades of oars.
The skinny lifeguard, raging at the sky,   5
Vomited sea, and fainted on the sand.

The cold simplicity of evening falls
Dead on my mind,
And underneath the piles the water
Leaps up, leaps up, and sags down slowly, farther   10
Than seagulls disembodied in the drag
Of oil and foam.

Plucking among the oyster shells a man
Stares at the sea, that stretches on its side.
Now far along the beach, a hungry dog   15
Announces everything I knew before:
Obliterate naiads weeping underground,
Where Homer's tongue thickens with human howls.

I would do anything to drag myself
Out of this place: 20
Root up a seaweed from the water,
To stuff it in my mouth, or deafen me,
Free me from all the force of human speech;
Go drown, almost.

Warm in the pleasure of the dawn I came   25
To sing my song
And look for mollusks in the shallows,
The whorl and coil that pretty up the earth,
While far below us, flaring in the dark,
The stars go out.   30

What did I do to kill my time today,
After the woman ranted in the cold,
The mellow sea, the sound blown dark as wine?
After the lifeguard rose up from the waves
Like a sea-lizard with the scales washed off?   35
Sit there, admiring sunlight on a shell?

Abstract with terror of the shell, I stared
Over the waters where
God brooded for the living all one day.
Lonely for weeping, starved for a sound of mourning,   40
I bowed my head, and heard the sea far off
Washing its hands.

James Wright (b. 1927)

Logical Organization

With the development of imagery goes a progression of the thought implied, but in some poems the thought dominates the structure and the poem progresses like a logical proposition, the speaker not merely meditating but working to a logical conclusion. Such poems may or may not contain words that usually signal logical coherence (*if, because, since, therefore*), but they will always make the reader feel the pressure of the conclusion.

Easter Hymn

If in that Syrian garden, ages slain,
You sleep, and know not you are dead in vain,
Nor even in dreams behold how dark and bright
Ascends in smoke and fire by day and night
The hate you died to quench and could but fan,   5
Sleep well and see no morning, son of man.

But if, the grave rent and the stone rolled by,
At the right hand of majesty on high
You sit, and sitting so remember yet
Your tears, your agony and bloody sweat,   10
Your cross and passion and the life you gave,
Bow hither out of heaven and see and save.

A. E. Housman (1859–1936)

when serpents bargain for the right to squirm

when serpents bargain for the right to squirm
and the sun strikes to gain a living wage—
when thorns regard their roses with alarm
and rainbows are insured against old age

when every thrush may sing no new moon in   5
if all screech-owls have not okayed his voice
—and any wave signs on the dotted line
or else an ocean is compelled to close

when the oak begs permission of the birch
to make an acorn—valleys accuse their   10
mountains of having altitude—and march
denounces april as a saboteur

then we'll believe in that incredible
unanimal mankind(and not until)

e. e. cummings (1894–1962)

Poetry of Departures

Sometimes you hear, fifth-hand,
As epitaph:
He chucked up everything
And just cleared off,
And always the voice will sound   5
Certain you approve
This audacious, purifying,
Elemental move.

And they are right, I think.
We all hate home   10
And having to be there:
I detest my room,
Its specially-chosen junk,
The good books, the good bed,
And my life, in perfect order: 15
So to hear it said

He walked out on the whole crowd
Leaves me flushed and stirred,
Like *Then she undid her dress*
Or *Take that you bastard;*   20
Surely I can, if he did?
And that helps me stay
Sober and industrious.
But I'd go today,

Yes, swagger the nut-strewn roads,   25
Crouch in the fo'c'sle
Stubbly with goodness, if
It weren't so artificial,
Such a deliberate step backwards
To create an object: 30
Books; china; a life
Reprehensibly perfect.

                              Philip Larkin (b. 1922)

QUESTIONS

1. "Poetry of Departures" is structured upon a series of turns of thought within its logical organization, the speaker reversing himself as he considers reasons for giving up one life for another unknown one. Where are these turns of thought?
2. Explain the precision and freshness of the following word choices: "epitaph," "audacious," "purifying," "elemental," and "reprehensibly."

On the Move

"Man, you gotta Go."

The blue jay scuffling in the bushes follows
Some hidden purpose, and the gust of birds
That spurts across the field, the wheeling swallows,
Have nested in the trees and undergrowth.
Seeking their instinct, or their poise, or both,   5
One moves with an uncertain violence
Under the dust thrown by a baffled sense
Or the dull thunder of approximate words.

On motorcycles, up the road, they come:
Small, black, as flies hanging in heat, the Boys,   10
Until the distance throws them forth, their hum
Bulges to thunder held by calf and thigh.
In goggles, donned impersonality,
In gleaming jackets trophied with the dust,
They strap in doubt—by hiding it, robust—   15
And almost hear a meaning in their noise.

Exact conclusion of their hardiness
Has no shape yet, but from known whereabouts
They ride, direction where the tires press.
They scare a flight of birds across the field: 20
Much that is natural, to the will must yield.
Men manufacture both machine and soul,
And use what they imperfectly control
To dare a future from the taken routes.

It is a part solution, after all.   25
One is not necessarily discord
On earth; or damned because, half animal,
One lacks direct instinct, because one wakes
Afloat on movement that divides and breaks.
One joins the movement in valueless world,   30
Choosing it, till, both hurler and the hurled,
One moves as well, always toward, toward.

A minute holds them, who have come to go:
The self-defined, astride the created will
They burst away; the towns they travel through   35
Are home for neither bird nor holiness,
For birds and saints complete their purposes.
At worst, one is in motion; and at best,
Reaching no absolute, in which to rest,
One is always nearer by not keeping still.   40

Thom Gunn (b. 1929)

Organization through Imagery

Most poetry employs imagery to develop its feeling and thought, but some poems in their general organization develop a single image or a series of images with a cumulative effect or contrast two images. Their structure would seem to be merely descriptive or pictorial, but the poet cannot work as the painter does, presenting all his pictorial details at once; he would rarely want to. His control of the order of the reader's perception allows him to develop the interplay of image and idea in ways not available to the painter. Development through imagery may be as simple as the structure of the "haiku," where a statement is put next to an image, or far more complex, but we follow such poems by watching how the developing image defines the statement of attitude. In such a poem there is no narrative skeleton of order, and logical order, if present, is merely implied. All four of the poems below could be reduced to a logical statement, but the basis of the organization and of our interest in them is the developing imagery.

Little Exercise

for Thomas Edwards Wanning

Think of the storm roaming the sky uneasily
like a dog looking for a place to sleep in,
listen to it growling.

Think how they must look now, the mangrove keys
lying out there unresponsive to the lightning   5
in dark, coarse-fibred families,

where occasionally a heron may undo his head,
shake up his feathers, make an uncertain comment
when the surrounding water shines.

Think of the boulevard and the little palm trees   10
all stuck in rows, suddenly revealed
as fistfuls of limp fish-skeletons.

It is raining there. The boulevard
and its broken sidewalks with weeds in every crack
are relieved to be wet, the sea to be freshened.   15

Now the storm goes away again in a series
of small, badly lit battle-scenes,
each in "Another part of the field."

Think of someone sleeping in the bottom of a row-boat
tied to a mangrove root or the pile of a bridge;   20
think of him as uninjured, barely disturbed.

Elizabeth Bishop (b. 1911)

Casino

Only their hands are living, to the wheel attracted,
are moved, as deer trek desperately towards a creek
   through the dust and scrub of a desert, or gently,
      as sunflowers turn to the light,

and, as night takes up the cries of feverish children,   5
the cravings of lions in dens, the loves of dons,
   gathers them all and remains the night, the
      Great room is full of their prayers.

To a last feast of isolation self-invited,
they flock, and in a rite of disbelief are joined;   10
   from numbers all their stars are-recreated,
      the enchanted, the worldly, the sad.

Without, calm rivers flow among the wholly living
quite near their trysts, and mountains part them, and birds,
   deep in the greens and moistures of summer,   15
      sing towards their work.

But here no nymph comes naked to the youngest shepherd,
the fountain is deserted, the laurel will not grow;
   the labyrinth is safe but endless, and broken
      is Ariadne's thread,   20

as deeper in these hands is grooved their fortune: lucky
were few, and it is possible that none was loved,
   and what was god-like in this generation
      was never to be born.

                    W. H. Auden (1907–1973)

The Portrait

   She speaks always in her own voice
   Even to strangers; but those other women
   Exercise their borrowed, or false, voices
   Even on sons and daughters.

   She can walk invisibly at noon   5
   Along the high road; but those other women
   Gleam phosphorescent—broad hips and gross fingers—
   Down every lampless alley.

She is wild and innocent, pledged to love
Through all disaster; but those other women   10
Decry her for a witch or a common drab
And glare back when she greets them.

Here is her portrait, gazing sidelong at me,
The hair in disarray, the young eyes pleading:
'And you, love? As unlike those other men   15
As I those other women?'

Robert Graves (b. 1895)

A Black Man Talks of Reaping

I have sown beside all waters in my day.
I planted deep, within my heart the fear
that wind of fowl would take the grain away.
I planted safe against this stark, lean year.

I scattered seed enough to plant the land   5
in rows from Canada to Mexico
but for my reaping only what the hand
can hold at once is all that I can show.

Yet what I sowed and what the orchard yields
my brother's sons are gathering stalk and root;   10
small wonder then my children glean in fields
they have not sown, and feed on bitter fruit.

Arna Bontemps (1902–1973)

Poetic Forms

Song

Poets continue to write poems they call "songs," not because they
necessarily expect them to be sung but to suggest a tradition of the
song as old as poetry itself, to allude to a short, emotional, simple
lyric poem that was sung. The term "lyric" still suggests the Apol-
lonian lyre that accompanied Greek singers. Medieval troubadours
and Minnesangers sang their poetry. In the English tradition the term
"song" suggests the Elizabethan song of a poet who was composer

as well, or wrote to fit his poem to a known tune, or wrote in one of many stanzaic forms suitable for musical accompaniment. Simplicity and ease are the characteristics most admired in the typical Elizabethan song, but these qualities occur along with intricate patterns of meter, turns of thought, and delicately balanced contrasts.

The song has a dual development, one in the court, the other in the streets. The court tradition is polite, polished, and balanced in phrasing, refined in the feelings expressed. The street song and ballad are full of violent incident, coarse phrasing, and ungentle feeling, but they have a vitality that had a continuing influence in extending the range and realism of poetry.

Song: Sigh no more, ladies

Sigh no more, ladies, sigh no more!
   Men were deceivers ever,
One foot in sea, and one on shore;
   To one thing constant never.
      Then sigh not so,   5
      But let them go,
And be you blithe and bonny,
Converting all your sounds of woe
Into Hey nonny, nonny.

Sing no more ditties, sing no moe,   10
   Of dumps so dull and heavy!
The fraud of men was ever so,
   Since summer first was leavy.
      Then sigh not so,
      But let them go,   15
And be you blithe and bonny,
Converting all your sounds of woe
Into Hey nonny, nonny.

        William Shakespeare (1564–1616)

Song: Ask me no more

Ask me no more where Jove bestows,
When June is past, the fading rose;
For in your beauty's orient deep
These flowers, as in their causes, sleep.

Ask me no more whither do stray   5
The golden atoms of the day;
For, in pure love, heaven did prepare
Those powders to enrich your hair.

Ask me no more whither doth haste
The nightingale, when May is past;   10
For in your sweet dividing throat
She winters, and keeps warm her note.

Ask me no more where those stars light
That downwards fall in dead of night;
For in your eyes they sit, and there   15
Fixed become, as in their sphere.

Ask me no more if east or west
The phoenix builds her spicy nest;
For unto you at last she flies,
And in your fragrant bosom dies.   20

Thomas Carew (c. 1595–1639)

QUESTIONS

1. Upon what repetitions is the structure based? What implied contrasts recur in the details of the structure?
2. Is there any progression in the poem as a whole? Might the last stanza have been placed elsewhere?
3. What archetypal suggestions occur in the imagery?
4. Explain the structuring of all aspects of sound in the poem.
5. Despite the extravagance of the praise of his lady, indicate word choices disciplined to a formal, impersonal style.

Swing Low, Sweet Chariot

Swing low, sweet chariot,
Comin' for to carry me home,
Swing low, sweet chariot,
Comin' for to carry me home.

I looked over Jordan and what did I see,   5
Comin' for to carry me home,
A band of angels, comin' after me,
Comin' for to carry me home.

If you get there before I do,
Comin' for to carry me home,   10
Tell all my friends I'm comin' too,
Comin' for to carry me home.

Swing low, sweet chariot,
Comin' for to carry me home,
Swing low, sweet chariot,   15
Comin' for to carry me home.

Anonymous: Traditional Spiritual

The Weary Blues

Droning a drowsy syncopated tune,
Rocking back and forth to a mellow croon,
    I heard a Negro play.
Down on Lenox Avenue the other night
By the pale dull pallor of an old gas light   5
    He did a lazy sway. . . .
    He did a lazy sway. . . .
To the tune o' those Weary Blues.
With his ebony hands on each ivory key
He made that poor piano moan with melody.   10
    O Blues!
Swaying to and fro on his rickety stool
He played that sad raggy tune like a musical fool.
    Sweet Blues!
Coming from a black man's soul.   15
    O Blues!
In a deep song voice with a melancholy tone
I heard that Negro sing, that old piano moan—
    "Ain't got nobody in all this world,
    Ain't got nobody but ma self.   20
    I's gwine to quit ma frownin'
    And put ma troubles on the shelf."
Thump, thump, thump, went his foot on the floor.
He played a few chords then he sang some more—
    "I got the Weary Blues   25
    And I can't be satisfied.
    Got the Weary Blues
    And can't be satisfied—
    I ain't happy no mo'
    And I wish that I had died."   30

And far into the night he crooned that tune.
The stars went out and so did the moon.
The singer stopped playing and went to bed
While the Weary Blues echoed through his head.
He slept like a rock or a man that's dead.   35

Langston Hughes (1902–1967)

Christ Climbed Down

Christ climbed down
from His bare Tree
this year
and ran away to where
there were no rootless Christmas trees   5
hung with candycanes and breakable stars

Christ climbed down
from His bare Tree
this year
and ran away to where   10
there were no gilded Christmas trees
and no tinsel Christmas trees
and no tinfoil Christmas trees
and no pink plastic Christmas trees
and no gold Christmas trees   15
and no black Christmas trees
and no powderblue Christmas trees
hung with electric candles
and encircled by tin electric trains
and clever cornball relatives   20

Christ climbed down
from His bare Tree
this year
and ran away to where
no intrepid Bible salesmen   25
covered the territory
in two-tone cadillacs

NOTE

This poem is one of seven originally conceived for jazz accompaniment and should be considered primarily as an oral message rather than as a poem written for the printed page.

and where no Sears Roebuck creches
complete with plastic babe in manger
arrived by parcel post   30
the babe by special delivery
and where no televised Wise Men
praised the Lord Calvert Whiskey

Christ climbed down
from His bare Tree   35
this year
and ran away to where
no fat handshaking stranger
in a red flannel suit
and a fake white beard   40
went around passing himself off
as some sort of North Pole saint
crossing the desert to Bethlehem
Pennsylvania
in a Volkswagen sled   45
drawn by rollicking Adirondack reindeer
with German names
and bearing sacks of Humble Gifts
from Saks Fifth Avenue
for everybody's imagined Christ child   50

Christ climbed down
from His bare Tree
this year
and ran away to where
no Bing Crosby carollers   55
groaned of a tight Christmas
and where no Radio City angels
iceskated wingless
thru a winter wonderland
into a jinglebell heaven   60
daily at 8:30
with Midnight Mass matinees

Christ climbed down
from His bare Tree
this year   65
and softly stole away into
some anonymous Mary's womb again
where in the darkest night
of everybody's anonymous soul
He awaits again   70

an unimaginable
and impossibly
Immaculate Reconception
the very craziest
of Second Comings   75

Lawrence Ferlinghetti (b. 1919)

Sonnet

Among the English poetic forms the sonnet is unique. It is neither an indefinitely flowing form, like blank verse, nor a stanzaic form, with its repetition of an established pattern; it is instead a strict form of fourteen iambic pentameter lines with a set rhyme scheme.

The sonnet originated in Italy, was imported into England in the sixteenth century, gained enormous popularity, and has flourished, with some interruption, down to the present. Several other poetic forms were imported into England at about the same time, most of them, like the sonnet, quite stylized; but none of them attained such a vogue, such endurance, such popularity as the sonnet. (One of these, the villanelle, is illustrated on pages 144–45 by Dylan Thomas' "Do Not Go Gentle into That Good Night.") The subject of the sonnet was originally love. The Petrarchan or Italian sonnet consists of two parts both in terms of its content and its rhyme scheme: the first eight lines, or octave, and the latter six, or sestet. The octave and the sestet normally contrast with one another, with the sestet providing a countermovement to the octave, often made very evident by such an initial word as "but," "then," or "hence." The rhyme scheme of the Petrarchan sonnet is among the most demanding in English: *abbaabba* for the octave and *cdcdcd* or *cdecde* for the sestet.

When the sonnet was imported into England, some sonneteers retained the original rigid Italian form, but others changed its concept. Shakespeare's sonnets deal with their subjects in four parts instead of two, with the rhyme scheme reflecting the structure: *abab cdcd efef gg*. The four parts make possible more frequent shifts and variations of perspective and tone climaxed by the concluding couplet. Other English poets worked other variations on the Italian form and widened the subject matter to include social, political, religious, and philosophical themes. All of these variations are called the English or, frequently inexactly, the Shakespearian sonnet. In English poetry both the Italian sonnet and the English sonnet have continued to be written through the years. Some sonnets even exhibit some of the characteristics of both forms.

Sonnet: Three things there be

Three things there be that prosper up apace
And flourish, whilst they grow asunder far,
But on a day, they meet all in one place,
And when they meet, they one another mar;
And they be these: the wood, the weed, the wag.   5
The wood is that which makes the gallow tree,
The weed is that which strings the hangman's bag,
The wag, my pretty knave, betokeneth thee.
Mark well, dear boy, whilst these assemble not,
Green springs the tree, hemp grows, the wag is wild;   10
But when they meet, it makes the timber rot,
It frets the halter, and it chokes the child.
Then bless thee, and beware, and let us pray
We part not with thee at this meeting day.

Sir Walter Ralegh (1552?–1618)

Sonnet: Since brass, nor stone

Since brass, nor stone, nor earth, nor boundless sea,
But sad mortality o'er-sways their power,
How with this rage shall beauty hold a plea,
Whose action is no stronger than a flower?
O! how shall summer's honey breath hold out   5
Against the wrackful siege of batt'ring days,
When rocks impregnable are not so stout,
Nor gates of steel so strong, but Time decays?
O fearful meditation! where, alack,
Shall Time's best jewel from Time's chest lie hid?   10
Or what strong hand can hold his swift foot back?
Or who his spoil of beauty can forbid?
O, none, unless this miracle have might,
That in black ink my love may still shine bright.

William Shakespeare (1564–1616)

Sonnet: Nuns fret not

Nuns fret not at their convent's narrow room;
And hermits are contented with their cells;
And students with their pensive citadels;
Maids at the wheel, the weaver at his loom,
Sit blithe and happy; bees that soar for bloom,   5
High as the highest Peak of Furness-fells,
Will murmur by the hour in foxglove bells:
In truth the prison, into which we doom
Ourselves, no prison is: and hence for me,
In sundry moods, 'twas pastime to be bound   10
Within the Sonnet's scanty plot of ground;
Pleased if some Souls (for such there needs must be)
Who have felt the weight of too much liberty,
Should find brief solace there, as I have found.

William Wordsworth (1770–1850)

NOTE

Furness-fells (6): mountains in England.

Sonnet: Oft have I seen

Oft have I seen at some cathedral door
  A laborer, pausing in the dust and heat,
  Lay down his burden, and with reverent feet
  Enter, and cross himself, and on the floor
Kneel to repeat his paternoster o'er;   5
  Far off the noises of the world retreat;
  The loud vociferations of the street
  Become an undistinguishable roar.
So, as I enter here from day to day,
  And leave my burden at this minster gate,   10
  Kneeling in prayer, and not ashamed to pray,
The tumult of the time disconsolate
  To inarticulate murmurs dies away,
  While the eternal ages watch and wait.

Henry Wadsworth Longfellow (1807–1882)

Ballad

The "ballad" is a narrative poem composed either in quatrains of four-stress lines or in quatrains with the four-stress line alternating with a three- or two-stress line. The "popular ballad" was sung long before it was written down; while many assume the ballad to have developed in the late Middle Ages, the written versions go back only until the late seventeenth century. The versions vary greatly because the oral tradition permitted margin for faulty memory, innovations, and improvements. The subject matter, like that of most popular literature, is love, violence, death, and encounters with the supernatural, but some popular ballads have a high literary quality. They tell their narrative, which usually begins in the middle of its events, with great compression, discipline, and attention to vivid detail. In addition, the best versions of the popular ballad have a high degree of objectivity.

The term "literary ballad" refers to ballads written by identifiable authors, while the author of the popular ballad is anonymous. The literary ballad is usually more subjective and orderly. Two examples of literary ballads are "Is My Team Plowing" (page 6) and "La Belle Dame Sans Merci" (pages 56–57). The refrain and the question and answer technique are frequently used in both the popular and the literary ballad.

Sir Patrick Spens

The king sits in Dumferling town,
    Drinking the blude-reid° wine: blood red
"O whar will I get a guid° sailòr   good
    To sail this ship of mine?"

Up and spake an eldern° knicht,   5   elderly
    Sat at the king's richt knee:
"Sir Patrick Spens is the best sailòr
    That sails upon the sea."

The king has written a braid° letter,   broad
    And signed it wi' his hand,   10
And sent it to Sir Patrick Spens,
    Was walking on the sand.

The first line that Sir Patrick read,
    A loud lauch lauched he;
The next line that Sir Patrick read,   15
    The tear blinded his ee.°   eye

"O wha is this has done this deed,
   This ill deed done to me,
To send me out this time o' the year,
   To sail upon the sea?   20

"Make haste, make haste, my merry men all,
   Our guid ship sails the morn."
"O say na sae,° my master dear,   so
   For I fear a deadly storm.

"Late, late yestreen I saw the new moon   25
   Wi' the auld° moon in her arm,   old
And I fear, I fear, my dear mastèr,
   That we will come to harm."

O our Scots nobles were richt laith:°   loth
   To weet° their cork-heeled shoon;°   30   wet, shoes
But lang owre° a' the play were played,   before
   Their hats they swam aboon.°   above

O lang, lang, may their ladies sit
   Wi' their fans into their hand,
Or e'er they see Sir Patrick Spens   35
   Come sailing to the land.

O lang, lang, may the ladies stand
   Wi' their gold kems° in their hair,   combs
Waiting for their ain° dear lords,   own
   For they'll see thame na mair.°   40   no more

Half o'er, half o'er to Aberdour
   It's fifty fadom deep.
And there lies guid Sir Patrick Spens,
   Wi' the Scots lords at his feet.

                  Anonymous

Lord Randal

"O where ha you been, Lord Randal, my son?
And where ha you been, my handsome young man?"
"I ha been at the greenwood; mother, mak my bed soon,
For I'm wearied wi hunting, and fain wad lie down."

"An wha met ye there, Lord Randal, my son?   5
And wha met you there, my handsome young man?"
"O I met wi my true-love; mother, mak my bed soon,
For I'm wearied wi hunting, and fain wad lie down."

"And what did she give you, Lord Randal, my son?
And what did she give you, my handsome young man?"   10
"Eels fried in a pan; mother, mak my bed soon,
For I'm wearied wi huntin, and fain wad lie down."

"An wha gat your leavins, Lord Randal, my son?
And wha gat your leavins, my handsome young man?"
"My hawks and my hounds; mother, mak my bed soon,   15
For I'm wearied wi huntin, and fain wad lie down."

"And what becam of them, Lord Randal, my son?
And what becam of them, my handsome young man?"
"They stretched their legs out and died; mother, mak my bed soon,
For I'm wearied wi huntin, and fain wad lie down."   20

"O I fear you are poisoned, Lord Randal, my son!
I fear you are poisoned, my handsome young man!"
"O yes, I am poisoned; mother, mak my bed soon,
For I'm sick at the heart, and I fain wad lie down."

Anonymous

The Twa Corbies

As I was walking all alane,°	alone
I heard two corbies° making a mane;°	two ravens, moan
The tane unto the t' other say,	
"Where sall we gang° and dine today?"	go
"In behind yon auld fail° dyke, 5	turf
I wot there lies a new-slain knight;	
And naebody kens° that he lies there	knows
But his hawk, his hound, and lady fair.	
"His hound is to the hunting gane,°	gone
His hawk to fetch the wild-fowl hame,° 10	home
His lady's ta'en another mate,	
So we may make our dinner sweet.	
"Ye'll sit on his white hause-bane,°	neck bone
And I'll pick out his bonny blue een;°	eyes
Wi' ae° lock o' his golden hair, 15	one
We'll theek° our nest when it grows bare.	thatch
"Mony a one for him makes mane,	
But nane sall ken where he is gane;	
O'er his white banes when they are bare,	
The wind sall blaw for evermair." 20	

Anonymous

Barbara Allan

It was in and about the Martinmas time,
    When the green leaves were a falling,
That Sir John Graeme, in the West Country,
    Fell in love with Barbara Allan.

He sent his man down through the town,   5
    To the place where she was dwelling:
"O haste and come to my master dear,
    Gin° ye be Barbara Allan."   *if*

O hooly,° hooly rose she up,   *slowly*
    To the place where he was lying,   10
And when she drew the curtain by,
    "Young man, I think you're dying."

"O it's I'm sick, and very, very sick,
    And 't is a' for° Barbara Allan:"   *all for*
"O the better for me ye's° never be,   15   *you shall*
    Tho your heart's blood were a spilling.

"O dinna ye mind, young man," said she,
    "When ye was in the tavern a drinking,
That ye made the healths gae° round and round,   *go*
    And slighted Barbara Allan?"   20

He turned his face unto the wall,
    And death was with him dealing:
"Adieu, adieu, my dear friends all,
    And be kind to Barbara Allan."

And slowly, slowly raise she up,   25
    And slowly, slowly left him,
And sighing said, she coud not stay,
    Since death of life had reft him.

She had not gane° a mile but twa,°   *gone, two*
    When she heard the dead-bell ringing,   30
And every jow° that the dead-bell geid,°   *stroke, gave*
    It cry'd, Woe to Barbara Allan!

"O mother, mother, make my bed!
    O make it saft° and narrow!   *soft*
Since my love died for me to-day,   35
    I'll die for him to-morrow."

Anonymous

6 Diction

Verbal Precision

One of the pleasures of reading good poetry comes from discovering that the poet has found precisely the right word to make his point. Verbal precision comes partly from context and partly from the choice of words rich in connotative nuance that no other word would render. Though there is no great denotative difference between describing a person reasonably overweight as "heavy" or "fat," there is obviously a great connotative difference. If it suits the tone of the speaker to be unpleasant about another person, "fat" is the appropriate word. When Shakespeare has Caesar, who correctly mistrusts Cassius, describe him as having a "lean and hungry look," Caesar's tone is caught precisely. In this context the words suggest Cassius to be a person so mean-spirited that he eats little or digests badly—a discontented man, a scavenger for opportunities. We might associate "a lean and hungry look" with a hungry dog, a metaphor that is probably part of Caesar's intention. Out of context "lean" has little connotative precision or richness: "skinny" or "slim" are more precise and richer, though entirely wrong for this context, the first too comical ("a skinny and hungry look"?) and the second too flattering. But "lean" in association with "hungry" precisely defines Caesar's attitude. Cassius is dangerous. "Lean" implies more agility, and therefore a more lethal threat, than "skinny" does.

The following poem illustrates the way in which verbal precision is achieved by the interaction of common words chosen to express the exact nuance.

123

After great pain, a formal feeling comes

After great pain, a formal feeling comes—
The Nerves sit ceremonious, like Tombs—
The stiff Heart questions was it He, that bore,
And Yesterday, or Centuries before?

The Feet, mechanical, go round—   5
Of Ground, or Air, or Ought—
A Wooden way
Regardless grown,
A Quartz contentment, like a stone—

This is the Hour of Lead—   10
Remembered, if outlived,
As Freezing persons, recollect the Snow—
First—Chill—then Stupor—then the letting go—

Emily Dickinson (1830–1886)

The first two lines of Emily Dickinson's poem contain two arresting words, "formal" and "ceremonious." They are arresting because they reverse our usual assumption that the end of pain is freedom, a sigh of relief and celebration. "Formal" and "ceremonious" suggest a period of respect before celebration or release from constraint. They suggest images of people sitting at solemn, formal occasions, perhaps in churches at funerals. Dickinson then develops that impression with a simile, "like tombs." The suggestion of death in "tombs" is developed next in the questions raised by the "stiff" heart. After great pain we feel vulnerable, fear the return of pain, and try to understand it. If we fear that the pain may be an intimation of our own mortality, our nerves are most likely to "sit ceremonious" as we consider our fate. Was this pain part of some divine plan ("was it He that bore?"), and if so, was the plan made yesterday or centuries ago? Such questions distract the speaker. She starts walking around mechanically in a "quartz contentment."

QUESTIONS

1. Quartz is a rock-like crystal but murky and opaque, heavy and usually colorless. Why a "quartz" contentment? Why not "marble" to go with tombs?
2. Why is the speaker contented at all, and, since she is, why "like a stone?"

3. Line 10 tempts the misreading "the hour of the dead." Why is it preferable as it is?
4. Since the speaker has survived her great pain, why does the final simile present an image of persons dying in the snow? Why not an image of dying from thirst in a desert?
5. How precisely stated and how necessary are the three stages of death in the final line?
6. What difference does it make whether the plan was made yesterday or centuries before?

Dead Boy

The little cousin is dead, by foul subtraction,
A green bough from Virginia's aged tree,
And none of the county kin like the transaction,
Nor some of the world of outer dark, like me.

A boy not beautiful, nor good, nor clever,   5
A black cloud full of storms too hot for keeping,
A sword beneath his mother's heart—yet never
Woman bewept her babe as this is weeping.

A pig with a pasty face, so I had said,
Squealing for cookies, kinned by poor pretense   10
With a noble house. But the little man quite dead,
I see the forbears' antique lineaments.

The elder men have strode by the box of death
To the wide flag porch, and muttering low send round
The bruit of the day. O friendly waste of breath!   15
Their hearts are hurt with a deep dynastic wound.

He was pale and little, the foolish neighbors say;
The first-fruits, saith the Preacher, the Lord hath taken;
But this was the old tree's late branch wrenched away,
Grieving the sapless limbs, the shorn and shaken.   20

John Crowe Ransom (1888–1974)

QUESTIONS

1. In the first stanza of Ransom's "Dead Boy" the child's death is described by two curious words, "subtraction" and "transaction," and the words are emphasized by their rhyming. Only in the last line of the stanza, where the speaker reveals that he belongs to "the world of outer dark," meaning that he is not kin to this aristocratic Virginia family, do we find a hint of why he uses such impersonal terms. Why does he use them?
2. The speaker is deeply moved. The family has lost a son, and because he admires the family he feels their loss. His speech therefore assumes, in stanzas three through five, a regal character appropriate to the death of a prince. By setting this speech, with the key words "antique" and "dynastic," alongside colloquialisms such as "pig with a pasty face" and "Squealing for cookies," Ransom keeps the reader reminded of his speaker's twofold attitude. What is this attitude?
3. What does "bruit" mean, and why does Ransom use this word instead of another, more familiar one?
4. What do the archaic words "saith" and "hath," in the last stanza, contribute to the poem?
5. The phrase "outer dark" in the first stanza recalls the "outer darkness" in St. Matthew's account of Christ's parable of the wedding feast—Matthew 22:1–14, in the King James version of the Bible. Do you think Ransom intended this similarity, and if he did, what does he gain by it? That is, how does the position of the speaker in the poem resemble that of the wedding guest? Are there other phrases in the poem that echo passages from the Bible?
6. The word "pretense" in stanza three makes a nice, unexpected rhyme with "lineaments." But being related to the word "pretender," it may serve still another function. Does the dictionary's definition of "pretender" suggest what that function might be and how it relates to other words in the poem?
7. In the eighteenth and nineteenth centuries, writers often employed what is known as poetic diction—high-sounding phrases for familiar things. Thus they might call fish "the finny tribe," or woman "the gentler sex." When, in stanza four, Ransom calls a coffin "the box of death," is he resorting to poetic diction, possibly for the sake of a rhyme with "breath"? Or is he saying something that cannot be said as effectively in any other way?
8. The last stanza of the poem is dominated by the metaphor of the tree. How has the diction of the preceding stanzas led up to this metaphor?

Long-Legged Fly

That civilisation may not sink,
Its great battle lost,
Quiet the dog, tether the pony
To a distant post;
Our master Caesar is in the tent   5
Where the maps are spread,
His eyes fixed upon nothing,
A hand under his head.
Like a long-legged fly upon the stream
His mind moves upon silence.   10

That the topless towers be burnt
And men recall that face,
Move most gently if move you must
In this lonely place.
She thinks, part woman, three parts a child,   15
That nobody looks; her feet
Practise a tinker shuffle
Picked up on a street.
Like a long-legged fly upon the stream
Her mind moves upon silence.   20

That girls at puberty may find
The first Adam in their thought,
Shut the door of the Pope's chapel,
Keep those children out.
There on that scaffolding reclines   25
Michael Angelo.
With no more sound than the mice make
His hand moves to and fro.
Like a long-legged fly upon the stream
His mind moves upon silence.   30

                    William Butler Yeats (1865–1939)

NOTES AND QUESTIONS

1. An earlier version of line 6 reads, "Where the military maps are spread." Why did Yeats drop the word "military"?
2. Line 8 earlier read, "A hand supporting the bloody head." Would it have been better?
3. *topless towers* (11): an allusion to Marlowe's lines: "Was this the face that launched a thousand ships / And burnt the topless towers of Ilium?" What is the effect of the allusion?

Neutral Tones

We stood by a pond that winter day,
And the sun was white, as though chidden of God,
And a few leaves lay on the starving sod;
   —They had fallen from an ash, and were gray.

Your eyes on me were as eyes that rove   5
Over tedious riddles of years ago;
And some words played between us to and fro
   On which lost the more by our love.

The smile on your mouth was the deadest thing
Alive enough to have strength to die;   10
And a grin of bitterness swept thereby
   Like an ominous bird a-wing. . . .

Since then, keen lessons that love deceives,
And wrings with wrong, have shaped to me
Your face, and the God-curst sun, and a tree,   15
   And a pond edged with grayish leaves.

Thomas Hardy (1840–1928)

Freshness and Vividness

Fresh language arrests attention and directs it to new and unexplored areas of the subject. While in the debased language of politics and advertising, words mean less than they seem to and will not bear close scrutiny, good poetry revitalizes the language, teaching by its own example the importance of the precise and fresh phrase and the vivid image. The fresh word choice can demand attention by its novelty as Cummings' coinage "manunkind" does (page 130), or the fresh word choice may be part of very simple phrasing unusual in its context as in "After great pain a *formal* feeling comes." The vivid image can be as extravagant as Macbeth's "The multitudinous seas incarnadine" or as simple as Wordsworth's "violet by a mossy stone." It can be quoted until its freshness is lost as Wordsworth's has been or remain astonishing despite quotation as Macbeth's has. Vividness occurs in the image, but freshness can occur in abstract language as well—as "Pied Beauty" and "pity this busy monster, manunkind" illustrate. Most often the fresh and vivid word or image or phrase will involve the unexpected and not the expected turn of thought, but sometimes, usually with the greatest poets, we find a great commonplace idea so inevitably phrased, often without imagery at all, that it is quoted through the centuries.

Upon Julia's Clothes

Whenas in silks my Julia goes,
Then, then, methinks, how sweetly flows
The liquefaction of her clothes.

Next, when I cast mine eyes, and see
That brave vibration, each way free,   5
O, how that glittering taketh me!

                    Robert Herrick (1591–1674)

Success is counted sweetest

Success is counted sweetest
By those who ne'er succeed,
To comprehend a nectar
Requires sorest need.

Not one of all the purple Host   5
Who took the Flag today
Can tell the definition
So clear of Victory

As he defeated—dying—
On whose forbidden ear   10
The distant strains of triumph
Burst agonized and clear!

                    Emily Dickinson (1830–1886)

Sonnet: My mistress' eyes

My mistress' eyes are nothing like the sun,
Coral is far more red than her lips' red.
If snow be white, why then her breasts are dun,
If hairs be wires, black wires grow on her head.
I have seen roses damasked, red and white,   5
But no such roses see I in her cheeks.
And in some perfumes is there more delight
Than in the breath that from my mistress reeks.
I love to hear her speak, yet well I know
That music hath a far more pleasing sound.   10

I grant I never saw a goddess go,
My mistress, when she walks, treads on the ground.
And yet, by Heaven, I think my love as rare
As any she belied with false compare.

William Shakespeare (1564–1616)

Pied Beauty

Glory be to God for dappled things—
    For skies of couple-colour as a brinded cow;
        For rose-moles all in stipple upon trout that swim;
Fresh-firecoal chestnut-falls; finches' wings;
    Landscape plotted and pieced—fold, fallow, and plough;   5
        And áll trádes, their gear and tackle and trim.

All things counter, original, spare, strange;
    Whatever is fickle, freckled (who knows how?)
        With swift, slow; sweet, sour; adazzle, dim;
He fathers-forth whose beauty is past change: 10
                Praise him.

Gerard Manley Hopkins (1844–1889)

pity this busy monster,manunkind,

pity this busy monster,manunkind,

not.   Progress is a comfortable disease:
your victim(death and life safely beyond)

plays with the bigness of his littleness
—electrons deify one razorblade   5
into a mountainrange;lenses extend

unwish through curving wherewhen till unwish
returns on its unself.
                A world of made
is not a world of born—pity poor flesh   10

and trees,poor stars and stones,but never this
fine specimen of hypermagical

ultraomnipotence.   We doctors know
a hopeless case if—listen:there's a hell
of a good universe next door;let's go   15

e. e. cummings (1894–1962)

Orchids

They lean over the path,
Adder-mouthed,
Swaying close to the face,
Coming out, soft and deceptive;
Limp and damp, delicate as a young bird's tongue;   5
Their fluttery fledgling lips
Move slowly,
Drawing in the warm air.

And at night,
The faint moon falling through whitewashed glass,   10
The heat going down
So their musky smell comes even stronger,
Drifting down from their mossy cradles:
So many devouring infants!
Soft luminescent fingers,   15
Lips neither dead nor alive,
Loose ghostly mouths
Breathing.

                    Theodore Roethke (1908–1963)

Aftermath

Compelled by calamity's magnet
They loiter and stare as if the house
Burnt-out were theirs, or as if they thought
Some scandal might any minute ooze
From a smoke-choked closet into light;   5
No deaths, no prodigious injuries
Glut these hunters after an old meat,
Blood-spoor of the austere tragedies.

Mother Medea in a green smock
Moves humbly as any housewife through   10
Her ruined apartments, taking stock
Of charred shoes, the sodden upholstery:
Cheated of the pyre and the rack,
The crowd sucks her last tear and turns away.

                    Sylvia Plath (1932–1963)

Irony: Hyperbole, Understatement, Paradox

Irony appeals to the reader through some kind of surprise, contrast, extravagance, discrepancy, incongruity or contradiction. The effect of irony may be comic or tragic, but more commonly its effect is simply to shift perspective to the realistic. The detachment that irony makes possible undercuts the sentimental, the naive, the pompous, and the didactic. To attempt to say directly what irony has achieved indirectly is to discover how much has been avoided of the tiresome and trite.

Dramatic Irony

We most frequently encounter irony as dramatic irony in the fictions of film, television, plays, novels, and short stories. In such fictions as in poems with a narrative element, dramatic irony occurs in the incongruity between what happens and what was expected or between the audience's superior knowledge of the actual nature of the situation and what a character thinks the situation is. "My Last Duchess" by Robert Browning is rich in these dramatic ironies. The Renaissance Italian duke, the speaker of the whole monologue, speaks of himself proudly and self-righteously, but we see beneath the surface of his words that he is villainous; he speaks unfavorably about his deceased wife, but ironically she comes through to us favorably even in *his* words. In the course of the poem we come to suspect that he has had her murdered, but we do not suspect until almost the end the additional dramatic irony that he has been saying all this to a representative of the family of the girl whom he now wants to marry. Just try to imagine "My Last Duchess" transformed into "His Last Duchess," recounted straightforwardly in third person narrative; if the narrator knew the Duke's faults and reported them to the reader, all the dramatic irony would be lost.

My Last Duchess

Ferrara

That's my last Duchess painted on the wall,
Looking as if she were alive. I call
That piece a wonder, now: Frà Pandolf's hands
Worked busily a day, and there she stands.
Will't please you sit and look at her? I said   5
"Frà Pandolf" by design, for never read
Strangers like you that pictured countenance,
The depth and passion of its earnest glance,
But to myself they turned (since none puts by
The curtain I have drawn for you, but I)   10
And seemed as they would ask me, if they durst,
How such a glance came there; so, not the first
Are you to turn and ask thus. Sir, 'twas not
Her husband's presence only, called that spot
Of joy into the Duchess' cheek; perhaps   15
Frà Pandolf chanced to say, "Her mantle laps
Over my lady's wrist too much," or "Paint
Must never hope to reproduce the faint
Half-flush that dies along her throat": such stuff
Was courtesy, she thought, and cause enough   20
For calling up that spot of joy. She had
A heart—how shall I say?—too soon made glad,
Too easily impressed: she liked whate'er
She looked on, and her looks went everywhere.
Sir, 'twas all one! My favor at her breast,   25
The dropping of the daylight in the West,
The bough of cherries some officious fool
Broke in the orchard for her, the white mule
She rode with round the terrace—all and each
Would draw from her alike the approving speech,   30
Or blush, at least. She thanked men,—good! but thanked
Somehow—I know not how—as if she ranked
My gift of a nine-hundred-years-old name

NOTES

Ferrara (title): the capital of a province in northern Italy. *Frà Pandolf*
(3): a fictitious artist, but it should be noted that Browning makes him
a monk.

With anybody's gift. Who'd stoop to blame
This sort of trifling? Even had you skill   35
In speech—(which I have not)—to make your will
Quite clear to such an one, and say, "Just this
Or that in you disgusts me; here you miss,
Or there exceed the mark"—and if she let
Herself be lessoned so, nor plainly set   40
Her wits to yours, forsooth, and made excuse,
—E'en then would be some stooping; and I choose
Never to stoop. Oh sir, she smiled, no doubt,
Whene'er I passed her; but who passed without
Much the same smile? This grew; I gave commands;   45
Then all smiles stopped together. There she stands
As if alive. Will't please you rise? We'll meet
The company below, then. I repeat,
The Count your master's known munificence
Is ample warrant that no just pretence   50
Of mine for dowry will be disallowed;
Though his fair daughter's self, as I avowed
At starting, is my object. Nay, we'll go
Together down, sir. Notice Neptune, though,
Taming a sea-horse, thought a rarity,   55
Which Claus of Innsbruck cast in bronze for me!

                              Robert Browning (1812–1889)

The Star in the Hills

A star hit in the hills behind our house
up where the grass turns brown touching the sky.

Meteors have hit the world before, but this was near,
and since TV; few saw, but many felt the shock.
The state of California owns that land   5
(and out from shore three miles), and any stars
that come will be roped off and viewed on week days 8 to 5.

A guard who took the oath of loyalty and denied
any police record told me this:
"If you don't have a police record yet   10
you could take the oath and get a job
if California should be hit by another star."

"I'd promise to be loyal to California
and to guard any stars that hit it," I said,
"or any place three miles out from shore,   15
unless the star was bigger than the state—
in which case I'd be loyal to *it*."

But he said no exceptions were allowed,
and he leaned against the state-owned meteor
so calm and puffed a cork-tip cigarette   20
that I looked down and traced my foot in the dust
and thought again and said, "Ok—any star."

William Stafford (b. 1914)

Verbal Irony

Since few short poems are basically narrative or dramatic, they lend themselves less to dramatic irony than to verbal irony. Like all irony, verbal irony works through extravagance, discrepancy, incongruity, or contradiction. The extremes of verbal irony are sarcasm, which is more hostile and obvious than most irony, and innuendo, which works by subtle suggestion rather than by indirect statement. Three common kinds of verbal irony are hyperbole (overstatement), understatement, and paradox.

Hyperbole (overstatement).   Overstatement is common in ordinary speech but not always with an ironical intention. Exaggeration to improve a dull tale may have no ironical intention, but the frequency with which it occurs attests to the naturalness of the impulse to exaggerate. The statement, "She is as big as the side of a house" is neither true nor kind, and being trite, it has nothing to do with literary hyperbole. Hyperbole displays wit as well as exaggeration. In the balcony scene Romeo's impetuosity is underscored with tragic irony when he declares to Juliet:

> Alack, there lies more peril in thine eye
> Than twenty of their swords!

Understatement.   Understatement occurs when the speaker's words deliberately say less than his attitude warrants. "What a day!" is a common understatement. The speaker in Andrew Marvell's "To His Coy Mistress" concludes a section of his plea to his mistress with understatement.

> The grave's a fine and private place,
> But none, I think, do there embrace.

Paradox. Paradox is a form of irony that arrests attention by presenting an apparent contradiction ("cold passion"). Like other forms of irony it works by surprise and incongruity, and like them its aim is a realistic point not directly stated but made emphatic by the demand it makes upon the reader to resolve the apparent contradiction. In a well-known modern poem the speaker observes "the silent, eloquent gestures" of fruit tree branches in bloom. Since eloquence denotes fluency of speech, there is a paradox in calling the silent branches eloquent; the branches in bloom say something about their beauty that requires no words. John Donne, speaking to God in "A Hymn to God the Father," says, "When Thou has done, Thou hast not done": when God has forgiven him the sins he is presently conscious of, God is still not finished.

On a Girdle

That which her slender waist confined
Shall now my joyful temples bind;
No monarch but would give his crown,
His arms might do what this has done.

It was my heaven's extremest sphere,   5
The pale which held that lovely deer.
My joy, my grief, my hope, my love,
Did all within this circle move.

A narrow compass, and yet there
Dwelt all that's good and all that's fair;   10
Give me but what this riband bound;
Take all the rest the sun goes round!

Edmund Waller (1606–1687)

My life closed twice before its close

My life closed twice before its close;
It remains to see
If Immortality unveil
A third event to me,

So huge, so hopeless to conceive   5
As these that twice befell.
Parting is all we know of heaven,
And all we need of hell.

Emily Dickinson (1830–1886)

Puss! Puss!

—Oh, Auntie, isn't he a beauty! And is he a gentleman or a lady?
—Neither, my dear! I had him fixed. It saves him from so many
  undesirable associations.

D. H. Lawrence (1885–1930)

Acquainted with the night

I have been one acquainted with the night.
I have walked out in rain—and back in rain.
I have outwalked the furthest city light.

I have looked down the saddest city lane.
I have passed by the watchman on his beat   5
And dropped my eyes, unwilling to explain.

I have stood still and stopped the sound of feet
When far away an interrupted cry
Came over houses from another street,

But not to call me back or say good-by;   10
And further still at an unearthly height
One luminary clock against the sky

Proclaimed the time was neither wrong nor right.
I have been one acquainted with the night.

Robert Frost (1874–1963)

Bells for John Whiteside's Daughter

There was such speed in her little body,
And such lightness in her footfall,
It is no wonder her brown study
Astonishes us all.

Her wars were bruited in our high window.   5
We looked among orchard trees and beyond
Where she took arms against her shadow,
Or harried unto the pond

The lazy geese, like a snow cloud
Dripping their snow on the green grass,   10
Tricking and stopping, sleepy and proud,
Who cried in goose, Alas,

For the tireless heart within the little
Lady with rod that made them rise
From their noon apple-dreams and scuttle   15
Goose-fashion under the skies!

But now go the bells, and we are ready,
In one house we are sternly stopped
To say we are vexed at her brown study,
Lying so primly propped.   20

John Crowe Ransom (1888–1974)

Tell all the Truth but tell it slant

Tell all the Truth but tell it slant—
Success in Circuit lies
Too bright for our infirm Delight
The Truth's superb surprise
As Lightning to the Children eased   5
With explanation kind
The Truth must dazzle gradually
Or every man be blind—

Emily Dickinson (1830–1886)

A Hymn to God the Father

Wilt Thou forgive that sin where I begun,
  Which is my sin, though it were done before?
Wilt Thou forgive those sins through which I run,
  And do them still, though still I do deplore?
    When Thou hast done, Thou hast not done,   5
      For I have more.

Wilt Thou forgive that sin by which I have won
  Others to sin? and made my sin their door?
Wilt Thou forgive that sin which I did shun
  A year or two, but wallowed in a score?   10
    When Thou hast done, Thou hast not done,
      For I have more.

I have a sin of fear, that when I have spun
  My last thread, I shall perish on the shore;
Swear by Thyself that at my death Thy Sun   15
  Shall shine as it shines now, and heretofore;
    And, having done that, Thou hast done,
      I have no more.

John Donne (1572?–1631)

7 Style

Varieties of Style

The great themes of poetry remain the same—love, the family, guilt, personal identity, mutability, and death, the universal concerns of all persons—but the conditions under which life is experienced change for each generation. The anxieties of being young are the same for almost everyone, but each person feels the stress and the pleasures of youth in an entirely individual way. The individual experiences a unique form of the universal archetypal experience, and literature comes into being when the style of the writer gives his individual definition to the archetype. Usually the voice of the speaker is expressed in a style characteristic not only of the speaker but also of the author—or in one of several styles characteristic of the author's development. Just as the changes in our tone of voice express our own changes in mood, poets express many attitudes of their own through changes in the voice of the speaker. But most poets also develop a personal style with characteristics evident in all of their poems. Style is a term used to denote the author's habitual manner of selecting and ordering words and his preference for certain rhythms, attitudes, and subjects.

A writer's style will to some extent reflect his generation and the cultural tradition he is part of, but his own psyche and taste, including his own disposition toward conformity or revolt, will be critical in how he uses the tradition he inherits and the style he creates. John Crowe Ransom's "Dead Boy" in the previous chapter, in its dry, impersonal style, is working ironically against the excessive sentimentality of nineteenth century poems about dead children. Most of modern poetry is an example of the freedom claimed from the constraints of meter and inherited proprieties of diction and subject. But every poet develops in his own way a style to express the attitudes that can become his only when he has found the style to express them, a style that, though nourished by tradition, is a fresh and personal departure from it.

Critical descriptions of style are often confusing to the uninitiated because they seem to be contradictory. One poet is praised for the naturalness and simplicity of his style and another for the opposite qualities—for elegance, wit, density of interactions between image and idea, metrical dexterity, and a playful intelligence too quick to follow in one reading. One poet is admired for dealing with plain, household truth clearly stated and another for forging through his own passion and wit a style so complex that only an educated reader can see the necessity for it. Of the latter kind of style we may ask why the difficulties of the style were necessary.

The truth about the truth is, as Oscar Wilde pointed out, that it is never pure and rarely simple. This statement is even truer of the emotions. One may think that he has a pure and simple anger or love when, in fact, these emotions are the result of a complex psychic history. If one is to state his attitudes truly, it would seem to be necessary to develop a style to handle great complexity. While some poets have done that, others have trimmed their style to focus on something elemental in their own and everyman's experience. Both ways to a poem are admired when they work. What matters is how well the end is achieved. Does the elaborate style communicate a true complexity, or is it merely ornamental? Does the elaboration of the point in stylistic ingenuity increase the effectiveness of the poem, or does it become merely repetitious? Does a mannered exaggeration and extravagance in metaphor only require a more sophisticated taste than most readers have developed, or is the result really excessive and unnecessarily confusing? With plainer, direct, and understated styles we may feel that too much is hidden. Why did the poet who exhibits such ability to be clear require that his poem be closely examined to render its significance? We may answer that nothing renders its significance until it is examined. We may then examine the poem, see the kind of significance it was designed to have, and take pleasure in its subtleties and design. Or we may decide that there is very little there.

To understand how style functions in a poem is to see that the poem would be a different poem if it were written in another style. Examining its style is essential to any understanding of the nature of the experience the poem is designed to create. The following series of questions should help you to come to that understanding, not just about the poems in this chapter but about all others as well. Because styles differ greatly, some questions are more useful than others for studying different poems.

Questions for Studying Style

1. Where has the poet gained a direct and natural effect in tone, structure, and word choice? Where has he deviated from the natural and direct word, phrase, or word order to achieve another effect? What has he gained by this deviation?

2. To what extent has the poet succeeded in arresting attention and intriguing curiosity by the unexpected image or turn of thought?

3. To what extent is the style concrete (dense with images). To what extent is it abstract?

4. To what extent is the style disciplined to conciseness and implication? To what extent is its value rather in the richness and amplitude with which it develops its thought?

5. To what extent is the style, including the things the speaker observes, intellectual and impersonal? To what extent is it personal, passionate, and unrestrained? Insofar as restraint of some kind is inevitable in poetry, where are the restraints in the latter style? How do the disciplines and restraints of the style differ from those of other styles?

6. To what extent is the style new, something that no other poet has created? To what extent is it traditional?

7. A poem prepares the reader for its effects, structuring details to build to ironies, turns of thought, and conclusions. What is distinctive about how the poet you are studying structures his poem? How does he use the line ending to gain special attention for words through their placement, either at the end of one line or the beginning of the next?

8. Commonly there is an interplay between the musical effect and the colloquial effect of a poem even though one dominates. Which effect dominates the sound? How is the effect of the sound related to the speaker and his attitude?

9. How clear is the poem? If you find it unclear, to what extent is the ambiguity a result of an ambivalence in the speaker's at-

titude? Why did the poet create an ambivalent speaker? What in the actual nature of the situation might justify the poem's ambiguity? What would be lost if the poem were made clearer? What in the style is designed to communicate the speaker's ambivalence?

10. Serious subjects may be treated in a great variety of styles. Are the word choices and tone dignified and graceful, reflecting the seriousness of the subject, or do they work ironically and playfully with it?

11. To what extent does the style in its total effect and in its incidental achievements appeal to the senses, to the emotions, to the intellect?

12. A poet takes pleasures in writing in certain ways—making unusual rhymes, for example, or contrasting colloquial and sophisticated diction, simple and complex syntax. What in his style seems to be most enjoyable to him—or, perhaps, to you?

Poem

As the cat
climbed over
the top of

the jamcloset
first the right   5
forefoot

carefully
then the hind
stepped down

into the pit of   10
the empty
flowerpot

William Carlos Williams (1883–1963)

QUESTIONS

1. What effect is achieved by the short lines?
2. Why does Williams not allow us to see a specific cat—"pale yellow alley" or "sleek Siamese"?
3. Is the poem merely about cats, or is it also possible to see an image of how the careful plans of humans may lead to unintended ends?

4. Show where the simplicity of the style is crafted to create comic effects.
5. In what other lines might "carefully" be placed? Why is it best where it is?

To a Snail

If "compression is the first grace of style,"
you have it. Contractility is a virtue
as modesty is a virtue.
It is not the acquisition of any one thing
that is able to adorn,   5
or the incidental quality that occurs
as a concomitant of something well said,
that we value in style,
but the principle that is hid:
in the absence of feet, "a method of conclusions";   10
"a knowledge of principles,"
in the curious phenomenon of your occipital horn.

                    Marianne Moore (1887–1972)

QUESTIONS

1. Marianne Moore's style is often praised for the poise with which she welds opinion, emotion and precise phrasing. What opinions are here? What evidence can you see of precise phrasing?
2. The speaker makes a statement, logically organized, to a snail. What is that statement?
3. What qualities of style does the speaker prefer and how does the snail symbolize them?

Her final Summer was it

Her final Summer was it—
And yet We guessed it not—
If tenderer industriousness
Pervaded Her, We thought

A further force of life   5
Developed from within—
When Death lit all the shortness up
It made the hurry plain—

We wondered at our blindness
When nothing was to see   10
But Her Carrara Guide post—
At Our Stupidity—

When duller than our dullness
The Busy Darling lay—
So busy was she—finishing—   15
So leisurely—were We—

Emily Dickinson (1830–1886)

Rose Aylmer

Ah what avails the sceptered race,
   Ah what the form divine!
What every virtue, every grace!
   Rose Aylmer, all were thine.
Rose Aylmer, whom these wakeful eyes   5
   May weep, but never see,
A night of memories and of sighs
   I consecrate to thee.

Walter Savage Landor (1775–1864)

Song

Summer is over upon the sea.
The pleasure yacht, the social being,
that danced on the endless polished floor,
stepped and side-stepped like Fred Astaire,
is gone, is gone, docked somewhere ashore.   5

The friends have left, the sea is bare
that was strewn with floating, fresh green weeds.
Only the rusty-sided freighters
go past the moon's marketless craters
and the stars are the only ships of pleasure.   10

Elizabeth Bishop (b. 1911)

Do Not Go Gentle into That Good Night

Do not go gentle into that good night,
Old age should burn and rave at close of day;
Rage, rage against the dying of the light.

Though wise men at their end know dark is right,
Because their words had forked no lightning they   5
Do not go gentle into that good night.

Good men, the last wave by, crying how bright
Their frail deeds might have danced in a green bay,
Rage, rage against the dying of the light.

Wild men who caught and sang the sun in flight,   10
And learn, too late, they grieved it on its way,
Do not go gentle into that good night.

Grave men, near death, who see with blinding sight
Blind eyes could blaze like meteors and be gay,
Rage, rage against the dying of the light.   15

And you, my father, there on the sad height,
Curse, bless, me now with your fierce tears, I pray.
Do not go gentle into that good night.
Rage, rage against the dying of the light.

                                        Dylan Thomas (1914–1953)

NOTES AND QUESTIONS

1. The "villanelle" is a fixed form consisting of five tercets and a quatrain. The entire form is strictly linked together by its use of only two rhymes, the tercets rhyming *aba* and the quatrain *abaa*. How has Thomas managed to avoid artificiality with this French form and gain the dignified effect for which this poem is greatly admired?
2. What sound patterns other than the rhyme scheme control the poem's form?
3. *blind* (14): Thomas' father was blind, and, an unbeliever, he was also blind to holy light. What other words are used with more than one meaning, perhaps an archetypal meaning?

plato told

plato told

him:he couldn't
believe it(jesus

told him;he
wouldn't believe   5
it)lao

tsze
certainly told
him,and general
(yes   10

mam)
sherman;
and even
(believe it
or   15

not)you
told him:i told
him;we told him
(he didn't believe it,no

sir)it took   20
a nipponized bit of
the old sixth

avenue
el;in the top of his head:to tell

him   25

e. e. cummings (1894–1962)

NOTE

Before Pearl Harbor, when the Sixth Avenue elevated was torn down in New York, the scrap metal was sold to the Japanese, here called the Nipponese, who converted it to weaponry.

Felix Randal

Felix Randal the farrier, O is he dead then? my duty all ended,
Who have watched his mould of man, big-boned and hardy-
handsome
Pining, pining, till time when reason rambled in it and some
Fatal four disorders, fleshed there, all contended?

Sickness broke him. Impatient, he cursed at first, but
mended   5
Being anointed and all; though a heavenlier heart began some
Months earlier, since I had our sweet reprieve and ransom
Tendered to him. Ah well, God rest him all road ever he
offended!

This seeing the sick endears them to us, us too it endears.
My tongue had taught thee comfort, touch had quenched thy
tears,   10
Thy tears that touched my heart, child, Felix, poor Felix Randal;

How far from then forethought of, all thy more boisterous years,
When thou at the random grim forge, powerful amidst peers,
Didst fettle for the great grey drayhorse his bright and bat-
tering sandal!

Gerard Manley Hopkins (1844–1889)

Afton Water

Flow gently, sweet Afton! among thy green braes,
Flow gently, I'll sing thee a song in thy praise;
My Mary's asleep by thy murmuring stream,
Flow gently, sweet Afton, disturb not her dream.

Thou stock dove whose echo resounds through the glen   5
Ye wild whistling blackbirds in yon thorny den,
Thou green-crested lapwing, thy screaming forbear,
I charge you, disturb not my slumbering fair.

How loftly, sweet Afton, thy neighboring hills,
Far marked with the courses of clear, winding rills;   10
There daily I wander as noon rises high,
My flocks and my Mary's sweet cot in my eye.

How pleasant thy banks and green valleys below,
Where, wild in the woodlands, the primroses blow;
There oft, as mild ev'ning weeps over the lea,   15
The sweet-scented birk shades my Mary and me.

Thy crystal stream, Afton, how lovely it glides,
And winds by the cot where my Mary resides;
How wanton thy waters her snowy feet lave,
As, gathering sweet flowerets, she stems thy clear wave.   20

Flow gently, sweet Afton, among thy green braes,
Flow gently, sweet river, the theme of my lays;
My Mary's asleep by thy murmuring stream,
Flow gently, sweet Afton, disturb not her dream.

                                        Robert Burns (1759–1796)

The Pulley

  When God at first made man,
Having a glass of blessings standing by,
"Let us," said He, "pour on him all we can.
Let the world's riches, which dispersèd lie,
  Contract into a span."   5

  So strength first made a way;
Then beauty flowed, then wisdom, honor, pleasure.
When almost all was out, God made a stay,
Perceiving that, alone of all his treasure,
  Rest in the bottom lay.   10

  "For if I should," said He,
"Bestow this jewel also on my creature,
He would adore My gifts instead of Me,
And rest in nature, not the God of nature;
  So both should losers be.   15

  "Yet let him keep the rest,
But keep them with repining restlessness.
Let him be rich and weary, that at least
If goodness lead him not, yet weariness
  May toss him to My breast."   20

                                        George Herbert (1593–1633)

Preludes

I

The winter evening settles down
With smell of steaks in passageways.
Six o'clock.
The burnt-out ends of smoky days.
And now a gusty shower wraps   5
The grimy scraps
Of withered leaves about your feet
And newspapers from vacant lots;
The showers beat
On broken blinds and chimney-pots,   10
And at the corner of the street
A lonely cab-horse steams and stamps.

And then the lighting of the lamps.

II

The morning comes to consciousness
Of faint stale smells of beer   15
From the sawdust-trampled street
With all its muddy feet that press
To early coffee-stands.

With the other masquerades
That time resumes,   20
One thinks of all the hands
That are raising dingy shades
In a thousand furnished rooms.

III

You tossed a blanket from the bed,
You lay upon your back, and waited;   25
You dozed, and watched the night revealing
The thousand sordid images
Of which your soul was constituted;
They flickered against the ceiling.
And when all the world came back   30
And the light crept up between the shutters
And you heard the sparrows in the gutters,
You had such a vision of the street
As the street hardly understands;

Sitting along the bed's edge, where   35
You curled the papers from your hair,
Or clasped the yellow soles of feet
In the palms of both soiled hands.

IV

His soul stretched tight across the skies
That fade behind a city block,   40
Or trampled by insistent feet
At four and five and six o'clock;
And short square fingers stuffing pipes,
And evening newspapers, and eyes
Assured of certain certainties,   45
The conscience of a blackened street
Impatient to assume the world.

I am moved by fancies that are curled
Around these images, and cling:
The notion of some infinitely gentle   50
Infinitely suffering thing.

Wipe your hand across your mouth, and laugh;
The worlds revolve like ancient women
Gathering fuel in vacant lots.

                    T. S. Eliot (1888–1965)

View of a Pig

The pig lay on a barrow dead.
It weighed, they said, as much as three men.
Its eyes closed, pink white eyelashes.
Its trotters stuck straight out.

Such weight and thick pink bulk   5
Set in death seemed not just dead.
It was less than lifeless, further off.
It was like a sack of wheat.

I thumped it without feeling remorse.
One feels guilty insulting the dead,   10
Walking on graves. But this pig
Did not seem able to accuse.

It was too dead. Just so much
A poundage of lard and pork.
Its last dignity had entirely gone.   15
It was not a figure of fun.

Too dead now to pity.
To remember its life, din, stronghold
Of earthly pleasure as it had been,
Seemed a false effort, and off the point.   20

Too deadly factual. Its weight
Oppressed me—how could it be moved?
And the trouble of cutting it up!
The gash in its throat was shocking, but not pathetic.

Once I ran at a fair in the noise   25
To catch a greased piglet
That was faster and nimbler than a cat,
Its squeal was the rending of metal.

Pigs must have hot blood, they feel like ovens.
Their bite is worse than a horse's—   30
They chop a half-moon clean out.
They eat cinders, dead cats.

Distinctions and admirations such
As this one was long finished with.
I stared at it a long time. They were going to scald it,   35
Scald it and scour it like a doorstep.

                         Ted Hughes (b. 1930)

In All These Acts

*Cleave the wood and thou shalt find Me, lift the rock and I am
there!*

                    —The Gospel According to Thomas

Dawn cried out: the brutal voice of a bird
Flattened the seaglaze. Treading that surf
Hunch-headed fishers toed small agates,
Their delicate legs, iridescent, stilting the ripples.
Suddenly the cloud closed. They heard big wind   5
Boom back on the cliff, crunch timber over along the ridge.
They shook up their wings, crying; terror flustered their pinions.

Then hemlock, tall, torn by the roots, went crazily down,
The staggering gyrations of splintered kindling.
Flung out of bracken, fleet mule deer bolted;   10
But the great elk, caught midway between two scissoring logs,
Arched belly-up and died, the snapped spine
Half torn out of his peeled back, his hind legs
Jerking that gasped convulsion, the kick of spasmed life,
Paunch plowed open, purple entrails   15
Disgorged from the basketwork ribs
Erupting out, splashed sideways, wrapping him,
Gouted in blood, flecked with the brittle silver of bone.
Frenzied, the terrible head
Thrashed off its antlered fuzz in that rubble   20
And then fell still, the great tongue
That had bugled in rut, calling the cow-elk up from the glades,
Thrust agonized out, the maimed member
Bloodily stiff in the stone-smashed teeth . . .

                            Far down below,   25
The mountain torrent, that once having started
Could never be stopped, scooped up that avalanchial wrack
And strung it along, a riddle of bubble and littered duff
Spun down its thread. At the gorged river mouth
The sea plunged violently in, gasping its potholes,   30
Sucked and panted, answering itself in its spume.
The river, spent at last, beating driftwood up and down
In a frenzy of capitulation, pumped out its life,
Destroying itself in the mother sea,
There where the mammoth sea-grown salmon   35
Lurk immemorial, roe in their hulls, about to begin.
They will beat that barbarous beauty out
On those high-stacked shallows, those headwater claims,
Back where they were born. Along that upward-racing trek
Time springs through all its loops and flanges,   40
The many-faced splendor and the music of the leaf,
The copulation of beasts and the watery laughter of drakes,
Too few the grave witnesses, the wakeful, vengeful beauty,
Devolving itself of its whole constraint,
Erupting as it goes.   45

                In all these acts
Christ crouches and seethes, pitched forward
On the crucifying stroke, juvescent, that will spring Him

Out of the germ, out of the belly of the dying buck,
Out of the father-phallus and the torn-up root.   50
These are the modes of His forth-showing,
His serene agonization. In the clicking teeth of otters
Over and over He dies and is born,
Shaping the weasel's jaw in His leap
And the staggering rush of the bass.   55

William Everson (b. 1912)

Now

Imagine coastal spray, far movement, marsh,
And birdcall—not the little ones—
Cocked in the rock, reeds winnowing, just dawn,
Flocks in the sea like negatives of stars.
Picture the loving distance waking there—   5
Our blood infatuated with old bones—
Whacked grass impatient, wind glued on the gull,
And all the idiotic diving birds,
The weed-whipped, grain-grabbed, dipping dears,
Ready to rise. And there you are and I . . .   10

Robert Huff (b. 1924)

Translations Compared

The translation of poetry is a special kind of art. A literal translation of the words of a poem from one language to another will lose most of what was important in the original—the rhythm, the musical phrasing, the colloquial vigor of the natural phrasing, and all the connotative precision that is the source of implications and associations essential to the art of the original. As a result some poems seem to be untranslatable; others have been the basis of adaptations that catch an essential quality of the original at the price of a loss in literalness and of other elements as well. The good translator of poetry must be a poet himself so that the result is a poem, one that captures as many essential qualities as possible of the original.

Helen

It is I, O Azure, come from the caves below
To hear the waves clamber the loudening shores,
And see those barks again in the dawn's glow
Borne out of darkness, swept by golden oars.

My solitary hands call back the lords   5
Whose salty beards beguiled my finger-tips;
I wept. They sang the prowess of their swords
And what great bays fled sternward of their ships.

I hear the martial trumpets and the deep-
Sea conches cry a cadence to the sweeps;   10
The oarsmen's chantey holds the storm in sway;

And high on the hero prows the Gods I see,
Their antique smiles insulted by the spray,
Reaching their carved, indulgent arms to me.

                              Paul Valéry
                    translated by Richard Wilbur

Hélène la reine triste

Azur! c'est moi. Je viens des grottes de la mort
Entendre l'onde se rompre aux degrés sonores,
Et je revois les galères dans les aurores
Ressusciter de l'ombre au fil des rames d'or.

Mes solitaires mains appellent les monarques   5
Dont la barbe de sel amusait mes doigts purs;
Je pleurais. Ils chantaient leurs triomphes obscurs
Et les golfes enfuis des poupes de leurs barques,

J'entends les conques profondes et les clairons
Militaires rythmer le vol des avirons;   10
Le chant clair des rameurs enchaîne le tumulte,

Et les Dieux, à la proue héroïque exaltés
Dans leur sourire antique et que l'écume insulte,
Tendent vers moi leurs bras indulgents et sculptés.

                    Paul Valéry (1871–1945)

Helen

I am the blue! I come from the lower world
to hear the serene erosion of the surf;
once more I see the galleys bleed with dawn,
and shark with muffled rowlocks into Troy.
My solitary hands recall the kings;   5
I used to run my fingers through their beards;
I wept. They sang about their shady wars,
the great gulfs boiling sternward from their keels.
I hear the military trumpets, all that brass,
blasting commands to the frantic oars;   10
the rowers' metronome enchains the sea,
and high on beaked and dragon prows, the gods—
their fixed, archaic smiles stung by the salt—
reach out their carved, indulgent arms to me!

Paul Valéry
translated by Robert Lowell

Ars Poetica

Between shadow and space, between trimmings and damsels,
endowed with a singular heart and sorrowful dreams,
precipitously pallid, withered in the brow
and with a furious widower's mourning for each day of life,
ah, for each invisible water that I drink somnolently   5
and from every sound that I welcome trembling,
I have the same absent thirst and the same cold fever,
a nascent ear, an indirect anguish,
as if thieves or ghosts were coming,
and in a shell of fixed and profound expanse,   10
like a humiliated waiter, like a slightly raucous bell,
like an old mirror, like the smell of a solitary house
where the guests come in at night wildly drunk,
and there is a smell of clothes thrown on the floor, and an absence of
     flowers—
possibly in another even less melancholy way—   15
but the truth is that suddenly the wind that lashes my chest,

the nights of infinite substance fallen in my bedroom,
the noise of a day that burns with sacrifice,
ask me mournfully what prophecy there is in me,
and there is a swarm of objects that call without being
    answered,   20
and a ceaseless movement, and a bewildered man.

Pablo Neruda
translated by Donald D. Walsh

Arte Poética

Entre sombra y espacio, entre guarniciones y doncellas,
dotado de corazón singular y sueños funestos,
precipitadamente pálido, marchito en la frente
y con luto de viudo furioso por cada día de vida,
ay, para cada agua invisible que bebo soñolientamente   5
y de todo sonido que acojo temblando,
tengo la misma sed ausente y la misma fiebre fría,
un oído que nace, una angustia indirecta,
como si llegaran ladrones o fantasmas,
y en una cáscara de extensión fija y profunda,   10
como un camarero humillado, como una campana un poco ronca,
como un espejo viejo, como un olor de casa sola
en la que los huéspedes entran de noche perdidamente ebrios,
y hay un olor de ropa tirada al suelo, y una ausencia de flores.
—posiblemente de otro modo aún menos melancólico—,   15
pero, la verdad, de pronto, el viento que azota mi pecho,
las noches de substancia infinita caídas en mi dormitorio,
el ruido de un día que arde con sacrificio
me piden lo profético que hay en mí, con melancolía,
y un golpe de objetos que llaman sin ser respondidos   20
hay, y un movimiento sin tregua, y un nombre confuso.

Pablo Neruda (1904–1973)

The Art of Poetry

Between shadow and space, between ornaments and maidens,
endowed with singular heart and doleful dreams,
precipitously paling, furrowed of brow
and in mourning like a widower raging over each day of life,
with an "ah, me" for each unseen water I drink somnolently   5
and every sound I take unto me trembling,

I have the same absent thirst and the same frosty fever,
an ear being born, an indirect anguish,
as if thieves or phantoms were about to appear,
and in a shell of fixed and deep extension,   10
like a servant humiliated, like a somewhat husky bell,
like an ancient mirror, like the odor of an empty house
into which guests enter at nighttime lost in drink
and there's an odor of clothes thrown on the floor and an absence of
    flowers
—possibly some other way even less melancholy—   15
but, in truth, all at once the wind that lashes my chest,
the nights of infinite substance fallen in my bedroom,
the sound of a day ardent with sacrifice
requires of me what there is in me of prophet, with melancholy,
and a rush of objects that call, unanswered,   20
is there, and a movement without surcease, and a confused name.

Pablo Neruda
translated by James Graham-Luján

NOTES AND QUESTIONS

1. *sueños funestos* (2): most literally translates "funereal dreams" but
   that phrase has inappropriate connotations of death in English.
   Which translator has solved the translator's problem better?
2. *ay* (5): is a sound of lament in the Spanish. Which translator has
   best preserved the tone of lament?
3. *arde* (18): is close to "ardent" in English. Which translation is
   better?
4. *con melancolía* (19): an ambiguous phrase. Does it modify the
   verb *piden* or the noun *profético*? Which translation seems prefer-
   able?
5. *nombre* (21): a noun meaning "name" in English. One translator
   has used another version, possibly faulty, employing the word
   hombre, "man." Which do you prefer?

Sentimentality and Didacticism

Most poetry deals with sentiments (feelings and attitudes)
of the speaker or poet, but the term "sentimentality" denotes an
indulgence in sentiments that are either not genuine or, if sincere, are
overstated. The sentimental poem asks a response from the reader

in excess of what seems appropriate for the situation as it is presented. Sentimentality may appear as a single word choice or pervade the entire conception of the poem.

To express sentiment is in itself a wholly valid function of many poems: the intoxication and exhilaration of the sunny days in Dickinson's "I taste a Liquor never brewed" or the joyousness in Thomas' "Fern Hill" are two examples. In Part Three, the subject or theme is constant throughout each section, but, in poem after poem, widely or subtly varying sentiments and attitudes are expressed. To distinguish between sentimentality and genuine sentiment may be difficult because, just as individuals change in their own taste, the nature and intensity of a whole people's sentiments may change from one historical period to the next. What seemed true sentiments for earlier ages may sometimes sound hollow to us. For example, the passionate theocentricity of some earlier religious poems may seem like indulgent sentimentality and didacticism to some modern disbelievers.

Sentimentality and didacticism may often coexist in a poem. Much poetry has an instructive quality, but "didacticism," when used as a derogatory term, denotes that the instructive element of the poem has become excessive, or that the effect achieved owes little to the important elements of poetry. Faulty didacticism appears in the appeal to popular stock responses in the language of politics and conventional morality. The distinction between good poetry with a didactic element and a poem excessively didactic is a matter of form and style. In poetry the meaning ought to be intrinsic or implied. However, if the ideas are stated directly, at least the form and language ought to deliver those ideas with nuance, force, precision, and freshness.

All poetry has meaning in terms of the speaker's attitude toward the experience he presents, even poems that work with an ironic discrepancy between the speaker's attitude and the reader's. Some very good poetry has a specifically didactic intention, as, for example, the antiwar poems in Part Three (pp. 286–93). Didacticism begins to seem a fault when the ideas are trite or moralistic or when the poetry becomes an ornamental means of presenting ideas that could be expressed more precisely in prose. A jingling rhyme and a jog-trot meter leading to an obvious ethical or political moral will not make a good poem no matter how popular it may be with people of particular persuasions who tap their foot happily to its beat.

On His Mistress Drowned

Sweet stream, that does with equal pace
Both thyself fly, and thyself chase,
    Forbear awhile to flow,
    And listen to my woe.
Then go, and tell the sea that all its brine   5
    Is fresh, compar'd to mine;
Inform it that the gentle dame,
Who was the life of all my flame,
    In th' glory of her bud
    Has pass'd the fatal flood.   10
Death by this only stroke triumphs above
    The greatest power of love:
    Alas, alas! I must give o'er,
    My sighs will let me add no more.

Go on, sweet stream, and henceforth rest   15
    No more than does my troubled breast;
And if my sad complaints have made thee stay,
    These tears, these tears shall mend thy way.

                            Thomas Sprat (1635–1713)

Little Trotty Wagtail

Little trotty wagtail, he went in the rain,
And tittering, tottering sideways he ne'er got straight again,
He stooped to get a worm, and looked up to get a fly,
And then he flew away ere his feathers they were dry.

Little trotty wagtail, he waddled in the mud,   5
And left his little footmarks, trample where he would.
He waddled in the water-pudge, and waggle went his tail,
And chirrup up his wings to dry upon the garden rail.

Little trotty wagtail, you nimble all about,
And in the dimpling water-pudge you waddle in and out;   10
Your home is nigh at hand, and in the warm pigsty,
So, little Master Wagtail, I'll bid you a good-bye.

                            John Clare (1793–1864)

Don't Go In

It is lighted, we know, like a palace,
    That fair, gilded temple of sin;
It has signs on the walls; let us read them:
    "The best of wine, brandy, and gin."
(As if human stomachs could need them!)   5
    My son, oh, my son, don't go in.

Though it giveth its beautiful color,
    Though it gleams in the cup like a rose,
Though it seeks like a serpent to charm you,
    And glitters and glimmers and glows,   10
Like the bright, wily serpent 'twill harm you
    And rob you of earthly repose.

It will tarnish your glorious manhood
    And sow the vile seeds of disgrace.
Then, why deal with this terrible danger?   15
    Why enter this crime-haunted place?
Much better to pass it a stranger
    Than God's whole image deface.

Much better to gird on the armor
    To fight life's great battle and win,   20
Than to lay down your all on the altar
    That burns in this temple of sin.
So, strike for the right and not falter—
    My son, oh, my son, don't go in.

                    Mrs. Kidder (a temperance
                        advocate, c. 1880)

from **Night Thoughts**

Death, the great counsellor, who man inspires
With ev'ry nobler thought and fairer deed!
Death, the deliverer, who rescues man!
Death, the rewarder, who the rescu'd crowns!
Death, that absolves my birth; a curse without it!   5
Rich death, that realizes all my cares,
Toils, virtues, hopes; without it a chimera!
Death, of all pain the period, not of joy;
Joy's source, and subject, still subsist unhurt;
One, in my soul; and one, in her great sire;   10

Tho' the four winds were warring for my dust.
Yes, and from winds, and waves, and central night,
Tho' prison'd there, my dust too I reclaim
(To dust when drop proud nature's proudest spheres),
And live entire. Death is the crown of life: 15
Were death denied, poor man would live in vain;
Were death denied, to live would not be life;
Were death denied, ev'n fools would wish to die.
Death wounds to cure: we fall; we rise; we reign!

Edward Young (1683–1765)

8 The Nature and Value of Poetry

Poetry and Rhetoric

Reading poetry is a particular kind of experience, and since its medium is language, it is primarily as language that it makes its impression. As the previous two chapters have suggested, what is impressive is not so much the freshness of the thought as the freshness of the phrasing and the personal style of the poet. The idea for a poem may be an image, a thought, a figure, or a phrase that begins to develop by getting linked with other elements. Robert Frost said his poems often began with the sound of a sentence. Sooner or later these elements become defined by their association with a speaker and his tone. On the other hand, rhetoric organizes ideas logically, as science does, to define and analyze and, as argument does, to persuade. The meaning of a piece of prose can be paraphrased without the loss of meaning and effect that occurs in attempts to paraphrase poetry.

However, it may be helpful in learning to read poetry to construct a prose statement, a paraphrase, of what the poem seems to say even though further study of the poem may require that the statement be revised: image, sound, style, and the speaker's tone will introduce contradictions, shades of meaning, and interactions omitted from the paraphrased statement. Paraphrase attempts to reproduce the poem's tone and organization and to include the implications of its images and symbols as well; but in paraphrase, the art and experience of the poem are lost. The literal precision of prose is substituted for the direct experience of the poem. The result with a good poem will be little more satisfactory than a paraphrase of your favorite popular song. That song will have some images and some ideas inevitably associated with them, but the paraphrase of it will not provide any of the satisfactions of the song itself.

What does "Swing Low, Sweet Chariot" mean? When we answer by saying that it expresses the speaker's desire to be carried to heaven in a chariot, we have not only ignored all the other elements that have made this song one of the most popular in the history of American song, but we have left the chariot unexplained. The image of the chariot attracts our attention. Where did the speaker get the idea that a chariot was the proper conveyance? This question is easily enough answered, but only in the context of its relationship to the whole song and the speaker's need to visualize a mysterious, desired event. Much of the song's great appeal defies paraphrase, because its appeal comes from the enactment and evocation of a mood, even though some ideas are inevitably associated with it.

Or consider an anonymous, early English lyric from the oral tradition.

Western Wind

> Western wind, when wilt thou blow,
> The small rain down can rain?
> Christ, that my love were in my arms,
> And I in my bed again!

The poem resists paraphrase. Its literal meaning is the poem itself, and we need a different way of talking about how it means because the basis for its coherence differs from that of rhetoric. We need a way of talking about its effect, just as in the presence of any art we have an impulse not only to understand what we experienced but to explain why we liked it or did not. Here we link the wind to the rain and associate the rain with fertility, growth, spring, and rebirth. The second pair of lines confirms that association since its image is of lovers in bed, but the poem is an object of art, something made, created from experience to provide an experience for the reader or, in this case, the listener. It has archetypal themes and a fairly common subject, the lover's lament at being parted from his love. It is admired chiefly for its poetic form—its conciseness, its simplicity, its pure lyric cry. Its archetypal images and ideas interact in a way quite unlike the logical method of prose, and it is on that interaction that any discussion must focus.

Both poetry and song began in the natural human need to create artistic forms that gave shape and design to awareness and feeling. Early sculpture and wall painting filled the same need. It was not enough to report what happened, or even how it felt; the need went beyond the attempt to explain the apparently meaningless flux of experience, to the attempt to create something attractive to keep, to have around, something that might last. What we have left of the most ancient civilizations are monuments, art objects, functional objects often elaborately decorated, some history and philosophy, and some poetry. The history and the philosophy are rhetoric and attest to man's attempt to explore significance from the perspective of logic and chronology. Monuments, art, and poetry communicate in a different way.

Rhetoric strives for an unambiguous descriptive or persuasive effect. It tells us what the facts are and what we should think of them. Good poetry thrives on all the ambiguities and ironies that are a part of our experience with the facts. The mind has other operations than the rational. As a restless, illogical, and dynamic phenomenon it reacts, associationally and instinctively, to form the attitudes and images that enable us to assimilate experience emotionally as well as rationally. Poetry employs this ability of the mind to form images, to associate freely, and to cope with ambiguous, ambivalent, and even contradictory attitudes. In dealing with such feelings and attitudes the good poet must avoid self-indulgence and sentimentality on one hand and on the other those descriptive and didactic ideas more clearly and effectively expressed in prose.

Much poetry shares with prose an interest in ideas—or with the speaker's attitude toward ideas. While "Western Wind" is an example of the purely poetic poem requiring an emotional and not a cognitive response, at the opposite extreme are philosophical and political poems full of ideas. Every age has produced political and religious songs, satires, and poems that have clear didactic intentions. Many of them were bad poems and have been forgotten. Others are obscure today because social conditions have changed. Those of great poetic intensity survive: poems that work from images that continue to yield significance and contemporary relevance like William Blake's "London" that follows.

Most good poetry lies between these extremes of good didactic poetry and simple lyrics like "Western Wind." In the poetry of Shakespeare, Donne, Yeats, and Frost, the ideas are important. The ideas were produced as part of the poetic conception of men of great intelligence. But it is the poetry that has survived, delivering the ideas, through the centuries, with more precision of tone and more power than a precise prose statement might have done. The truth of this poetry is personal, something shaped by the poets' feeling and imagination as they defined their thought. Good poetry is created not by the mind alone, but, as William Butler Yeats says, by the blood, the imagination, and the intellect running together.

London

I wander thro' each charter'd street,
Near where the charter'd Thames does flow,
And mark in every face I meet
Marks of weakness, marks of woe.

In every cry of every Man,   5
In every Infant's cry of fear,
In every voice, in every ban,
The mind-forg'd manacles I hear.

How the Chimney-sweeper's cry
Every black'ning Church appalls;   10
And the hapless Soldier's sigh
Runs in blood down Palace walls.

But most thro' midnight streets I hear
How the youthful Harlot's curse
Blasts the new born Infant's tear,   15
And blights with plagues the Marriage hearse.

William Blake (1757–1827)

NOTES AND QUESTIONS

1. *charter'd* (1): the "charter'd streets" of the opening stanza still suggest something planned or restrictive, but for Blake they had an additional ironical meaning. Charters from the king guaranteed certain liberties, but by implication or specific reference they denied other liberties. Explain the tone of Blake's use of the term. Why is the term better than "dirty" of the original version?

2. *mind-forg'd manacles* (8): manacles are made by hands for the purpose of binding hands and feet. That the image has them forged by the mind suggests that reason made them. Why does the speaker say he *hears* them? What other auditory images occur in the poem? What characteristic do all the auditory images have in common?

3. *appalls* (10): the church of this poem is not appalled but indifferent. Work out the image of the church covered with a black pall and relate it to the chimney-sweeper's cry (9).

4. In the last stanza "blights" and "plagues" have vegetative associations. Why are these appropriate? What is suggested by the use of "hearse" instead of "carriage," "tear" instead of "ear"?

5. An idea is implied by the metaphors of the last stanza: Not only the marriage in the blackened church but the source of life itself, imaged in the infant, are blighted by the social evils that produced the harlot's curse. Such a bald statement suggests some of the difficulties of translating poems into statements. The greatness of the poem is in the densely implicative fusion of image and idea, and to ignore those implications, as well as certain ambiguities, is to ignore the most important part of the poem. What implications might be ignored by a statement derived from the last stanza?

6. Explain how the poem is organized to climax in the last stanza.

On Wenlock Edge

On Wenlock Edge the wood's in trouble;
   His forest fleece the Wrekin heaves;
The gale, it plies the saplings double,
   And thick on Severn snow the leaves.

'Twould blow like this through holt and hanger   5
   When Uricon the city stood:
'Tis the old wind in the old anger,
   But then it threshed another wood.

Then, 'twas before my time, the Roman
   At yonder heaving hill would stare: 10
The blood that warms an English yeoman,
   The thoughts that hurt him, they were there.

There, like the wind through woods in riot,
   Through him the gale of life blew high;
The tree of man was never quiet: 15
   Then 'twas the Roman, now 'tis I.

The gale, it plies the saplings double,
  It blows so hard, 'twill soon be gone:
To-day the Roman and his trouble
  Are ashes under Uricon.   20

              A. E. Housman (1859–1936)

After Apple-Picking

My long two-pointed ladder's sticking through a tree
Toward heaven still,
And there's a barrel that I didn't fill
Beside it, and there may be two or three
Apples I didn't pick upon some bough.   5
But I am done with apple-picking now.
Essence of winter sleep is on the night,
The scent of apples: I am drowsing off.
I cannot rub the strangeness from my sight
I got from looking through a pane of glass   10
I skimmed this morning from the drinking trough
And held against the world of hoary grass.
It melted, and I let it fall and break.
But I was well
Upon my way to sleep before it fell,   15
And I could tell
What form my dreaming was about to take.
Magnified apples appear and disappear,
Stem end and blossom end,
And every fleck of russet showing clear.   20
My instep arch not only keeps the ache,
It keeps the pressure of a ladder-round.
I feel the ladder sway as the boughs bend.
And I keep hearing from the cellar bin
The rumbling sound   25
Of load on load of apples coming in.
For I have had too much
Of apple-picking: I am overtired
Of the great harvest I myself desired.
There were ten thousand thousand fruit to touch,   30
Cherish in hand, lift down, and not let fall.
For all
That struck the earth,
No matter if not bruised or spiked with stubble,

Went surely to the cider-apple heap   35
As of no worth.
One can see what will trouble
This sleep of mine, whatever sleep it is.
Were he not gone,
The woodchuck could say whether it's like his   40
Long sleep, as I describe its coming on,
Or just some human sleep.

Robert Frost (1874–1963)

A Postcard from the Volcano

Children picking up our bones
Will never know that these were once
As quick as foxes on the hill;

And that in autumn, when the grapes
Made sharp air sharper by their smell   5
These had a being, breathing frost;

And least will guess that with our bones
We left much more, left what still is
The look of things, left what we felt

At what we saw. The spring clouds blow   10
Above the shuttered mansion-house,
Beyond our gate and the windy sky

Cries out a literate despair.
We knew for long the mansion's look
And what we said of it became   15

A part of what it is . . . Children,
Still weaving budded aureoles,
Will speak our speech and never know,

Will say of the mansion that it seems
As if he that lived there left behind   20
A spirit storming in blank walls,

A dirty house in a gutted world,
A tatter of shadows peaked to white,
Smeared with the gold of the opulent sun.

Wallace Stevens (1879–1955)

Value and Importance

Some poems are better than others and are recognized as such by people who have learned to enjoy them. At the same time, there are no absolute standards of poetic quality. Many of the poems that enraptured our grandparents have been forgotten; and many of our own favorites will be forgotten as well. At any given time, however, there is likely to be a fairly well-defined consensus on the worth of certain poems and on the importance of their authors. Readers, provided they are similar in experience and education, will rarely differ about whether the poem in question is great or bad. More likely, one will claim it to be great, the other good; or one will call it good, the other bad. We can distinguish between great and bad poetry almost as readily as we can distinguish great from bad cooking; but the great and the good, the good and the bad, may be so closely related that differences in personal taste and experience prevent our reaching the same conclusion.

The bad poem may be criticized for its faulty craftsmanship or for its confused and trite effects; and the good poem be praised for the integration of all its elements, the strength of its voice, and the freshness of image and phrase. Bad poetry may have a pretentious, imprecise or sentimental style or a content that is didactic, sentimental, or confusing. With good poetry interest is centered on the effect of the language, and in that effect the language is inseparable from the content.

The value of a good poem is that its language extends, shapes, and illuminates our experience. Even attitudes far from our own, such as the cynicism of the Duke in "My Last Duchess" or the visionary rapture of Dylan Thomas, become part of our own experience because of the artistry of their language. The voices are caught so precisely and vividly that, though such attitudes may be strange to us, we are convinced of their reality. Those voices, known to us only as a piece of language, become a part of our experience and knowledge.

To observe how any evaluation of the importance and truth of poetry depends on evaluating the experience we have with its language, consider for comparison two lines from Shakespeare's plays. First a line from Hamlet, who considers himself surrounded by enemies. Hamlet's observation, that "one may smile, and smile, and be a villain" has a particular kind of ambiguity. To Hamlet the observation applies to practically everybody; to us it applies, according to our experience, to fewer people. But to all readers the observation seems immediately to be true. It is, however, something we already knew and is of no particular interest for the knowledge it imparts. We value it for the pacing and conciseness of the language. In the larger context of *Hamlet* it tells us as much about Hamlet's emotional state and idealism as it does about his ability to perceive the truth. As part of *Hamlet* it has its place in the grand design of a great tragedy. By itself, however, it lacks the greatness of the following quotation from *King Lear:*

> When we are born, we cry that we are come
> To this great stage of fools.—

Lear's observation is more complex than Hamlet's; it is more densely metaphorical, more surprising, even audacious, and more comprehensive. It refers to more of man's experience; its frame of reference is larger, grander, and more spiritual. Even though its tone is elevated, its central image is drawn from common experience. It achieves a different order of truth than Hamlet's line achieves, and as a result more people would call it "great."

While we give immediate assent to the truth of Hamlet's line, we are not so quick to accept Lear's metaphor. It may be that babies taken from the womb cry from the pain of the cold air and the difficulties of learning to breathe, and it may be, as Freud suggests, that the baby taken from the womb senses a loss of security, but it is not literally true that babies cry *because* this is a great stage of fools. Lear speaks not just in metaphor but in madness, and our reflex is to keep a safe distance from such intensities of emotion. But the beauty of the line is amazing and haunting because its intensity is an essential part of its greatness. Its truth, being locked safely in metaphor, is not something we care to analyze as we would a rhetorical statement. It pushes beyond the boundaries of our conscious experience into the disorderly area of our unconscious fears and there the language shapes an insight. We validate its truth from experience we are not conscious of having had. The greatness of the line is in its magnitude, in its intensity and power, but chiefly in the ease with which our imagination is engaged to give comprehensive form to the anxieties and despairing moments of all men.

Poetry may be good in many ways—it may achieve its effect through an ingenious elaboration of a frivolous theme (Suckling's "The Constant Lover") or by a light treatment of a serious theme (Hardy's "The Ruined Maid") or by a serious treatment of a serious theme (Housman's "To an Athlete Dying Young"). As with good poetry, the truth of great poetry may be merely a personal and relative truth; our pleasure with both is in the expression achieved and the new awareness gained. But great poetry has other qualities illustrated in Lear's line. In the magnitude and intensity of Lear's line we witness a great poetic imagination create an artistic shape of enduring value and see intense universal experience shaped into comprehensible form.

Sonnet: Batter my heart

Batter my heart, three-personed God; for You
As yet but knock, breathe, shine, and seek to mend;
That I may rise and stand, o'erthrow me, and bend
Your force, to break, blow, burn, and make me new.
I, like an usurped town, to another due,   5
Labor to admit You, but Oh, to no end!
Reason, Your viceroy in me, me should defend,
But is captived, and proves weak or untrue.
Yet dearly I love You, and would be loved fain,
But am betrothed unto Your enemy: 10
Divorce me, untie or break that knot again,
Take me to You, imprison me, for I,
Except You enthrall me, never shall be free,
Nor ever chaste, except You ravish me.

                                    John Donne (1572?–1631)

NOTES AND QUESTIONS

1. *three-personed God* (1): the Father, the Son, and the Holy Ghost, the three persons of the Christian Trinity. Since the speaker is addressing God, what is unusual about the verbs he uses throughout?

2. Why is this sonnet, generally considered a great poem, impressive to nonbelievers as well as to believers? To what degree is the speaker's attitude universal? To what degree does the reader encounter a new experience?

3. *usurped town* (5): a town taken over by the enemy in war. Trace the development of the military figure of the usurped town throughout the poem. What other figure merges in line 9 with the usurped town? Trace the development of both figures in the sestet.

4. Most readers are impressed by the compression and energy of this sonnet. How has this effect been achieved?

Dover Beach

The sea is calm tonight.
The tide is full, the moon lies fair
Upon the straits; on the French coast the light
Gleams and is gone; the cliffs of England stand,
Glimmering and vast, out in the tranquil bay.   5
Come to the window, sweet is the night air!
Only, from the long line of spray
Where the sea meets the moon-blanched land,
Listen! you hear the grating roar
Of pebbles which the waves draw back, and fling,   10
At their return, up the high strand,
Begin, and cease, and then again begin,
With tremulous cadence slow, and bring
The eternal note of sadness in.

Sophocles long ago   15
Heard it on the Ægean, and it brought
Into his mind the turbid ebb and flow
Of human misery; we
Find also in the sound a thought,
Hearing it by this distant northern sea.   20

The Sea of Faith
Was once, too, at the full, and round earth's shore
Lay like the folds of a bright girdle furled.
But now I only hear
Its melancholy, long, withdrawing roar,   25
Retreating, to the breath
Of the night wind, down the vast edges drear
And naked shingles of the world.

Ah, love, let us be true
To one another! for the world, which seems   30
To lie before us like a land of dreams,
So various, so beautiful, so new,
Hath really neither joy, nor love, nor light,
Nor certitude, nor peace, nor help for pain;
And we are here as on a darkling plain,   35
Swept with confused alarms of struggle and flight,
Where ignorant armies clash by night.

                              Matthew Arnold (1822–1888)

The Dover Bitch: A Criticism of Life

for Andrews Wanning

So there stood Matthew Arnold and this girl
With the cliffs of England crumbling away behind them,
And he said to her, "Try to be true to me,
And I'll do the same for you, for things are bad
All over, etc., etc."   5
Well now, I knew this girl. It's true she had read
Sophocles in a fairly good translation
And caught that bitter allusion to the sea,
But all the time he was talking she had in mind
The notion of what his whiskers would feel like   10
On the back of her neck. She told me later on
That after a while she got to looking out
At the lights across the channel, and really felt sad,
Thinking of all the wine and enormous beds
And blandishments in French and the perfumes.   15
And then she got really angry. To have been brought
All the way down from London, and then be addressed
As a sort of mournful cosmic last resort
Is really tough on a girl, and she was pretty.
Anyway, she watched him pace the room   20
And finger his watch-chain and seem to sweat a bit,
And then she said one or two unprintable things.
But you mustn't judge her by that. What I mean to say is,
She's really all right. I still see her once in a while
And she always treats me right. We have a drink   25
And I give her a good time, and perhaps it's a year
Before I see her again, but there she is,
Running to fat, but dependable as they come.
And sometimes I bring her a bottle of *Nuit d'Amour*.

                                        Anthony Hecht (b. 1923)

The Darkling Thrush

I leant upon a coppice gate
    When Frost was spectre-gray,
And Winter's dregs made desolate
    The weakening eye of day.
The tangled bine-stems scored the sky   5

Like strings of broken lyres,
And all mankind that haunted nigh
Had sought their household fires.

The land's sharp features seemed to be
    The Century's corpse outleant,   10
His crypt the cloudy canopy,
    The wind his death-lament.
The ancient pulse of germ and birth
    Was shrunken hard and dry,
And every spirit upon earth   15
    Seemed fervourless as I.

At once a voice arose among
    The bleak twigs overhead
In a full-hearted evensong
    Of joy illimited;
An aged thrush, frail, gaunt, and small,
    In blast-beruffled plume,
Had chosen thus to fling his soul
    Upon the growing gloom.

So little cause for carolings   25
    Of such ecstatic sound
Was written on terrestrial things
    Afar or nigh around,
That I could think there trembled through
    His happy good-night air   30
Some blessed Hope, whereof he knew
    And I was unaware.

December 1900.

                        Thomas Hardy (1840–1928)

NOTES AND QUESTIONS

1. *coppice gate* (1): a gate between a pasture or field and a copse of
   trees.
2. What is the significance of the date at the end? How is it related
   to the imagery?
3. Explain the following line: "The ancient pulse of germ and birth
   was shrunken hard and dry." Is it a better line than most in the
   poem?

4. Why does Hardy have the speaker describe the bird as aged, frail, gaunt and small? Might the bird have been a normally healthy bird? Why does the bird sing? Is the bird somewhat awkward as a device?
5. How much is clear, how much ambivalent, and how much ambiguous in the ending?

The Second Coming

Turning and turning in the widening gyre
The falcon cannot hear the falconer;
Things fall apart; the centre cannot hold;
Mere anarchy is loosed upon the world,
The blood-dimmed tide is loosed, and everywhere   5
The ceremony of innocence is drowned;
The best lack all conviction, while the worst
Are full of passionate intensity.

Surely some revelation is at hand;
Surely the Second Coming is at hand.   10
The Second Coming! Hardly are those words out
When a vast image out of *Spiritus Mundi*
Troubles my sight: somewhere in sands of the desert
A shape with lion body and the head of a man,
A gaze blank and pitiless as the sun,   15
Is moving its slow thighs, while all about it
Reel shadows of the indignant desert birds.
The darkness drops again; but now I know
That twenty centuries of stony sleep
Were vexed to nightmare by a rocking cradle,   20
And what rough beast, its hour come round at last,
Slouches towards Bethlehem to be born?

                    William Butler Yeats (1865–1939)

NOTES AND QUESTIONS

1. *The Second Coming* (title): the Biblical Antichrist (Revelation 4:7, Daniel 7:4, and Ezekiel 1:10) depicted in images of beasts and men, but the title also alludes ironically to Christ's Second Com-

ing (Revelation 19:11–16). Yeats viewed history as occurring in cycles of twenty centuries; those since the birth of Christ, being nearly elapsed, will give way to a "Savage God" whom Yeats refers to elsewhere. What images in the poem suggest the nature of this new god?

2. *Spiritus Mundi* (12): World Spirit, Yeats' own term, refers to an archetypal and non-Christian concept of a collective human memory. It is defined by Yeats as a general storehouse of images. Which of the images associated here with the new god have archetypal significance? What archetypal cycles, rituals, fears, and desires are implied by word choices and events in the poem?

3. *lion . . . man* (14): both man and beast, whereas Christ was man and God. What other details contrast the new savage god with Christ?

4. Those who argue the poem's greatness cite certain phrasing often quoted and certain images. What phrasing, what images, and what verbs seem particularly effective?

5. On the eve of World War II Yeats wrote to a friend:

> Communist, Fascist, nationalist, clerical, anti-clerical, are all responsible according to the number of their victims. I have not been silent; I have used the only vehicle I possess—verse. If you have my poems by you, look up a poem called "The Second Coming." It was written some sixteen or seventeen years ago and foretold what is happening. I have written of the same thing again and again since . . .

The poem really applies to far more than just to any recent war. What else in modern lifes does it apply to?

Sonnet Pair

Sonnet: No longer mourn for me

No longer mourn for me when I am dead
Than you shall hear the surly sullen bell
Give warning to the world that I am fled
From this vile world, with vilest worms to dwell.
Nay, if you read this line, remember not   5
The hand that writ it, for I love you so
That I in your sweet thoughts would be forgot
If thinking on me then should make you woe.
O, if, I say, you look upon this verse
When I, perhaps, compounded am with clay,   10

Do not so much as my poor name rehearse,
But let your love even with my life decay,
Lest the wise world should look into your moan
And mock you with me after I am gone.

William Shakespeare (1564–1616)

Sonnet: When I have seen by time's fell hand

When I have seen by time's fell hand defaced
The rich-proud cost of outworn buried age;
When sometime lofty towers I see down-razed,
And brass eternal slave to mortal rage;
When I have seen the hungry ocean gain   5
Advantage on the kingdom of the shore,
And the firm soil win of the watery main,
Increasing store with loss and loss with store;
When I have seen such interchange of state,
Or state itself confounded to decay,   10
Ruin hath taught me thus to ruminate:
That time will come and take my love away.
This thought is as a death, which cannot choose
But weep to have that which it fears to lose.

William Shakespeare (1564–1616)

QUESTIONS

1. How does the subject of the imagery in the second sonnet differ from that of the first?
2. Compare how the quatrains are marked for the reader in each sonnet by the opening words, and show how the subject of the quatrains develops in a more complex and profound way in the second.
3. Which sonnet makes better use of such literary means as alliteration, paradox, hyperbole, and irony?
4. Where is the phrasing in the second sonnet strongest and most memorable?
5. Mark Van Doren (*Introduction to Poetry*, New York: Hill and Wang, 1968) has called the first of these two sonnets perfect, the second great. Argue the perfection of the first sonnet and its deficiency compared to the greatness of the second.

PART TWO *Four Poets*

John Donne

(1572?–1631)

In the centuries since John Donne's time, the social fabric, customs, attitudes, religious beliefs and allegiances, even the very language itself, have changed enormously. Donne, like almost all poets, spoke to and for his own age, and he will speak to us more meaningfully if we attune our ears to the voices, the cries, and the church bells of the turn of the century—the dawn of the *seventeenth* century. Because he deals with universals, the constant concerns of men of all times, Donne has continued to speak to succeeding ages. He speaks mostly of love—of erotic love and of spiritual love—at first as poet and priest of Apollo and later as poet and priest of his own Christian God.

To begin to form a taste for Donne, consider two little epigrams:

Antiquary[1]

If in his study he hath so much care
To'hang all old strange things, let his wife beware.

A Lame Beggar

I am unable, yonder beggar cries,
To stand or move; if he say true, he lies.

---

[1] The spelling and punctuation have been largely modernized in all of the Donne poems. The unusual use of the apostrophe, as in "To'hang" has been retained because it is related to Donne's sense of the meter.

Here we experience Donne's *humor,* which exists mainly in his cynical love poems; his *wit,* in the earlier sense of the term—mental agility, turns and thrusts; his delight in a *pun,* as in the word "lies"; and his fondness for *paradox,* as in "if he say true, he lies."

Donne wrote love poems that range in tone from cynical sexual frankness, full of wit and humor, to passionate spirituality. "The Sun Rising" illustrates a stage between these extremes where there is both wit and passion.

The Sun Rising

    Busy old fool, unruly sun,
    Why dost thou thus
Through windows and through curtains call on us?
Must to thy motions lovers' seasons run?
    Saucy pedantic wretch, go chide   5
    Late schoolboys and sour prentices,
    Go tell court-huntsmen that the king will ride,
    Call country ants to harvest offices;
Love, all alike, no season knows, nor clime,
Nor hours, days, months, which are the rags of time.   10

    Thy beams, so reverend and strong
    Why shouldst thou think?
I could eclipse and cloud them with a wink,
But that I would not lose her sight so long;
    If her eyes have not blinded thine,   15
    Look, and to-morrow late tell me
    Whether both the'Indias of spice and mine
    Be where thou left'st them, or lie here with me.
Ask for those kings whom thou saw'st yesterday,
And thou shalt hear, all here in one bed lay.   20

    She'is all states, and all princes I;
    Nothing else is.
Princes do but play us; compared to this,
All honor's mimic, all wealth alchemy.
    Thou, sun, art half as happy'as we,   25
    In that the world's contracted thus;
    Thine age asks ease, and since thy duties be
    To warm the world, that's done in warming us.
Shine here to us, and thou art everywhere;
This bed thy center is, these walls thy sphere.   30

We see at once the difference between Donne's age and ours in his references to "prentices" (apprentices), "court-huntsmen," "the King," "the'Indias of spice and mine" (the East Indies famous for spices and the West Indies for the mining of gold), and "alchemy" (as used here, a glittering nothing). More importantly we also see a poetic style that at first seems mannered, that of a group later to be called the "metaphysical poets." Metaphysical poetry is so called not so much for its subject matter, which varies, but for its style: paradox, outrageous hyperbole, subtlety of thought, and imagery that is not merely sensory but that appeals to the intellect and refers to all fields of knowledge as they existed at the time. The distinguishing characteristic of the metaphysical style is the "metaphysical conceit," a startling exaggeration of metaphors and rhetorical figures which appeals less to the reader's realistic perception of image and logic than to his ability to extend them imaginatively and intellectually. We find all of these features in "The Sun Rising."

Jack Donne, as he was called at the time, was probably still a young man about town when he wrote "The Sun Rising." He composed his poem for someone with whom he was very much in love—possibly for Ann More, with whom he eloped in 1601 and who bore him seventeen children, of whom five were still-born. Regardless of who inspired the poet, the poem is about the speaker's attitude toward a beloved. Yet the speaker does not address her, but the sun. Nothing less than the sun is made the conceit for expressing the magnitude of his love. Donne plays against the convention of addressing the sun respectfully, as Hyperion. He calls it a "busy old fool," "unruly," and a "saucy pedantic wretch" because it awakens him and his love, and he finally asserts that if the sun would confine itself within the lovers' room, with its center in their bed, it would be everywhere. The lovers' love is as great as all space, as mighty as all kings. The presentation of the sun—at first in images of its rising and moving around the world, and finally in the concept of it confined within the lovers' room—illustrates the audacity of the metaphysical conceit in initially appealing to the senses, but ultimately to the intellect.

"The Sun Rising" is also studded with hyperboles, paradoxes, and sudden shifts of thrust—all hallmarks of metaphysical poetry. In the second stanza, for example, the speaker voices a hyperbole when he says that he could eclipse the beams of the sun and cloud them with a wink—except that (sudden shift!) he does not wish to lose sight of his beloved for so long a time as it takes to wink. Then, with further hyperbole, still pursuing the motif of "sight," he suggests that the brilliance of the eyes of his beloved may have blinded the sun's eyes. A paradox exists in the notion that all wealth is alchemy and even more strikingly in the thought that if the sun were confined to the lovers' room it would be everywhere. The exaggeration intrinsic to every hyperbole and the seeming contradiction in every paradox are always surprising, but it is the intensity of the exaggeration and the outrageousness of the seeming contradiction that are characteristic of metaphysical poetry generally, and of Donne's especially.

The seventeenth century in England was beset by religious turmoil, in its earlier years chiefly the struggles between the supporters of the Church of England and those of the Church of Rome. Donne, descended from a longtime Roman Catholic family, was a member of that church through his earlier life, but shifted his allegiance to the Church of England, in which he was ordained in 1615 and was appointed Dean of St. Paul's in 1621. In his religious poetry, though, Donne's God is not significantly Roman or Anglican. He is the Christian God, probably conceived of intellectually and philosophically by Donne in the light of his omnivorous reading, but known to Donne with great personal feeling.

Since virtually none of Donne's poetry was published until two years after his death, very little is known about the dates of composition; but his lighter, rather cynical love poems probably date from his earlier years, when he read law at the London Inns of Court, went on an expedition to Cadiz, and was seeking preferment at court. His more serious love poems and his religious poems probably date from his middle and later years. Not so much variety is discernible in his religious poems as in his love poems.

The poems of Donne on the following pages are arranged in a hypothetical order from the worldly to the spiritual. "Song: Go and catch a falling star" proclaims the nonexistence of a faithful woman. "Love's Deity" treats the mischief of unreciprocated love. "The Sun Rising" would stand about here in this arrangement. "Lovers' Infiniteness" and "The Canonization" show Donne's nearest approach to the conventional sincere love poem. "The Ecstasy" and "A Valediction: Forbidding Mourning" deal with the spiritual aspect of the love between man and woman. Finally, in "Sonnet: At the round earth's imagined corners," "Sonnet: Wilt thou love God," and "A Hymn to God the Father," we see Donne's very personal love of his God.

As much as customs, attitudes, belief, knowledge—all things—have changed in the three and a half centuries between Donne's time and ours, his reputation, since T. S. Eliot's rediscovery of him, is assured. Our concept of the Divine may have changed and our knowledge of science and of nature may be greater, but even for most agnostics and atheists among us, Donne's poetry still speaks with more genius and passion than most other poetry.

Just how John Donne saw himself in his role as poet we cannot say exactly. But in his religious poems at least, he must have recognized the profundity and intensity of his own insights and feelings; and to give voice to these he created passionate personae and a style universally praised for the authority with which it speaks of his intense spiritual experience. In his love poems he emerges as the same kind of figure, a person of uncommon insights into and feelings about love, which he again communicates with uncommon imagination, subtlety, and feeling. This is very close to the classical concept of the role of the poet as a person differing from others not only in his ability to manipulate language, but in his whole being—clairvoyant, sage, seer, maker, minister to his audience. In a sense every poet must at times seem egotistical, simply because of his awareness of his "special" nature. Donne must have seen himself as poet in much the same way as he saw the lovers in "A Valediction: Forbidding Mourning," as very different from "ordinary" men.

Song

Go and catch a falling star,
    Get with child a mandrake root,
Tell me where all past years are,
    Or who cleft the Devil's foot,
Teach me to hear mermaids singing,   5
    Or to keep off envy's stinging,
        And find
        What wind
Serves to advance an honest mind.

If thou be'st born to strange sights,   10
    Things invisible to see,
Ride ten thousand days and nights,
    Till age snow white hairs on thee,
Thou, when thou return'st, wilt tell me
    All strange wonders that befell thee,   15
        And swear
        Nowhere
Lives a woman true, and fair.

If thou findst one, let me know,
    Such a pilgrimage were sweet.   20
Yet do not; I would not go,
    Though at next door we might meet;

> Though she were true, when you met her,
> And last, till you write your letter,
> Yet she   25
> Will be
> False, ere I come, to two, or three.

NOTES AND QUESTIONS

1. *mandrake* (2): mandragora, a plant whose root, shaped roughly
   like the human body, had been superstitiously thought to be
   efficacious in promoting human fertility. In the first stanza the
   speaker enjoins the listener to do seven things that are presented
   specifically and concretely; how might he have conveyed the
   same message in a brief, abstract, unpoetical sentence?
2. Is line 11 a paradox? Is the contradiction seeming or real?
3. The stanzaic pattern is intricate. What effects are achieved by
   the brevity of lines 7 and 8? By the rhyming of lines 7, 8 and 9?
   By the feminine rhymes of lines 5 and 6? Over-all?

Love's Deity

> I long to talk with some old lover's ghost,
>   Who died before the god of love was born:
> I cannot think that he who then loved most
>   Sunk so low as to love one which did scorn.
> But since this god produced a destiny,   5
> And that vice-nature, custom, lets it be,
>   I must love her that loves not me.
>
> Sure, they which made him god meant not so much,
>   Nor he, in his young godhead, practised it.
> But when an even flame two hearts did touch,   10
>   His office was indulgently to fit
> Actives to passives. Correspondency
> Only his subject was; it cannot be
>   Love, till I love her that loves me.
>
> But every modern god will now extend   15
>   His vast prerogative, as far as Jove.
> To rage, to lust, to write to, to commend,
>   All is the purlieu of the god of love.
> Oh were we wakened by this tyranny

To ungod this child again, it could not be   20
I should love her who loves not me.

Rebel and atheist too, why murmur I,
    As though I felt the worst that love could do?
Love might make me leave loving, or might try
    A deeper plague, to make her love me too,   25
Which, since she loves before, I'm loth to see;
Falsehood is worse than hate; and that must be,
    If she whom I love should love me.

NOTES AND QUESTIONS

1. *vice-nature* (6): standing in the place of or substituting for nature. *Actives to passives* (12): males to corresponding females. *will* (15): wishes to. *Jove* (16): mythologically, the highest god, who rules over the gods. *before* (26): already (someone else).
2. The first three stanzas of "Love's Deity" are about the common seventeenth century subject of the contrariness with which an individual always falls in love—with someone who does not reciprocate the love and who loves someone else. The speaker blames this situation on the "god of love" (Cupid), and says (stanza one) that it was not so bad before this god was born or (stanza two) while he was still young, but that (stanza three) now that this god has grown powerful he has become a tyrant. Why does the speaker call himself (stanza four) a rebel? An atheist?

Lovers' Infiniteness

If yet I have not all thy love,
Dear, I shall never have it all;
I cannot breathe one other sigh to move,
Nor can entreat one other tear to fall;
And all my treasure, which should purchase thee,   5
Sighs, tears, and oaths, and letters, I have spent.
Yet no more can be due to me,
Than at the bargain made was meant.
If then thy gift of love were partial,
That some to me, some should to others fall,   10
    Dear, I shall never have thee all.

Or if then thou gavest me all,
All was but all which thou hadst then;

But if in thy heart, since, there be or shall
New love created be, by other men,   15
Which have their stocks entire, and can in tears,
In sighs, in oaths, in letters, outbid me,
This new love may beget new fears,
For this love was not vowed by thee.
And yet it was, thy gift being general,   20
The ground, thy heart, is mine; whatever shall
    Grow there, dear, I should have it all.

Yet I would not have all yet;
He that hath all can have no more,
And since my love doth every day admit   25
New growth, thou shouldst have new rewards in store;
Thou canst not every day give me thy heart;
If thou canst give it, then thou never gavest it:
Love's riddles are, that though thy heart depart,
It stays at home, and thou with losing savest it: 30
But we will have a way more liberal
Than changing hearts, to join them, so we shall
    Be one, and one another's All.

NOTES AND QUESTIONS

1. This poem is, among other things, a play on "infiniteness" and on the word "all." How does the concept of "all" change from stanza to stanza?
2. The speaker resolves his quandary in the last three lines. If he and his beloved will quit giving and receiving their "all's" by simply becoming *one*, then they will be "one another's All." Identify and resolve the paradoxes in lines 28–30.
3. Does the poem as a whole seem relatively concrete or abstract? Trace the mercantile imagery and consider its appropriateness.

The Canonization

For God's sake, hold your tongue, and let me love,
    Or chide my palsy, or my gout,
My five gray hairs, or ruined fortune flout,
    With wealth your state, your mind with arts improve,
        Take you a course, get you a place,   5
        Observe his honor, or his grace,

Or the King's real, or his stamped face
   Contemplate; what you will, approve,
   So you will let me love.

Alas, alas, who's injured by my love?   10
   What merchant's ships have my sighs drowned?
Who says my tears have overflowed his ground?
   When did my colds a forward spring remove?
     When did the heats which my veins fill
     Add one more to the plaguy bill?   15
Soldiers find wars, and lawyers find out still
   Litigious men, which quarrels move,
   Though she and I do love.

Call us what you will, we are made such by love;
   Call her one, me another fly,   20
We're tapers too, and at our own cost die,
   And we in us find the eagle and the dove.
     The phoenix riddle hath more wit
     By us; we two being one, are it.
So, to one neutral thing both sexes fit.   25
   We die and rise the same, and prove
   Mysterious by this love.

We can die by it, if not live by love,
   And if unfit for tombs and hearse
Our legend be, it will be fit for verse;   30
   And if no piece of chronicle we prove,
     We'll build in sonnets pretty rooms;
     As well a well-wrought urn becomes
The greatest ashes, as half-acre tombs,
   And by these hymns, all shall approve   35
   Us *canonized* for Love.

And thus invoke us: "You, whom reverend love
   Made one another's hermitage;
You, to whom love was peace, that now is rage;
   Who did the whole world's soul extract, and drove   40
     Into the glasses of your eyes
     (So made such mirrors, and such spies,
That they did all to you epitomize)
   Countries, towns, courts: beg from above
   A pattern of your love!"   45

NOTES AND QUESTIONS

1. *stamped* (7): stamped on coins. *approve* (8): do; try. *plaguy bill* (15): roster of plague victims. *fly* (20): insect (which may fly into a candle, to its death). *die* (21): slang in Donne's time for the sexual act. *wit* (23): sense. *rooms* (32): in Italian, stanzas. *drove* (40): crammed.
2. Cleanth Brooks in his *The Well-Wrought Urn* said of "The Canonization":

> . . . the poet daringly treats profane love as if it were divine love. The canonization is not that of a pair of holy anchorites who have renounced the world and the flesh. The hermitage of each is the other's body; but they do renounce the world, and so their title to sainthood is cunningly argued. The poem then is a parody of Christian sainthood. . . .

Argue that Brooks' comment involves both metaphor and paradox.

The Ecstasy

Where, like a pillow on a bed,
    A pregnant bank swelled up, to rest
The violet's reclining head,
    Sat we two, one another's best.

Our hands were firmly cemented   5
    With a fast balm, which thence did spring;
Our eye-beams twisted, and did thread
    Our eyes, upon one double string;

So to intergraft our hands, as yet
    Was all the means to make us one,   10
And pictures in our eyes to get
    Was all our propagation.

As, 'twixt two equal armies, Fate
    Suspends uncertain victory,
Our souls (which to advance their state   15
    Were gone out) hung 'twixt her and me.

And whilst our souls negotiate there,
    We like sepulchral statues lay;
All day, the same our postures were,
    And we said nothing, all the day.   20

If any, so by love refined
    That he souls' language understood,
And by good love were grown all mind,
    Within convenient distance stood,

He (though he knew not which soul spake,   25
    Because both meant, both spake the same)
Might thence a new concoction take,
    And part far purer than he came.

This Ecstasy doth unperplex,
    We said, and tell us what we love;   30
We see by this it was not sex;
    We see we saw not what did move:

But as all several souls contain
    Mixture of things, they know not what,
Love these mixed souls doth mix again,   35
    And makes both one, each this and that.

A single violet transplant,
    The strength, the color, and the size,
(All which before was poor, and scant)
    Redoubles still, and multiplies.   40

When love, with one another so
    Interinanimates two souls,
That abler soul, which thence doth flow,
    Defects of loneliness controls.

We then, who are this new soul, know   45
    Of what we are composed, and made,
For the atomies of which we grow
    Are souls, whom no change can invade.

But oh, alas, so long, so far
    Our bodies why do we forbear?   50
They're ours, though they're not we, we are
    The intelligences, they the sphere.

We owe them thanks because they thus
    Did us to us at first convey,
Yielded their forces, sense, to us,   55
    Nor are dross to us, but allay.

On man heaven's influence works not so,
    But that it first imprints the air;

So soul into the soul may flow,
 Though it to body first repair. 60

As our blood labors to beget
 Spirits as like souls as it can,
Because such fingers need to knit
 That subtle knot which makes us man:

So must pure lovers' souls descend 65
 To affections, and to faculties,
Which sense may reach and apprehend,
 Else a great Prince in prison lies.

To our bodies turn we then, that so
 Weak men on love revealed may look; 70
Love's mysteries in souls do grow,
 But yet the body is his book,

And if some lover, such as we,
 Have heard this dialogue of one,
Let him still mark us, he shall see 75
 Small change, when we're to bodies gone.

A Valediction: Forbidding Mourning

As virtuous men pass mildly away,
 And whisper to their souls to go,
Whilst some of their sad friends do say,
 "The breath goes now," and some say, "No,"

So let us melt, and make no noise, 5
 No tear-floods, nor sigh-tempests move;
'Twere profanation of our joys
 To tell the laity our love.

Moving of the earth brings harms and fears,
 Men reckon what it did and meant; 10
But trepidation of the spheres,
 Though greater far, is innocent.

Dull sublunary lovers' love
 (Whose soul is sense) cannot admit
Absence, because it doth remove 15
 Those things which elemented it.

But we, by a love so much refined
   That our selves know not what it is,
Inter-assured of the mind,
   Care less, eyes, lips, and hands to miss.   20

Our two souls therefore, which are one,
   Though I must go, endure not yet
A breach, but an expansion,
   Like gold to airy thinness beat.

If they be two, they are two so   25
   As stiff twin compasses are two:
Thy soul, the fixed foot, makes no show
   To move, but doth, if the other do;

And though it in the center sit,
   Yet when the other far doth roam,   30
It leans, and hearkens after it,
   And grows erect, as that comes home.

Such wilt thou be to me, who must,
   Like the other foot, obliquely run;
Thy firmness makes my circle just,   35
   And makes me end where I begun.

NOTES AND QUESTIONS

1. *Moving* (9): quaking. *trepidation* (11): quaking. *spheres* (11): according to the Ptolemaic earth-centered cosmology, the celestial spheres. *innocent* (12): innocuous, harmless; therefore in an antonymous relationship with "harms" in line 9 and resulting in a notable antithesis of lines 11–12 and lines 9–10. *sublunary* (13): beneath the moon, earthly, nonspiritual. *elemented* (16): composed. *mind* (19): mind or spirit. *stiff twin compasses* (26): the two-legged draftsman's compass.
2. The main idea of the first stanza is the old notion that the good die quietly; what is the relationship of the first stanza to the second?
3. Explain the figures in line 6.
4. Donne implies that "our love" in line 8 is the opposite of the meanings conveyed by "profanation" (7) and "laity" (8). What kind of love is "our love"?
5. The third stanza has no explicit relationship to the rest of the poem. What is the implied relationship?

6. Consider "Whose soul is sense" (14). What rhetorical or meta-phorical figure is contained in this expression? (Be sure to consider the precise meaning you are giving to "soul.")
7. Identify the figure in line 20.
8. Line 24 means "like gold beaten into gold leaf." Explain this simile in relation to the three preceding lines; in relation to the paradox in line 21.

Sonnet: At the round earth's imagined corners

At the round earth's imagined corners, blow
Your trumpets, angels, and arise, arise
From death, you numberless infinities
Of souls, and to your scattered bodies go,
All whom the flood did, and fire shall o'erthrow,   5
All whom war, dearth, age, agues, tyrannies,
Despair, law, chance, hath slain, and you whose eyes
Shall behold God and never taste death's woe.
But let them sleep, Lord, and me mourn a space,
For if above all these my sins abound,   10
'Tis late to ask abundance of Thy grace
When we are there; here on this lowly ground,
Teach me how to repent; for that's as good
As if Thou hadst sealed my pardon with Thy blood.

Sonnet: Wilt thou love God

Wilt thou love God, as He thee? then digest,
My soul, this wholesome meditation,
How God the Spirit, by angels waited on
In heaven, doth make His Temple in thy breast.
The Father, having begot a Son most blest,   5
And still begetting (for he ne'er begun),
Hath deigned to choose thee, by adoption,
Coheir to His glory and sabbath's endless rest;
And as a robbed man which by search doth find
His stol'n stuff sold must lose or buy it again,   10
The Son of glory came down, and was slain,
Us whom He had made, and Satan stol'n, to unbind.
'Twas much that man was made like God before,
But that God should be made like man, much more.

Other poems of John Donne in this book are:
"A Hymn to God the Father" (p. 138)
"The Bait" (p. 248)
"The Good-Morrow" (p. 316)
"Sonnet: Batter my heart" (p. 171)
"Sonnet: Death, be not proud" (p. 345)

William Butler Yeats

(1865–1939)

William Butler Yeats read John Donne in the M. J. C. Grierson edition of 1912 and wrote to Grierson:

> Your notes [on Donne] tell me exactly what I want to know. Poems that I could not understand or could but understand are now clear and I notice that the more precise and learned the thought the greater the beauty, the passion; the intricacy and subtleties of his imagination are the length and depths of the furrow made by his passion. His pedantry and his obscenity—the rock and the loam of his Eden—but make me the more certain that one who is but a man like us all has seen God.[1]

Yeats, though he had earlier been strongly influenced by Spenser, Shelley, and Blake, had found in Donne's poetry qualities that were to distinguish his own later poetry: a fusion of the intellectual and the sensuous and an ability to use one's own experience to create the characters and situations of his poetry.

Yet Yeats' experience and his inherent poetic gift kept him from being dominated by the example of Donne, or of any other poet. Yeats was a provincial, born in Sandymount in northern Ireland, and therefore stood outside the culture that nourished the English poetic tradition. For years he tried to revive the ancient Irish myths, substituting their conventions for those of English poetry, as in the

---

[1] William Butler Yeats, *Letters of William Butler Yeats*, ed. Allan Wade (London: Macmillan, 1954), p. 570.

early "The Song of Wandering Aengus." In addition, he was passionately concerned with social and political events in the Ireland of his own time, particularly with the Revolution of 1916 and the creation of the Irish Free State in 1922, when he became a senator for six years—the "sixty-year-old smiling public man" of "Among School Children." Finally, in poems such as "John Kinsella's Lament for Mrs. Mary Moore" he takes as his characters the very poorest and most ignorant Irish men and women he had known, elevating their colloquial speech into sonorous and unforgettable poetry.

Yeats' experience was full of conflicting forces. He devoted much of his life to the development of an Irish literature and the development of the Abbey Theatre, but the literary figures from whom he learned most were all English. He was an ardent nationalist, but always somewhat removed from the blood and temper and irrationality of the battles of the independence movement, so that he is sometimes accused of being indifferent, distant, and aristocratic. He seems to have spent his happiest hours at Coole Park (see "The Wild Swans at Coole"), the estate of Lady Gregory, far from the bullets and the barricades. He was Irish but not Catholic. His grandfather had been a minister of the Church of Ireland, the Protestant minority church normally associated with the Irish of English background. His father, an apostate from that church, seems to have left his son, a fundamentally religious man, with no interest either in conventional Christianity or in any other organized religion—nor with any apparent guilt about having no part in it. But Yeats had a great interest in the occult—in mediums, spells, dreams, intuition, the insights of the mad, and the whole spirit-haunted world of Irish myth and folklore. His interest, his belief, in such things is commonly explained on the basis that a poet needs more for a frame of reference than a Christian apostate would have—politics, economics, materialism, a celebration of the flesh, and love. Love and beautiful women took a large part of his attention, but his serious, spiritual nature required something more, if only to place in a larger frame the myths and Catholic spiritual beliefs of those around him and to answer some need in himself to explain his own spiritual sense, the loss of the woman he loved, and his sense that in all loss and change a process, mysterious and inevitable, was taking place.

The conventionally Christian references that occur mixed in his poetry with personal, occult, and pagan symbols all suggest the spiritual shape given to his attitude and thought. There is little to suggest that "A Prayer for my Daughter" is a prayer to the Christian God but much to suggest the spiritual nature of the speaker. In "The Magi" (see page 45) he uses a familiar Christian theme to express a fatalistic view of mankind that no Christian could accept as true. For the most part, though, Yeats was content to ignore Christianity and to deal instead with his own attempt to reconcile his conflicting beliefs and feelings. The man of passion and the man of thought, the religious man and the nonbeliever, the Irishman and the cosmopolitan—somehow these opposing identities had to be harmonized. This sense of other selves is reflected in his idea of the Mask:

> There is a relation between discipline and the theatrical sense. If we cannot imagine ourselves as different from what we are and assume that second self, we cannot impose a discipline upon ourselves, though we may accept one from others. Active virtue as distinguished from the passive acceptance of a current code is therefore theatrical, consciously dramatic, the wearing of a mask. It is the condition of arduous full life. One constantly notices in very active natures a tendency to pose, or if the pose has become a second self, a preoccupation with the effect they are producing.
>
> . . .
>
> I think that all happiness depends on the energy to assume the mask of some other self; that all joyous or creative life is a re-birth as something not oneself, something which has no memory and is created in a moment and perpetually renewed. We put on a grotesque or solemn painted face to hide us from the terrors of judgment, invent an imaginative Saturnalia where one forgets reality, a game like that of a child, where one loses the infinite pain of self-realisation. Perhaps all the sins and energies of the world are but its flight from an infinite blinding beam.[2]

In a difficult prose work, *A Vision,* Yeats attempted to explain what he really believed. *A Vision* attempts an objective description of man's condition and his fate but shows man in constant conflict and change. All opposites exist in terms of each other. "Leda and the Swan" reflects the theory by showing both love and strife born of the same seed. In Greek mythology the union of Leda and Zeus, metamorphosed as a swan, gave birth to Helen, who in her life and in Yeats' poetry, represents love and strife. The swan is flesh and spirit, passionate and indifferent, creating love and strife. According

[2] William Butler Yeats, "Extracts from a Diary Kept in 1909," *The Autobiography of William Butler Yeats* (New York: Macmillan, 1953), pp. 285, 306.

to the larger view of history suggested in "The Second Coming," Leda's conception ended one two-thousand-year cycle of history and began another which was to end with Mary's conception, Mary's cycle to end as described in "The Second Coming."

Yeats read Donne at a time when his own style was changing from the manner of his early poetry in which the aim was to create "a vision of human perfection" and the style was visionary, languorous and metrically restrained (see "The Song of Wandering Aengus"). The period of change is marked by the loss of his dream of marrying Maud Gonne (who married another in 1903) and the publication of *Responsibilities* in 1914. During the first years of this period he wrote nothing at all. Afterwards his poetry is more energetic and colloquial, more concerned with the physical world of his own experience and moods than with the visionary, and based on the immediate drama of his personal life, with the speakers reflecting, as Donne's had, his own passion, situation, and intellect. The great late poetry of Yeats is often concerned with age. A sense of loss and inevitability creates in the tone of much of his later poetry an effect something like that of pagan tragedy. Losses accumulate, heroic strength is required, and behind it all a larger design like fate is suggested, as much pagan as Christian, inscrutable and indifferent but sustaining. In 1924 Yeats received the Nobel prize. He continued to write and revise up until his death, some of his greatest poems appearing in his final volume, *Last Poems,* 1939. "The Circus Animals' Desertion" summarizes his writing life. In "Under Ben Bulben" he wrote his epitaph.

> Cast a cold eye
> On life, on death.
> Horseman, pass by!

The Song of Wandering Aengus

> I went out to the hazel wood,
> Because a fire was in my head,
> And cut and peeled a hazel wand,
> And hooked a berry to a thread;
> And when white moths were on the wing,   5
> And moth-like stars were flickering out,
> I dropped the berry in a stream
> And caught a little silver trout.

When I had laid it on the floor
  I went to blow the fire aflame,   10
But something rustled on the floor,
  And some one called me by my name:
It had become a glimmering girl
  With apple blossom in her hair
Who called me by my name and ran   15
  And faded through the brightening air.

Though I am old with wandering
  Through hollow lands and hilly lands,
I will find out where she has gone,
  And kiss her lips and take her hands;   20
And walk among long dappled grass,
  And pluck till time and times are done
The silver apples of the moon,
  The golden apples of the sun.

NOTES AND QUESTIONS

1. "The Song of Wandering Aengus," one of Yeats' early poems, is
   full of the love of Irish myth that characterizes even his last and
   most sophisticated work. Aengus (usually spelled Angus) is the
   Irish god of love; his hazel wand (line 3) has magic powers, the
   hazel being a sacred tree of ancient Ireland.
2. This poem is what is sometimes called an art ballad, an attempt
   by a modern poet to work within the conventions of folk poetry.
   How in tone and technique does it resemble and differ from the
   popular ballad "Barbara Allan" (p. 122) and Keats' "La Belle
   Dame Sans Merci" (p. 56)?

The Wild Swans at Coole

The trees are in their autumn beauty,
  The woodland paths are dry,
Under the October twilight the water
  Mirrors a still sky;

Upon the brimming water among the stones   5
Are nine-and-fifty swans.

The nineteenth autumn has come upon me
Since I first made my count;
I saw, before I had well finished,
All suddenly mount   10
And scatter wheeling in great broken rings
Upon their clamorous wings.

I have looked upon those brilliant creatures,
And now my heart is sore.
All's changed since I, hearing at twilight,   15
The first time on this shore,
The bell-beat of their wings above my head,
Trod with a lighter tread.

Unwearied still, lover by lover,
They paddle in the cold   20
Companionable streams or climb the air;
Their hearts have not grown old;
Passion or conquest, wander where they will,
Attend upon them still.

But now they drift on the still water,   25
Mysterious, beautiful;
Among what rushes will they build,
By what lake's edge or pool
Delight men's eyes when I awake some day
To find they have flown away?   30

Leda and the Swan

A sudden blow: the great wings beating still
Above the staggering girl, her thighs caressed
By the dark web, her nape caught in his bill,
He holds her helpless breast upon his breast.

How can those terrified vague fingers push   5
The feathered glory from her loosening thighs?
And how can body, laid in that white rush,
But feel the strange heart beating where it lies?

A shudder in the loins engenders there
The broken wall, the burning roof and tower   10

And Agamemnon dead.
                    Being so caught up,
So mastered by the brute blood of the air,
Did she put on his knowledge with his power
Before the indifferent beak could let her drop?

NOTES AND QUESTIONS

1. In Greek mythology Leda, a mortal woman, was raped by the god
   Zeus in the form of a swan. From this union came Helen and
   Clytemnestra. Helen, by abandoning her husband Menelaus to go
   with Prince Paris to Troy, became the cause of the Trojan War.
   Clytemnestra, the wife of Agamemnon, murdered her husband
   after his return from the war and so initiated the tragedy re-
   counted in the *Oresteia* of Aeschylus. To Yeats the rape of Leda
   marked symbolically the beginning of a new age, the heroic age
   of classical antiquity; it was a "violent annunciation" contrasting
   with the Annunciation to Mary, which marked the beginning of
   Christianity. How does Yeats view this classical age? Note espe-
   .cially the question asked in the last two lines.
2. "Leda and the Swan" is a sonnet, a form Yeats rarely used. Com-
   pare the diction and cadence of "Leda and the Swan" with that of
   the much earlier "Song of Wandering Aengus." How has Yeats'
   style, as distinct from his thinking, changed during the years that
   separate the two poems?

Among School Children

I

I walk through the long schoolroom questioning;
A kind old nun in a white hood replies;
The children learn to cipher and to sing,
To study reading-books and history,
To cut and sew, be neat in everything   5
In the best modern way—the children's eyes
In momentary wonder stare upon
A sixty-year-old smiling public man.

II

I dream of a Ledaean body, bent
Above a sinking fire, a tale that she   10

Told of a harsh reproof, or trivial event
That changed some childish day to tragedy—
Told, and it seemed that our two natures blent
Into a sphere from youthful sympathy,
Or else, to alter Plato's parable,   15
Into the yolk and white of the one shell.

III

And thinking of that fit of grief or rage
I look upon one child or t'other there
And wonder if she stood so at that age—
For even daughters of the swan can share   20
Something of every paddler's heritage—
And had that colour upon cheek or hair,
And thereupon my heart is driven wild:
She stands before me as a living child.

IV

Her present image floats into the mind—   25
Did Quattrocento finger fashion it
Hollow of cheek as though it drank the wind
And took a mess of shadows for its meat?
And I though never of Ledaean kind
Had pretty plumage once—enough of that,   30
Better to smile on all that smile, and show
There is a comfortable kind of old scarecrow.

V

What youthful mother, a shape upon her lap
Honey of generation had betrayed,
And that must sleep, shriek, struggle to escape   35
As recollection or the drug decide,
Would think her son, did she but see that shape
With sixty or more winters on its head,
A compensation for the pang of his birth,
Or the uncertainty of his setting forth?   40

VI

Plato thought nature but a spume that plays
Upon a ghostly paradigm of things;

Solider Aristotle played the taws
Upon the bottom of a king of kings;
World-famous golden-thighed Pythagoras   45
Fingered upon a fiddle-stick or strings
What a star sang and careless Muses heard:
Old clothes upon old sticks to scare a bird.

VII

Both nuns and mothers worship images,
But those the candles light are not as those   50
That animate a mother's reveries,
But keep a marble or a bronze repose.
And yet they too break hearts—O Presences
That passion, piety or affection knows,
And that all heavenly glory symbolise—   55
O self-born mockers of man's enterprise;

VIII

Labour is blossoming or dancing where
The body is not bruised to pleasure soul,
Nor beauty born out of its own despair,
Nor blear-eyed wisdom out of midnight oil.   60
O chestnut-tree, great-rooted blossomer,
Are you the leaf, the blossom or the bole?
O body swayed to music, O brightening glance,
How can we know the dancer from the dance?

NOTES AND QUESTIONS

1. Yeats, now an aging senator, is inspecting a school, and the sight of the children reminds him of his youth, setting off a chain reaction of ideas that leads him to consider not only his own life but the meaning of life in general. *Ledaean body* (9): a body born of Leda, like Helen's (see "Leda and the Swan" p. 201); the reference is to Maud Gonne. *Plato's parable* (15): in Plato's *Symposium* sexual love is explained by the parable that male and female were originally parts of a single body that was later cut in two "as you might divide an egg with a hair"; the halves are reunited in the sexual act, though here the poet's "youthful sympathy" with Maud Gonne is said to have achieved this unity in a nonsexual way.

daughters of the swan (20): daughters of Leda. *Quattrocento* (26): the fifteenth century in Italian art, characterized by a thin, pale, intellectual ideal of beauty. *Plato* (41), *Aristotle* (43), *Pythagoras* (45): Yeats considers the theories of three philosophers who tried to explain the meaning of life and concludes that, despite their wisdom, they too ended up as scarecrows like himself—"Old clothes upon old sticks to scare a bird" (48).

2. In this poem the classroom serves the same purpose that the storm-threatened house serves in Yeats' earlier poem, "A Prayer for My Daughter" (p. 257): it is a specific setting that provides a steady source of imagery governing the direction of the poet's thinking. Thus, for example, in lines 43–44 Yeats imagines Aristotle not as the serene old philosopher but as the harassed tutor of Alexander the Great (the "king of kings"), whom he must discipline with an occasional thrashing (the "taws" is a leather strap). Find other direct references to childhood and education. How do they contribute to the view of life that Yeats expresses here?

3. The poem reaches its climax in the last two stanzas, where Yeats' meditation on childhood and old age and the value of human achievements turns first to anguish, then to ecstasy. "Man's enterprise" mocks him; the images he creates ("Presences") break his heart by representing an ideal that he himself cannot embody; the growth of wisdom is accompanied by the decline of physical power. In the blossoming chestnut-tree and the dancer, however, Yeats sees the symbols of perfection, of unqualified achievement. Why are these symbols especially effective? What do they have in common with one another?

Sailing to Byzantium

I

That is no country for old men. The young
In one another's arms, birds in the trees
—Those dying generations—at their song,
The salmon-falls, the mackerel-crowded seas,
Fish, flesh, or fowl, commend all summer long   5
Whatever is begotten, born, and dies.
Caught in that sensual music all neglect
Monuments of unageing intellect.

II

An aged man is but a paltry thing,
A tattered coat upon a stick, unless   10
Soul clap its hands and sing, and louder sing
For every tatter in its mortal dress,
Nor is there singing school but studying
Monuments of its own magnificence;
And therefore I have sailed the seas and come   15
To the holy city of Byzantium.

III

O sages standing in God's holy fire
As in the gold mosaic of a wall,
Come from the holy fire, perne in a gyre,
And be the singing-masters of my soul.   20
Consume my heart away; sick with desire
And fastened to a dying animal
It knows not what it is; and gather me
Into the artifice of eternity.

IV

Once out of nature I shall never take   25
My bodily form from any natural thing,
But such a form as Grecian goldsmiths make
Of hammered gold and gold enamelling
To keep a drowsy Emperor awake;
Or set upon a golden bough to sing   30
To lords and ladies of Byzantium
Of what is past, or passing, or to come.
        1927

NOTES AND QUESTIONS

1. *Byzantium* (title): the original name of Constantinople (present day Istanbul) which, toward the end of antiquity, evolved a gorgeous and highly stylized art, especially of mosaic and metalwork. Yeats regarded it as the ideal city, where a unity of religion, art, and practical life was achieved. In this poem he contrasts it with the Ireland of his own day, where he claims the things of the mind were disregarded so that it was therefore "no country for old men."

2. *O sages* (17): the poet appeals to the sages of Byzantium, asking
   them to teach him the spiritual joy he craves. But is he addressing
   a vision of the sages "in God's holy fire" and comparing them with
   those in a mosaic? Or is he addressing the sages in a mosaic as
   though they were visionary beings? Yeats' syntax leaves the matter
   ambiguous. Why?

3. *perne in a gyre* (19): a perne is a spindle, and the gyre is the
   spiral movement that Yeats believed to be the pattern of the cyclic
   phases of history, thought, and nature (see "The Second Coming,"
   p. 175). In its full meaning, the image is quite esoteric. How
   does Yeats translate it into a truly poetic image—one that can be
   understood by readers who are unfamiliar with his mystical
   theories?

4. *artifice of eternity* (24): usually the word *artifice* is used pejora-
   tively: the artificial is lifeless, false; we prefer the natural and the
   spontaneous. Yeats asks us to reverse our inclinations and acknowl-
   edge the artificial world of Byzantium as the supreme ideal, in-
   comparably superior to the messy naturalness of Ireland.

> I think that in early Byzantium, maybe never before or since in re-
> corded history, religious, aesthetic and practical life were one, that
> architects and artificers—though not, it may be, poets, for language
> had been the instrument of controversy and must have grown ab-
> stract—spoke to the multitude and the few alike. The painter, the
> mosaic worker, the worker in gold and silver, the illuminator of
> sacred books, were almost impersonal, almost perhaps without the
> consciousness of individual design, absorbed in their subject-matter
> and that the vision of a whole people. [Yeats' note]

Does his Byzantium have the appeal he wants it to have? If so,
why?

5. *such a form . . . make* (27): the form is that of an artificial sing-
   ing bird that was supposedly created to amuse the emperor of
   Byzantium. The poet imagines himself being reincarnated as this
   bird. Compare the symbolism of the bird with that of Byzantium
   as a whole. Which is the more daring symbol? Which is the more
   effective?

6. This poem and "Among School Children" are invariably cited as
   two of Yeats' greatest works. They were written in the same year,
   1926, and both are composed in ottava rima, originally an Italian
   form, an eight-line stanza in iambic pentameter rhyming *abababcc*.
   What other stylistic features do the two poems share?

A Dialogue of Self and Soul

I

My Soul. I summon to the winding ancient stair;
    Set all your mind upon the steep ascent,
    Upon the broken, crumbling battlement,
    Upon the breathless starlit air,
    Upon the star that marks the hidden pole;   5
    Fix every wandering thought upon
    That quarter where all thought is done:
    Who can distinguish darkness from the soul?

My Self. The consecrated blade upon my knees
    Is Sato's ancient blade, still as it was,   10
    Still razor-keen, still like a looking-glass
    Unspotted by the centuries;
    That flowering, silken, old embroidery, torn
    From some court-lady's dress and round
    The wooden scabbard bound and wound,   15
    Can, tattered, still protect, faded adorn.

My Soul. Why should the imagination of a man
    Long past his prime remember things that are
    Emblematical of love and war?
    Think of ancestral night that can,   20
    If but imagination scorn the earth
    And intellect its wandering
    To this and that and t'other thing,
    Deliver from the crime of death and birth.

My Self. Montashigi, third of his family, fashioned it   25
    Five hundred years ago, about it lie
    Flowers from I know not what embroidery—
    Heart's purple—and all these I set
    For emblems of the day against the tower
    Emblematical of the night,   30
    And claim as by a soldier's right
    A charter to commit the crime once more.

NOTE

Sato's ancient blade (10): an antique Japanese sword given to Yeats by a friend, Junzo Sato, used here as a symbol of life, the choice of rebirth over deliverance from rebirth.

My Soul. Such fullness in that quarter overflows
  And falls into the basin of the mind
  That man is stricken deaf and dumb and blind,   35
  For intellect no longer knows
  Is from the *Ought,* or *Knower* from the *Known—*
  That is to say, ascends to Heaven;
  Only the dead can be forgiven;
  But when I think of that my tongue's a stone.   40

II

My Self. A living man is blind and drinks his drop.
  What matter if the ditches are impure?
  What matter if I live it all once more?
  Endure that toil of growing up;
  The ignominy of boyhood; the distress   45
  Of boyhood changing into man;
  The unfinished man and his pain
  Brought face to face with his own clumsiness;
  The finished man among his enemies?—
  How in the name of Heaven can he escape   50
  That defiling and disfigured shape
  The mirror of malicious eyes
  Casts upon his eyes until at last
  He thinks that shape must be his shape?
  And what's the good of an escape   55
  If honour find him in the wintry blast?

  I am content to live it all again
  And yet again, if it be life to pitch
  Into the frog-spawn of a blind man's ditch,
  A blind man battering blind men;   60
  Or into that most fecund ditch of all,
  The folly that man does
  Or must suffer, if he woos
  A proud woman not kindred of his soul.

  I am content to follow to its source   65
  Every event in action or in thought;
  Measure the lot; forgive myself the lot!
  When such as I cast out remorse
  So great a sweetness flows into the breast
  We must laugh and we must sing,   70
  We are blest by everything,
  Everything we look upon is blest.

For Anne Gregory

'Never shall a young man,
Thrown into despair
By those great honey-coloured
Ramparts at your ear,
Love you for yourself alone   5
And not your yellow hair.'

'But I can get a hair-dye
And set such colour there,
Brown, or black, or carrot,
That young men in despair   10
May love me for myself alone
And not my yellow hair.'

'I heard an old religious man
But yesternight declare
That he had found a text to prove   15
That only God, my dear,
Could love you for yourself alone
And not your yellow hair.'

John Kinsella's Lament for Mrs. Mary Moore

A bloody and a sudden end,
    Gunshot or a noose,
For Death who takes what man would keep,
    Leaves what man would lose.
He might have had my sister,   5
    My cousins by the score,
But nothing satisfied the fool
    But my dear Mary Moore,
None other knows what pleasures man
    At table or in bed.   10
What shall I do for pretty girls
    Now my old bawd is dead?

Though stiff to strike a bargain,
    Like an old Jew man,
Her bargain struck we laughed and talked   15
    And emptied many a can;
And O! but she had stories,
    Though not for the priest's ear,

To keep the soul of man alive,
   Banish age and care,   20
And being old she put a skin
   On everything she said.
What shall I do for pretty girls
Now my old bawd is dead?

The priests have got a book that says   25
   But for Adam's sin
Eden's Garden would be there
   And I there within.
No expectation fails there,
   No pleasing habit ends,   30
No man grows old, no girl grows cold,
   But friends walk by friends.
Who quarrels over halfpennies
   That plucks the trees for bread?
What shall I do for pretty girls   35
Now my old bawd is dead?

The Circus Animals' Desertion

I

I sought a theme and sought for it in vain,
I sought it daily for six weeks or so.
Maybe at last, being but a broken man,
I must be satisfied with my heart, although
Winter and summer till old age began   5
My circus animals were all on show,
Those stilted boys, that burnished chariot,
Lion and woman and the Lord knows what.

II

What can I but enumerate old themes?
First that sea-rider Oisin led by the nose   10
Through three enchanted islands, allegorical dreams,
Vain gaiety, vain battle, vain repose,
Themes of the embittered heart, or so it seems,
That might adorn old songs or courtly shows;
But what cared I that set him on to ride,   15
I, starved for the bosom of his faery bride?

And then a counter-truth filled out its play,
The Countess Cathleen was the name I gave it;
She, pity-crazed, had given her soul away,
But masterful Heaven had intervened to save it.   20
I thought my dear must her own soul destroy,
So did fanaticism and hate enslave it,
And this brought forth a dream and soon enough
This dream itself had all my thought and love.

And when the Fool and Blind Man stole the bread   25
Cuchulain fought the ungovernable sea;
Heart-mysteries there, and yet when all is said
It was the dream itself enchanted me:
Character isolated by a deed
To engross the present and dominate memory.   30
Players and painted stage took all my love,
And not those things that they were emblems of.

III

Those masterful images because complete
Grew in pure mind, but out of what began?
A mound of refuse or the sweepings of a street,   35
Old kettles, old bottles, and a broken can,
Old iron, old bones, old rags, that raving slut
Who keeps the till. Now that my ladder's gone,
I must lie down where all the ladders start,
In the foul rag-and-bone shop of the heart.   40

NOTES AND QUESTIONS

1. To the very end of his life Yeats had difficulty finding themes for
   poetry, and this is a poem about not being able to write a poem.
   Desperate because of the failure of his imagination, Yeats calls
   to mind the characters, images, and symbols that have served him
   in the past: *Oisin* (10): a warrior-poet (pronounced *usheen*) of
   Irish myth whom Yeats celebrated in his earlier poems. *The
   Countess Cathleen* (18): a play by Yeats that tells of an Irish
   woman who sells her soul to the devil to save the peasants from
   starvation; her real-life model was the heroic but fanatic Maud
   Gonne. *the Fool, Blind Man, Cuchulain* (25–26): characters from
   another play by Yeats, *On Baile's Strand,* in which the hero Cu-
   chulain (pronounced *cuhoolin*), crazed with grief to discover that

he has unknowingly killed his own son, goes out to battle the sea. What does Yeats say were the reasons he wrote these works? Does he feel that his personal motivations influenced the works themselves?

2. No poet in English has written about old age more consistently and magnificently than Yeats. Compare the "old man" persona in this poem with those in "Sailing to Byzantium," "Among School Children," and "The Lamentation of the Old Pensioner" (pp. 338 and 339). What do the four personae have in common? How are they different?

Other poems of William Butler Yeats in this book are:
"A Prayer for My Daughter" (p. 257)
"Crazy Jane Talks with the Bishop" (p. 64)
"The Lamentation of the Old Pensioner" (p. 338)
"Long-Legged Fly" (p. 127)
"The Magi" (p. 45)
"No Second Troy" (p. 46)
"The Second Coming" (p. 175)
"When You Are Old" (p. 5)

Robert Frost

(1874–1963)

Robert Frost seems at first to be a regional poet—a New Englander. He was, but only in a sense. Both of his parents were from the Northeast, and, although he was born in San Francisco, where his father was a newspaper editor, at the age of eleven he was taken back to New England at the time of his father's death; there he spent most of the rest of his long life in New Hampshire, Vermont, and Massachusetts. Almost every one of his poems is clearly set in New England. Yet there was no restrictive localism; what he wrote transcended the setting.

Frost devoted almost all of his life to his role as poet. His first published poem appeared in his high school newspaper when he was sixteen. He continued to compose his poems, but he was about forty and living in England (1912–1915) before he gained recognition as a poet—being "discovered" by the English. His reputation then became secure, flourishing both in the United States and abroad, and he spent the next half century writing, giving public readings and lectures, and conversing. Four times winner of the Pulitzer Prize for Poetry (1924, 1931, 1937, 1943), recipient of formal felicitations from the Senate of the United States on his seventy-fifth birthday and again on his eighty-fifth, he had an enormous and broadly based popularity.

Frost was devoted to observing, thinking, reflecting, and conversing, but not conversing particularly with his fellow poets. Although during his stay in England he came to know his poet-contemporaries —Ezra Pound probably better than the others—he later described himself as a "lone wolf." The people Frost enjoyed talking with were his fellow human beings: at various times during his life his fellow farmers, his students, his audiences, his lecture hosts, his pullman-car porters. Even in his later years good talk would keep him awake and alert farther into the early hours than his fellow talkers (he would certainly have referred to them as "talkers," not "conversationalists"). These were the conversations from which he derived his sense of the sound of the language and that often served as the seed which, nourished by his imagination and reflection, would grow into a poem.

Among his comments on the sound of the language Frost said: "A sentence is a sound in itself on which other sounds called words may be strung. . . . The sentence-sounds are very definite entities. . . . They are as definite as words." Frost's ear for what he called "sentence-sounds" is an important key to his diction and style. The sentence-sounds that he heard were basically those of ordinary colloquial speech. Many of his lines consist entirely of monosyllabic words; uncommon words are rare, unless nature lore requires them, like "heal-all" in "Design." Frost instinctively disliked any syntactic artificiality; seldom is there an inversion of subject and predicate or any other syntactic irregularity even for poetic effect. The resulting quality is what makes commentators describe his style as "colloquial," "conversational," "rustic," "homespun"—a style that grew out of his ear for the sentence-sounds of natural speech.

Yet Frost was a versatile, though still flexible, traditional metrist. Of the poems that follow, the three longest, "The Death of the Hired Man," "Home Burial," and "The Wood-Pile," are all in blank verse dominated by speech rhythm. Three others are sonnets: "A Dream Pang" closest to the pristine Italian form; "Design," also an Italian sonnet, but with a rhyme pattern even more intense than that already required by the form (and wholly appropriate to the subject of design); and "The Oven Bird," a freely rhymed English type of sonnet. The remaining three poems are in varied stanzaic forms of four, five, or six lines, with a variety of meters and of rhymes. The wedding of traditional metrics and sentence-sounds is a popular feature of Frost's style.

The speaker in many of Frost's poems is Frost himself. In others the personae are people who resemble Frost in background and experience, close to nature and to simple, rural life. His subjects were therefore nature itself and rural characters and their relationships, hardships, and anecdotes. "The Hillside Thaw" (see page 33), though basically pure description, illustrates his strength as a close observer of nature and as a master of sustained tone and metaphor. Although "The Wood-Pile" pays equally close attention to nature, it illustrates the low-keyed tone he employs to depict a relentlessly indifferent nature as the basis on which men ironically build their courage and their dreams. Craftsmanship, consistently admired by

Frost, created a wood-pile, mysteriously abandoned, left to decay in a slow, inevitable, natural process. His clear look at the cold fact of nature's indifference is less understated in the dramatic dialogues of "The Death of The Hired Man" and "Home Burial."

The hallmarks of Frost's art are the low-keyed honesty of tone, the casual naturalness of the style, and the sense readers have of having felt at some time attitudes they find expressed for them in his poems. There is sentiment but no sentimentality, and the ideas in his best poems are a statement of the ambivalence all people feel when they look with complete honesty at themselves. This ambivalence is reflected in words he wrote for his epitaph. "I had a lover's quarrel with the world."

A Dream Pang

I had withdrawn in forest, and my song
Was swallowed up in leaves that blew alway;
And to the forest edge you came one day
(This was my dream) and looked and pondered long,
But did not enter, though the wish was strong: 5
You shook your pensive head as who should say,
"I dare not—too far in his footsteps stray—
He must seek me would he undo the wrong."

Not far, but near, I stood and saw it all,
Behind low boughs the trees let down outside;   10
And the sweet pang it cost me not to call
And tell you that I saw does still abide.
But 'tis not true that thus I dwelt aloof,
For the wood wakes, and you are here for proof.

Reluctance

Out through the fields and the woods
    And over the walls I have wended;
I have climbed the hills of view
    And looked at the world, and descended;
I have come by the highway home,   5
    And lo, it is ended.

The leaves are all dead on the ground,
    Save those that the oak is keeping
To ravel them one by one

And let them go scraping and creeping   10
Out over the crusted snow,
   When others are sleeping.

And the dead leaves lie huddled and still,
   No longer blown hither and thither;
The last lone aster is gone;   15
   The flowers of the witch hazel wither;
The heart is still aching to seek,
   But the feet question "Whither?"

Ah, when to the heart of man
   Was it ever less than a treason   20
To go with the drift of things,
   To yield with a grace to reason,
And bow and accept the end
   Of a love or a season?

The Death of the Hired Man

Mary sat musing on the lamp-flame at the table,
Waiting for Warren. When she heard his step,
She ran on tiptoe down the darkened passage
To meet him in the doorway with the news
And put him on his guard. "Silas is back."   5
She pushed him outward with her through the door
And shut it after her. "Be kind," she said.
She took the market things from Warren's arms
And set them on the porch, then drew him down
To sit beside her on the wooden steps.   10

"When was I ever anything but kind to him?
But I'll not have the fellow back," he said.
"I told him so last haying, didn't I?
If he left then, I said, that ended it.
What good is he? Who else will harbor him   15
At his age for the little he can do?
What help he is there's no depending on.
Off he goes always when I need him most.
He thinks he ought to earn a little pay,
Enough at least to buy tobacco with,   20
So he won't have to beg and be beholden.
'All right,' I say, 'I can't afford to pay
Any fixed wages, though I wish I could.'

'Someone else can.' 'Then someone else will have to.'
I shouldn't mind his bettering himself   25
If that was what it was. You can be certain,
When he begins like that, there's someone at him
Trying to coax him off with pocket money—
In haying time, when any help is scarce.
In winter he comes back to us. I'm done."   30

"Sh! not so loud: he'll hear you," Mary said.

"I want him to: he'll have to soon or late."

"He's worn out. He's asleep beside the stove.
When I came up from Rowe's I found him here,
Huddled against the barn door fast asleep,   35
A miserable sight, and frightening, too—
You needn't smile—I didn't recognize him—
I wasn't looking for him—and he's changed.
Wait till you see."

                    "Where did you say he'd been?"

"He didn't say. I dragged him to the house,   40
And gave him tea and tried to make him smoke.
I tried to make him talk about his travels.
Nothing would do: he just kept nodding off."

"What did he say? Did he say anything?"

"But little."

            "Anything? Mary, confess   45
He said he'd come to ditch the meadow for me."

"Warren!"

            "But did he? I just want to know."

"Of course he did. What would you have him say?
Surely you wouldn't grudge the poor old man
Some humble way to save his self-respect.   50
He added, if you really care to know,
He meant to clear the upper pasture, too.
That sounds like something you have heard before?
Warren, I wish you could have heard the way
He jumbled everything. I stopped to look   55
Two or three times—he made me feel so queer—
To see if he was talking in his sleep.

He ran on Harold Wilson—you remember—
The boy you had in haying four years since.
He's finished school, and teaching in his college.   60
Silas declares you'll have to get him back.
He says they two will make a team for work:
Between them they will lay this farm as smooth!
The way he mixed that in with other things.
He thinks young Wilson a likely lad, though daft   65
On education—you know how they fought
All through July under the blazing sun,
Silas up on the cart to build the load,
Harold along beside to pitch it on."

"Yes, I took care to keep well out of earshot."   70

"Well, those days trouble Silas like a dream.
You wouldn't think they would. How some things linger!
Harold's young college-boy's assurance piqued him.
After so many years he still keeps finding
Good arguments he sees he might have used.   75
I sympathize. I know just how it feels
To think of the right thing to say too late.
Harold's associated in his mind with Latin.
He asked me what I thought of Harold's saying
He studied Latin, like the violin,   80
Because he liked it—that an argument!
He said he couldn't make the boy believe
He could find water with a hazel prong—
Which showed how much good school had ever done him.
He wanted to go over that. But most of all   85
He thinks if he could have another chance
To teach him how to build a load of hay—"

"I know, that's Silas' one accomplishment.
He bundles every forkful in its place,
And tags and numbers it for future reference,   90
So he can find and easily dislodge it
In the unloading. Silas does that well.
He takes it out in bunches like big birds' nests.
You never see him standing on the hay
He's trying to lift, straining to lift himself."   95

"He thinks if he could teach him that, he'd be
Some good perhaps to someone in the world.
He hates to see a boy the fool of books.

Poor Silas, so concerned for other folk,
And nothing to look backward to with pride,   100
And nothing to look forward to with hope,
So now and never any different."

Part of a moon was falling down the west,
Dragging the whole sky with it to the hills.
Its light poured softly in her lap. She saw it   105
And spread her apron to it. She put out her hand
Among the harplike morning-glory strings,
Taut with the dew from garden bed to eaves,
As if she played unheard some tenderness
That wrought on him beside her in the night.   110
"Warren," she said, "he has come home to die:
You needn't be afraid he'll leave you this time."

"Home," he mocked gently.

                    "Yes, what else but home?
It all depends on what you mean by home.
Of course he's nothing to us, any more   115
Than was the hound that came a stranger to us
Out of the woods, worn out upon the trail."

"Home is the place where, when you have to go there,
They have to take you in."

                    "I should have called it
Something you somehow haven't to deserve."   120

Warren leaned out and took a step or two,
Picked up a little stick, and brought it back
And broke it in his hand and tossed it by.
"Silas has better claim on us you think
Than on his brother? Thirteen little miles   125
As the road winds would bring him to his door.
Silas has walked that far no doubt today.
Why doesn't he go there? His brother's rich,
A somebody—director in the bank."

"He never told us that."

                    "We know it, though."   130

"I think his brother ought to help, of course.
I'll see to that if there is need. He ought of right
To take him in, and might be willing to—

He may be better than appearances.
But have some pity on Silas. Do you think   135
If he had any pride in claiming kin
Or anything he looked for from his brother,
He'd keep so still about him all this time?"

"I wonder what's between them."

                       "I can tell you.
Silas is what he is—we wouldn't mind him—   140
But just the kind that kinsfolk can't abide.
He never did a thing so very bad.
He don't know why he isn't quite as good
As anybody. Worthless though he is,
He won't be made ashamed to please his brother."   145

"*I* can't think Si ever hurt anyone."

"No, but he hurt my heart the way he lay
And rolled his old head on that sharp-edged chair-back.
He wouldn't let me put him on the lounge.
You must go in and see what you can do.   150
I made the bed up for him there tonight.
You'll be surprised at him—how much he's broken.
His working days are done; I'm sure of it."

"I'd not be in a hurry to say that."

"I haven't been. Go, look, see for yourself.   155
But, Warren, please remember how it is:
He's come to help you ditch the meadow.
He has a plan. You mustn't laugh at him.
He may not speak of it, and then he may.
I'll sit and see if that small sailing cloud   160
Will hit or miss the moon."

                    It hit the moon.
Then there were three there, making a dim row,
The moon, the little silver cloud, and she.

Warren returned—too soon, it seemed to her—
Slipped to her side, caught up her hand and waited.   165

"Warren?" she questioned.

                    "Dead," was all he answered.

Home Burial

He saw her from the bottom of the stairs
Before she saw him. She was starting down,
Looking back over her shoulder at some fear.
She took a doubtful step and then undid it
To raise herself and look again. He spoke   5
Advancing toward her: "What is it you see
From up there always?—for I want to know."
She turned and sank upon her skirts at that,
And her face changed from terrified to dull.
He said to gain time: "What is it you see?"   10
Mounting until she cowered under him.
"I will find out now—you must tell me, dear."
She, in her place, refused him any help,
With the least stiffening of her neck and silence.
She let him look, sure that he wouldn't see,   15
Blind creature; and awhile he didn't see.
But at last he murmured, "Oh," and again, "Oh."

"What is it—what?" she said.

                              "Just that I see."

"You don't," she challenged. "Tell me what it is."

"The wonder is I didn't see at once.   20
I never noticed it from here before.
I must be wonted to it—that's the reason.
The little graveyard where my people are!
So small the window frames the whole of it.
Not so much larger than a bedroom, is it?   25
There are three stones of slate and one of marble,
Broad-shouldered little slabs there in the sunlight
On the sidehill. We haven't to mind *those*.
But I understand: it is not the stones,
But the child's mound——"

                              "Don't, don't, don't, don't,"
                         she cried.   30

She withdrew, shrinking from beneath his arm
That rested on the banister, and slid downstairs;
And turned on him with such a daunting look,
He said twice over before he knew himself:
"Can't a man speak of his own child he's lost?"   35

"Not you!—Oh, where's my hat? Oh, I don't need it!
I must get out of here. I must get air.—
I don't know rightly whether any man can."

"Amy! Don't go to someone else this time.
Listen to me. I won't come down the stairs."   40
He sat and fixed his chin between his fists.
"There's something I should like to ask you, dear."

"You don't know how to ask it."

                    "Help me, then."

Her fingers moved the latch for all reply.

"My words are nearly always an offense.   45
I don't know how to speak of anything
So as to please you. But I might be taught,
I should suppose. I can't say I see how.
A man must partly give up being a man
With womenfolk. We could have some arrangement   50
By which I'd bind myself to keep hands off
Anything special you're a-mind to name.
Though I don't like such things 'twixt those that love.
Two that don't love can't live together without them.
But two that do can't live together with them."   55
She moved the latch a little. "Don't—don't go.
Don't carry it to someone else this time.
Tell me about it if it's something human.
Let me into your grief. I'm not so much
Unlike other folks as your standing there   60
Apart would make me out. Give me my chance.
I do think, though, you overdo it a little.
What was it brought you up to think it the thing
To take your mother-loss of a first child
So inconsolably—in the face of love.   65
You'd think his memory might be satisfied—"

"There you go sneering now!"

                    "I'm not, I'm not!
You make me angry. I'll come down to you.
God, what a woman! And it's come to this,
A man can't speak of his own child that's dead."   70

"You can't because you don't know how to speak.
If you had any feelings, you that dug

With your own hand—how could you?—his little grave;
I saw you from that very window there,
Making the gravel leap and leap in air,   75
Leap up, like that, like that, and land so lightly
And roll back down the mound beside the hole.
I thought, Who is that man? I didn't know you.
And I crept down the stairs and up the stairs
To look again, and still your spade kept lifting.   80
Then you came in. I heard your rumbling voice
Out in the kitchen, and I don't know why,
But I went near to see with my own eyes.
You could sit there with the stains on your shoes
Of the fresh earth from your own baby's grave   85
And talk about your everyday concerns.
You had stood the spade up against the wall
Outside there in the entry, for I saw it."

"I shall laugh the worst laugh I ever laughed.
I'm cursed. God, if I don't believe I'm cursed."   90

"I can repeat the very words you were saying:
'Three foggy mornings and one rainy day
Will rot the best birch fence a man can build.'
Think of it, talk like that at such a time!
What had how long it takes a birch to rot   95
To do with what was in the darkened parlor?
You *couldn't* care! The nearest friends can go
With anyone to death, comes so far short
They might as well not try to go at all.
No, from the time when one is sick to death,   100
One is alone, and he dies more alone.
Friends make pretense of following to the grave,
But before one is in it, their minds are turned
And making the best of their way back to life
And living people, and things they understand.   105
But the world's evil. I won't have grief so
If I can change it. Oh, I won't, I won't!"

"There, you have said it all and you feel better.
You won't go now. You're crying. Close the door.
The heart's gone out of it: why keep it up?   110
Amy! There's someone coming down the road!"

"*You*—oh, you think the talk is all. I must go—
Somewhere out of this house. How can I make you—"

"If—you—do!" She was opening the door wider.
"Where do you mean to go? First tell me that.   115
I'll follow and bring you back by force. I *will!—*"

The Wood-Pile

Out walking in the frozen swamp one gray day,
I paused and said, "I will turn back from here.
No, I will go on farther—and we shall see."
The hard snow held me, save where now and then
One foot went through. The view was all in lines   5
Straight up and down of tall slim trees
Too much alike to mark or name a place by
So as to say for certain I was here
Or somewhere else: I was just far from home.
A small bird flew before me. He was careful   10
To put a tree between us when he lighted,
And say no word to tell me who he was
Who was so foolish as to think what *he* thought.
He thought that I was after him for a feather—
The white one in his tail; like one who takes   15
Everything said as personal to himself.
One flight out sideways would have undeceived him.
And then there was a pile of wood for which
I forgot him and let his little fear
Carry him off the way I might have gone,   20
Without so much as wishing him good-night.
He went behind it to make his last stand.
It was a cord of maple, cut and split
And piled—and measured, four by four by eight.
And not another like it could I see.   25
No runner tracks in this year's snow looped near it.
And it was older sure than this year's cutting,
Or even last year's or the year's before.
The wood was gray and the bark warping off it
And the pile somewhat sunken. Clematis   30
Had wound strings round and round it like a bundle.
What held it, though, on one side was a tree
Still growing, and on one a stake and prop,
These latter about to fall. I thought that only
Someone who lived in turning to fresh tasks   35
Could so forget his handiwork on which

He spent himself, the labor of his ax,
And leave it there far from a useful fireplace
To warm the frozen swamp as best it could
With the slow smokeless burning of decay.   40

The Road Not Taken

Two roads diverged in a yellow wood,
And sorry I could not travel both
And be one traveler, long I stood
And looked down one as far as I could
To where it bent in the undergrowth;   5

Then took the other, as just as fair,
And having perhaps the better claim,
Because it was grassy and wanted wear;
Though as for that, the passing there
Had worn them really about the same,   10

And both that morning equally lay
In leaves no step had trodden black.
Oh, I kept the first for another day!
Yet knowing how way leads on to way,
I doubted if I should ever come back.   15

I shall be telling this with a sigh
Somewhere ages and ages hence:
Two roads diverged in a wood, and I—
I took the one less traveled by,
And that has made all the difference.   20

The Oven Bird

There is a singer everyone has heard,
Loud, a mid-summer and a mid-wood bird,
Who makes the solid tree trunks sound again.
He says that leaves are old and that for flowers
Mid-summer is to spring as one to ten.   5
He says the early petal-fall is past,
When pear and cherry bloom went down in showers
On sunny days a moment overcast;
And comes that other fall we name the fall.

He says the highway dust is over all.   10
The bird would cease and be as other birds
But that he knows in singing not to sing.
The question that he frames in all but words
Is what to make of a diminished thing.

Stopping by Woods on a Snowy Evening

Whose woods these are I think I know.
His house is in the village, though;
He will not see me stopping here
To watch his woods fill up with snow.

My little horse must think it queer   5
To stop without a farmhouse near
Between the woods and frozen lake
The darkest evening of the year.

He gives his harness bells a shake
To ask if there is some mistake.   10
The only other sound's the sweep
Of easy wind and downy flake.

The woods are lovely, dark, and deep,
But I have promises to keep,
And miles to go before I sleep,   15
And miles to go before I sleep.

Design

I found a dimpled spider, fat and white,
On a white heal-all, holding up a moth
Like a white piece of rigid satin cloth—
Assorted characters of death and blight
Mixed ready to begin the morning right,   5
Like the ingredients of a witches' broth—
A snow-drop spider, a flower like a froth,
And dead wings carried like a paper kite.
What had that flower to do with being white,
The wayside blue and innocent heal-all?   10
What brought the kindred spider to that height,
Then steered the white moth thither in the night?
What but design of darkness to appall?—
If design govern in a thing so small.

NOTES AND QUESTIONS

1. *heal-all* (2): a low-growing plant normally bearing blue flowers and reputed to have healing powers.
2. "Design" is based on an observation, actual or imagined, of a minute phenomenon of nature; but the poem conveys a tone and an irony that lead to the questions in the sestet. What is that tone? What is the irony? Identify the words and phrases which, acting alone or reinforcing one another, create the tone and the irony.

Other poems of Robert Frost in this book are:
"A Time to Talk" (p. 26)
"Acquainted with the Night" (p. 137)
"After Apple-Picking" (p. 167)
"The Hillside Thaw" (p. 33)
"Revelation" (p. 297)
"The Span of Life" (p. 99)
"Storm Fear" (p. 333)

Sylvia Plath

(1932–1963)

In 1960 the first book of Sylvia Plath's poems, *The Colossus*, was published. Three years later she was dead, but no one writing poetry since her time has had quite the combination of popular and critical acclaim that she has had. She is still being discovered by great numbers of readers and her books continue to appear posthumously. Her second and best book of poems, *Ariel*, was published in 1966; transitional poems, written between the other two books, were published in *Crossing the Water* in 1971. Her novel, *The Bell Jar*, published in the United States in 1971, was a best seller. A complete collection of her poems has not yet appeared.

To focus upon the confessional nature of Plath's late *Ariel* poetry and to trace in it evidence of her immanent suicide is only one way to account for the astonishment the reader feels for the disturbing metaphors and juxtapositions in her poems. Because a field of poppies reminds one speaker of a woman in an ambulance "whose red heart blooms through her coat," some readers see the indulgence of a strange imagination instead of the austerities of the style. The style is disciplined to follow the associative patterns of thought and imagination in the minds of speakers whose situations are at various degrees removed from those of Sylvia Plath herself. Her own sensitivity is applied to them, but in a style disciplined to a dramatic presentation of their feelings, not to what Plath felt for or about them. In the dramatic presentation we are in the minds of these speakers; we see neither them nor their situations from the outside. Because their desperate and vulnerable situations are not stated but must be pieced together, some readers have difficulty with Plath. The difficulty is compounded because the style is further trimmed to simple juxtapositions between disturbing statements and vivid images.

229

But paradoxically, like much in the life of Sylvia Plath, in these austerely crafted poems, autobiographical facts are hinted and a psychic stress is clearly proclaimed. At the age of ten she lost her own father, and "The Colossus" describes a girl's feeling in her attempt to piece together the images, scattered like his bones, of her father: "Thirty years now I have labored . . . I am none the wiser." She was several years under thirty when she wrote this poem describing a girl's feeling, and at that particular time she was a happily married woman. "The world of her poetry," said her husband, Ted Hughes, "is one of emblematic visionary events, mathematical symmetries, clairvoyance and metamorphoses." One metamorphosis, several years later in one of her best poems, "Daddy," was to present the stream of consciousness of a girl whose father (who had died when she was ten) had been a Nazi Panzer officer guilty with all Nazis of millions of deaths. The love she feels for him results in the guilt she feels for loving a Nazi, and she must perform a ritual stabbing of a model she made of him and then prepare for suicide. In the mathematical balance between the inevitability of her love and the resulting necessity of her guilt, the poem has the symmetry of the necessity of guilt and punishment inherent in Greek tragedy. "Her psychic gifts, at almost any time," said Ted Hughes, "were strong enough to make her frequently wish to be rid of them." In the same year, the last year of her life, she wrote "Lady Lazarus," which deals more directly with suicide, its speaker resentful of being dragged back from death.

> Dying
> Is an art, like everything else.
> I do it exceptionally well.

These highly praised and much-anthologized poems, revealing a private and troubled self, obscure her other, more public, self. The official facts of her life and the images to be gathered from reports of her friends reveal a vivacious girl and young woman who moved from accomplishment to accomplishment. Although she missed a semester at college because of a suicide attempt, a subject of her novel *The Bell Jar,* the record shows her election to offices in high school and college; scholarships to Smith College, where she graduated *summa cum laude* in 1955; boyfriends and weekends at Princeton, Yale, and Harvard; and before graduation, poetry published in *Seventeen, Mademoiselle,* and *Harpers,* and many poetry prizes. After graduation she occasionally attended a course with Robert Lowell, who remembers "a brilliant tense presence embarrassed by restraint," and she spent two years on a Fulbright Fellowship at Cambridge University, where she met and married her husband and had two children.

Pregnancy is the subject of "Metaphors" and her first child the subject of "Morning Song." "Aftermath" (page 131) and "Spinster," each showing women described by an outside observer, illustrate her early style.

Spinster

Now this particular girl
During a ceremonious April walk
With her latest suitor
Found herself, of a sudden, intolerably struck
By the birds' irregular babel   5
And the leaves' litter.

By this tumult afflicted, she
Observed her lover's gestures unbalance the air,
His gait stray uneven
Through a rank wilderness of fern and flower.   10
She judged petals in disarray,
The whole season, sloven.

How she longed for winter then!—
Scrupulously austere in its order
Of white and black   15
Ice and rock, each sentiment within border,
And heart's frosty discipline
Exact as a snowflake.

But here—a burgeoning
Unruly enough to pitch her five queenly wits   20
Into vulgar motley—
A treason not to be borne. Let idiots
Reel giddy in bedlam spring:
She withdrew neatly.

And round her house she set   25
Such a barricade of barb and check
Against mutinous weather
As no mere insurgent man could hope to break
With curse, fist, threat
Or love, either.   30

The Colossus

I shall never get you put together entirely,
Pieced, glued, and properly jointed.
Mule-bray, pig-grunt and bawdy cackles
Proceed from your great lips.
It's worse than a barnyard.   5

Perhaps you consider yourself an oracle,
Mouthpiece of the dead, or of some god or other.
Thirty years now I have labored
To dredge the silt from your throat.
I am none the wiser.   10

Scaling little ladders with gluepots and pails of lysol
I crawl like an ant in mourning
Over the weedy acres of your brow
To mend the immense skull plates and clear
The bald, white tumuli of your eyes.   15

A blue sky out of the Oresteia
Arches above us. O father, all by yourself
You are pithy and historical as the Roman Forum.
I open my lunch on a hill of black cypress.
Your fluted bones and acanthine hair are littered   20

In their old anarchy to the horizon-line.
It would take more than a lightning-stroke
To create such a ruin.
Nights, I squat in the cornucopia
Of your left ear, out of the wind,   25

Counting the red stars and those of plum-color.
The sun rises under the pillar of your tongue.
My hours are married to shadow.
No longer do I listen for the scrape of a keel
On the blank stones of the landing.   30

NOTE

Oresteia (16): a trilogy of Greek tragedies by Aeschylus in which Electra
is a central figure. Electra mourns her father's death and must avenge it
with the aid of her brother, Orestes, by killing her mother.

Mirror

I am silver and exact. I have no preconceptions.
Whatever I see I swallow immediately
Just as it is, unmisted by love or dislike.
I am not cruel, only truthful—
The eye of a little god, four-cornered.   5
Most of the time I meditate on the opposite wall.
It is pink, with speckles. I have looked at it so long
I think it is a part of my heart. But it flickers.
Faces and darkness separate us over and over.

Now I am a lake. A woman bends over me,   10
Searching my reaches for what she really is.
Then she turns to those liars, the candles or the moon.
I see her back, and reflect it faithfully.
She rewards me with tears and an agitation of hands.
I am important to her. She comes and goes.   15
Each morning it is her face that replaces the darkness.
In me she has drowned a young girl, and in me an old woman
Rises toward her day after day, like a terrible fish.

Metaphors

I'm a riddle in nine syllables,
An elephant, a ponderous house,
A melon strolling on two tendrils.
O red fruit, ivory, fine timbers!
This loaf's big with its yeasty rising.   5
Money's new-minted in this fat purse.
I'm a means, a stage, a cow in calf.
I've eaten a bag of green apples,
Boarded the train there's no getting off.

Morning Song

Love set you going like a fat gold watch.
The midwife slapped your footsoles, and your bald cry
Took its place among the elements.

Our voices echo, magnifying your arrival. New statue.
In a drafty museum, your nakedness   5
Shadows our safety. We stand round blankly as walls.

I'm no more your mother
Than the cloud that distils a mirror to reflect its own slow
Effacement at the wind's hand.

All night your moth-breath   10
Flickers among the flat pink roses. I wake to listen:
A far sea moves in my ear.

One cry, and I stumble from bed, cow-heavy and floral
In my Victorian nightgown.
Your mouth opens clean as a cat's. The window square   15

Whitens and swallows its dull stars. And now you try
Your handful of notes;
The clear vowels rise like balloons.

Poppies in October

Even the sun-clouds this morning cannot manage such skirts.
Nor the woman in the ambulance
Whose red heart blooms through her coat so astoundingly—

A gift, a love gift
Utterly unasked for   5
By a sky

Palely and flamily
Igniting its carbon monoxides, by eyes
Dulled to a halt under bowlers.

O my God, what am I   10
That these late mouths should cry open
In a forest of frost, in a dawn of cornflowers.

The Hanging Man

By the roots of my hair some god got hold of me.
I sizzled in his blue volts like a desert prophet.

The nights snapped out of sight like a lizard's eyelid:
A world of bald white days in a shadeless socket.

A vulturous boredom pinned me in this tree.   5
If he were I, he would do what I did.

Daddy

You do not do, you do not do
Any more, black shoe
In which I have lived like a foot
For thirty years, poor and white,
Barely daring to breathe or Achoo.   5

Daddy, I have had to kill you.
You died before I had time—
Marble-heavy, a bag full of God,
Ghastly statue with one grey toe
Big as a Frisco seal   10

And a head in the freakish Atlantic
Where it pours bean green over blue
In the waters off beautiful Nauset.
I used to pray to recover you.
Ach, du.   15

In the German tongue, in the Polish town
Scraped flat by the roller
Of wars, wars, wars.
But the name of the town is common.
My Polack friend   20

Says there are a dozen or two.
So I never could tell where you
Put your foot, your root,
I never could talk to you.
The tongue stuck in my jaw.   25

It stuck in a barb wire snare.
Ich, ich, ich, ich,
I could hardly speak.
I thought every German was you.
And the language obscene   30

An engine, an engine
Chuffing me off like a Jew.
A Jew to Dachau, Auschwitz, Belsen.
I began to talk like a Jew.
I think I may well be a Jew.   35

The snows of the Tyrol, the clear beer of Vienna
Are not very pure or true.

With my gypsy ancestress and my weird luck
And my Taroc pack and my Taroc pack
I may be a bit of a Jew.   40

I have always been scared of *you,*
With your Luftwaffe, your gobbledygoo.
And your neat moustache
And your Aryan eye, bright blue.
Panzer-man, panzer-man, O You—   45

Not God but a swastika
So black no sky could squeak through.
Every woman adores a Fascist,
The boot in the face, the brute
Brute heart of a brute like you.   50

You stand at the blackboard, daddy,
In the picture I have of you,
A cleft in your chin instead of your foot
But no less a devil for that, no not
Any less the black man who   55

Bit my pretty red heart in two.
I was ten when they buried you.
At twenty I tried to die
And get back, back, back to you.
I thought even the bones would do.   60

But they pulled me out of the sack,
And they stuck me together with glue.
And then I knew what to do.
I made a model of you,
A man in black with a Meinkampf look   65

And a love of the rack and the screw.
And I said I do, I do.
So daddy, I'm finally through.
The black telephone's off at the root,
The voices just can't worm through.   70

If I've killed one man, I've killed two—
The vampire who said he was you
And drank my blood for a year,
Seven years, if you want to know.
Daddy, you can lie back now.   75

There's a stake in your fat black heart
And the villagers never liked you.
They are dancing and stamping on you.
They always *knew* it was you.
Daddy, daddy, you bastard, I'm through. 80

NOTES AND QUESTIONS

1. *Nauset* (13): a beach on the east coast of Cape Cod. The speaker has moved from an image of her father on the Pacific, when they watched the Frisco seals, to the Atlantic, where only his head was visible in the water. Explain the relationships among images of his size in stanza two.
2. *Ach, du* (15): Ah, you. Cite the evidence of the speaker's psychic conflict thus far in the poem. What more customary tradition is suggested by her keeping his black shoe?
3. *Dachau, Auschwitz, Belsen* (33): Nazi concentration camps. Why does she call the German language an engine? Why does she claim to be a Jew?
4. *Taroc pack* (39): a pack of cards used by gypsies to tell fortunes. Why does she have a Taroc pack? Why does she associate gypsies with Jews? With herself?
5. *Luftwaffe* (42): the Nazi air force. *Panzer-man* (45): a member of the tank corps that overran first Poland then most of Europe. *Meinkampf* (65): the title of Hitler's autobiography. These words have developed a horrible symbolic significance. Does every woman adore a fascist?
6. The enigma of line 71, "If I've killed one man, I've killed two," suggests her inability to kill the father image by stabbing the model she made of her father. Why is it probable that she has not killed the lover (the vampire) either? Why has she assumed that the lover has betrayed her?

Lady Lazarus

I have done it again.
One year in every ten
I manage it—

A sort of walking miracle, my skin
Bright as a Nazi lampshade,   5
My right foot

A paperweight,
My face a featureless, fine
Jew linen.

Peel off the napkin   10
O my enemy.
Do I terrify?—

The nose, the eye pits, the full set of teeth?
The sour breath
Will vanish in a day.   15

Soon, soon the flesh
The grave cave ate will be
At home on me

And I a smiling woman.
I am only thirty.   20
And like the cat I have nine times to die.

This is Number Three.
What a trash
To annihilate each decade.

What a million filaments.   25
The peanut-crunching crowd
Shoves in to see

Them unwrap me hand and foot—
The big strip tease.
Gentleman, ladies,   30

These are my hands,
My knees.
I may be skin and bone,

Nevertheless, I am the same, identical woman.
The first time it happened I was ten.   35
It was an accident.

The second time I meant
To last it out and not come back at all.
I rocked shut

As a seashell.   40
They had to call and call
And pick the worms off me like sticky pearls.

Dying
Is an art, like everything else.
I do it exceptionally well.   45

I do it so it feels like hell.
I do it so it feels real.
I guess you could say I've a call.

It's easy enough to do it in a cell.
It's easy enough to do it and stay put.   50
It's the theatrical

Comeback in broad day
To the same place, the same face, the same brute
Amused shout:

"A miracle!"   55
That knocks me out.
There is a charge

For the eyeing of my scars, there is a charge
For the hearing of my heart—
It really goes.   60

And there is a charge, a very large charge,
For a word or a touch
Or a bit of blood

Or a piece of my hair or my clothes.
So, so, Herr Doktor.   65
So, Herr Enemy.

I am your opus,
I am your valuable,
The pure gold baby

That melts to a shriek.   70
I turn and burn.
Do not think I underestimate your great concern.

Ash, ash—
You poke and stir.
Flesh, bone, there is nothing there—   75

A cake of soap,
A wedding ring,
A gold filling.

Herr God, Herr Lucifer,
Beware   80
Beware.

Out of the ash
I rise with my red hair
And I eat men like air.

Another poem of Sylvia Plath's in this book is "Aftermath" (p. 131).

PART THREE

Poetic Themes

Love

Traditional

Greek Wit

To His Mistress

You deny me: and to what end?
There are no lovers, dear, in the under world,
No love but here: only the living know
The sweetness of Aphrodite—
                                    but below,   5
But in Acheron, careful virgin, dust and ashes
Will be our only lying down together.

> Asklepiades (Third Century, B.C.)
> paraphrased by Dudley Fitts

Remonstrance

So I am your 'darling girl'!
                              Your tears
Say so, and the sleights your hands play,
You are conventionally jealous, and your kisses
Suggest a lover who knows just what he wants.   5

I am the more confused, then,
For when I whisper 'Here I am, take me, come,'
You fuss, cough, and adjourn the session *sine die.*

Are you a Lover or a Senator?

> Philodemos The Epicurean (First Century, B.C.)
> paraphrased by Dudley Fitts

Courtly Love

The tradition of courtly love poetry derives from the troubadours of southern France in the twelfth century, when the speaker idealized his beloved and was ennobled by loving an unattainable, ideal, but indifferent woman. In the English Renaissance the tradition is represented in many poems, chiefly sonnets, that develop two dilemmas of the lover: although the lover's love is ideal it is sensual as well, and although only his lady can cure him, she will not.

How Can the Heart Forget Her?

At her fair hands how have I grace entreated
With prayers oft repeated!
Yet still my love is thwarted:
Heart, let her go, for she'll not be converted—
    Say, shall she go?   5
    O no, no, no, no, no!
She is most fair, though she be marble-hearted.

How often have my sighs declared my anguish,
Wherein I daily languish!
Yet still she doth procure it: 10
    Say, shall she go?
    O no, no, no, no, no!
She gave the wound, and she alone must cure it.

But shall I still a true affection owe her,
Which prayers, sighs, tears do show her,   15
And shall she still disdain me?
Heart, let her go, if they no grace can gain me—
    Say, shall she go?
    O no, no, no, no, no!
She made me hers, and hers she will retain me.   20

But if the love that hath and still doth burn me
No love at length return me,
Out of my thoughts I'll set her:
    Say, shall she go?
    O no, no, no, no, no!   25
Fix'd in the heart, how can the heart forget her?

        Anonymous: A conventional lover's complaint
        from Davison's *Poetical Rhapsody,* 1602

Sonnet: Fair is my love

Fair is my love, and cruel as she's fair;
Her brow shades frowns, although her eyes are sunny,
Her smiles are lightning, though her pride despair,
And her disdains are gall, her favours honey.
A modest maid, decked with a blush of honor,   5
Whose feet do tread green paths of youth and love,
The wonder of all eyes that look upon her,
Sacred on earth, designed a saint above.
Chastity and Beauty, which were deadly foes,
Live, reconcilèd friends, within her brow;   10
And had she pity to conjoin with those,
Then who had heard the plaints I utter now?
For had she not been fair and thus unkind,
My muse had slept, and none had known my mind.

        Samuel Daniel (1562–1619)

When I Was Fair and Young

When I was fair and young, and favor gracèd me,
  Of many was I sought, their mistress for to be;
But I did scorn them all, and answered them therefore,
  Go, go, go, seek some otherwhere,
    Importune me no more!   5

How many weeping eyes I made to pine with woe,
  How many sighing hearts, I have no skill to show;
Yet I the prouder grew, and answered them therefore,
  Go, go, go, seek some otherwhere,
    Importune me no more!   10

Then spake fair Venus' son, that proud victorious boy,
    And said: Fine dame, since that you be so coy,
I will so pluck your plumes that you shall say no more,
    Go, go, go, seek some otherwhere,
        Importune me no more!   15

When he had spake these words, such change grew in my breast
    That neither night nor day since that, I could take any rest.
Then lo! I did repent that I had said before,
    Go, go, go, seek some otherwhere,
        Importune me no more!   20

Elizabeth I (1533–1603)

Pastoral Love

The pastoral poem employs a set of conventions derived from the *Idyls* (little pictures) of Theocritus and the *Eclogues* of Virgil. The Renaissance English fashion in the pastoral presented a romantic view of country life written by a sophisticated city poet concerned to present an ideal of natural human relationships in a beautiful and tranquil natural world. In the pastoral elegy, the pastoral conventions gave dignity to the subject of death. The pastoral love poem presented as artificially simple the loves of shepherds and shepherdesses in an ideally sunny natural setting, a picture in sharp contrast to the complexity of real life and love.

The Passionate Shepherd to His Love

Come live with me and be my love,
And we will all the pleasures prove
That valleys, groves, hills, and fields,
Woods, or steepy mountain yields.

And we will sit upon the rocks,   5
Seeing the shepherds feed their flocks,
By shallow rivers to whose falls
Melodious birds sing madrigals.

And I will make thee beds of roses
And a thousand fragrant posies,   10
A cap of flowers, and a kirtle
Embroidered all with leaves of myrtle;

A gown made of the finest wool
Which from our pretty lambs we pull;
Fair lined slippers for the cold   15
With buckles of the purest gold;

A belt of straw and ivy buds,
With coral clasps and amber studs:
And if these pleasures may thee move,
Come live with me, and be my love.   20

The shepherds' swains shall dance and sing
For thy delight each May morning:
If these delights thy mind may move,
Then live with me and be my love.

Christopher Marlowe (1564–1593)

The Nymph's Reply to the Shepherd

If all the world and love were young,
And truth in every shepherd's tongue,
These pretty pleasures might me move
To live with thee and be thy love.

Time drives the flocks from field to fold   5
When rivers rage and rocks grow cold,
And Philomel becometh dumb;
The rest complains of cares to come.

The flowers do fade, and wanton fields
To wayward winter reckoning yields;   10
A honey tongue, a heart of gall,
Is fancy's spring, but sorrow's fall.

Thy gowns, thy shoes, thy beds of roses,
Thy cap, thy kirtle, and thy posies
Soon break, soon wither, soon forgotten—   15
In folly ripe, in reason rotten.

Thy belt of straw and ivy buds,
Thy coral clasps and amber studs,
All these in me no means can move
To come to thee and be thy love.   20

But could youth last and love still breed,
Had joys no date nor age no need,
Then these delights my mind might move
To live with thee and be thy love.

Sir Walter Ralegh (1552?–1618)

The Bait

Come live with me, and be my love,
And we will some new pleasures prove
Of golden sands, and crystal brooks:
With silken lines, and silver hocks.

There will the river whispering run   5
Warmed by thy eyes, more than the sun.
And there the enamored fish will stay,
Begging themselves they may betray.

When thou wilt swim in that live bath,
Each fish, which every channel hath,   10
Will amorously to thee swim,
Gladder to catch thee, than thou him.

If thou to be so seen be'st loath
By sun, or moon, thou dark'nest both,
And if myself have leave to see,   15
I need not their light, having thee.

Let others freeze with angling reeds,
And cut their legs with shells and weeds,
Or treacherously poor fish beset,
With strangling snare or windowy net: 20

Let coarse bold hands, from slimy nest
The bedded fish in banks out-wrest;
Or curious traitors, sleave-silk flies,
Bewitch poor fishes' wand'ring eyes.

For thee, thou need'st no such deceit   25
For thou thyself art thine own bait;
That fish that is not catched thereby,
Alas, is wiser far than I.

John Donne (1572?–1631)

I Care Not for These Ladies

I care not for these ladies,
That must be wooed and prayed:
Give me kind Amaryllis,
The wanton country maid.
Nature art disdaineth,   5
Her beauty is her own.
   Her when we court and kiss,
   She cries, "Forsooth, let go!"
   But when we come where comfort is,
   She never will say no.   10

If I love Amaryllis,
She gives me fruit and flowers:
But if we love these ladies,
We must give golden showers.
Give them gold, that sell love,   15
Give me the nut-brown lass,
   Who, when we court and kiss,
   She cries, "Forsooth, let go!"
   But when we come where comfort is,
   She never will say no.   20

These ladies must have pillows,
And beds by strangers wrought;
Give me a bower of willows,
Of moss and leaves unbought,
And fresh Amaryllis,   25
With milk and honey fed;
   Who, when we court and kiss,
   She cries, "Forsooth, let go!"
   But when we come where comfort is,
   She never will say no.   30

        Thomas Campion (1567–1620)

Cavalier Wit

The term "Cavalier" denotes a group loyal to Charles I (1625–1649). As a poetic style in love poems, it denotes the gallant and witty manner of the speaker in poems with a tight logical structure and a short rhythmic line. The speaker's gallantry, however, does not preclude frankness. The wit of the cavalier speaker is based upon the ease, sometimes the flippant manner, with which he discusses his physical interest in his lady, a subject the courtly lover could not approach except in poems late in the tradition.

To the Virgins, to Make Much of Time

Gather ye rose-buds while ye may,
    Old Time is still a-flying;
And this same flower that smiles today
    Tomorrow will be dying.

The glorious lamp of heaven, the Sun,   5
    The higher he's a-getting;
The sooner will his race be run,
    And nearer he's to setting.

That age is best which is the first,
    When youth and blood are warmer;   10
But being spent, the worse, and worst
    Times, still succeed the former.

Then be not coy, but use your time;
    And while ye may, go marry;
For having lost but once your prime,   15
    You may for ever tarry.

                Robert Herrick (1591–1674)

Song: Why so pale and wan

Why so pale and wan, fond lover?
    Prithee, why so pale?
Will, when looking well can't move her,
    Looking ill prevail?
    Prithee, why so pale?   5

Why so dull and mute, young sinner?
    Prithee, why so mute?
Will, when speaking well can't win her,
    Saying nothing do't?
    Prithee, why so mute?   10

Quit, quit, for shame; this will not move,
    This cannot take her.

If of herself she will not love,
    Nothing can make her:
    The devil take her!   15
        Sir John Suckling (1609–1642)

To Lucasta, Going to the Wars

Tell me not, Sweet, I am unkind,
    That from the nunnery
Of thy chaste breast and quiet mind
    To war and arms I fly.

True, a new mistress now I chase,   5
    The first foe in the field;
And with a stronger faith embrace
    A sword, a horse, a shield.

Yet this inconstancy is such
    As thou too shall adore;   10
I could not love thee, Dear, so much,
    Loved I not Honor more.
        Richard Lovelace (1618–1657)

Modern

Sonnet: If thou must love me

If thou must love me, let it be for nought
Except for love's sake only. Do not say
"I love her for her smile—her look—her way
Of speaking gently,—for a trick of thought
That falls in well with mine, and certes brought   5
A sense of pleasant ease on such a day"—
For these things in themselves, Beloved, may
Be changed, or change for thee,—and love so wrought,
May be unwrought so. Neither love me for
Thine own dear pity's wiping my cheeks dry,—   10
A creature might forget to weep, who bore
Thy comfort long, and lose thy love thereby!
But love me for love's sake, that evermore
Thou mayst love on, through love's eternity.
        Elizabeth Barrett Browning (1806–1861)

Sonnet: I, being born a woman

I, being born a woman and distressed
By all the needs and notions of my kind,
Am urged by your propinquity to find
Your person fair, and feel a certain zest
To bear your body's weight upon my breast: 5
So subtly is the fume of life designed,
To clarify the pulse and cloud the mind,
And leave me once again undone, possessed.
Think not for this, however, the poor treason
Of my stout blood against my staggering brain,   10
I shall remember you with love, or season
My scorn with pity,—let me make it plain:
I find this frenzy insufficient reason
For conversation when we meet again.

                                        Edna St. Vincent Millay (1892–1950)

I Knew a Woman

I knew a woman, lovely in her bones,
When small birds sighed, she would sigh back at them;
Ah, when she moved, she moved more ways than one:
The shapes a bright container can contain!
Of her choice virtues only gods should speak,   5
Or English poets who grew up on Greek
(I'd have them sing in chorus, cheek to cheek).

How well her wishes went! She stroked my chin,
She taught me Turn, and Counter-turn, and Stand;
She taught me Touch, that undulant white skin;   10
I nibbled meekly from her proffered hand;
She was the sickle; I, poor I, the rake,
Coming behind her for her pretty sake
(But what prodigious mowing we did make).

Love likes a gander, and adores a goose: 15
Her full lips pursed, the errant note to seize;
She played it quick, she played it light and loose;
My eyes, they dazzled at her flowing knees;
Her several parts could keep a pure repose,
Or one hip quiver with a mobile nose   20
(She moved in circles, and those circles moved).

Let seed be grass, and grass turn into hay:
I'm martyr to a motion not my own;
What's freedom for? To know eternity.
I swear she cast a shadow white as stone.   25
But who would count eternity in days?
These old bones live to learn her wanton ways:
(I measure time by how a body sways).

> Theodore Roethke (1908–1963)

Sonnet: Far from Eden

Far from Eden, and with sullen eyes,
far from the orchard of our awful loss,
past love she went, to boredom, then to lies,
to stand here, sullen (centuries from the Cross),
to stand, rude and resentful of my call.   5
But final things are never very good:
I let her go. With appetites we maul
our innocence; we burn the sacred wood.

Steps going down, and many a weary mile,
tread doleful Adams when they learn to cry,   10
since only God goes gentle all the while,
since women hate those who have known them sly,
with tears, with desperate orisons, we learn
to genuflect where flaming seraphs burn.

> James Graham-Luján (b. 1912)

Love Poem

My clumsiest dear, whose hands shipwreck vases,
At whose quick touch all glasses chip and ring,
Whose palms are bulls in china, burs in linen,
And have no cunning with any soft thing

Except all ill-at-ease fidgeting people: 5
The refugee uncertain at the door
You make at home; deftly you steady
The drunk clambering on his undulant floor.

Unpredictable dear, the taxi drivers' terror,
Shrinking from far headlights pale as a dime   10
Yet leaping before red apoplectic streetcars—
Misfit in any space. And never on time.

A wrench in clocks and the solar system. Only
With words and people and love you move at ease.
In traffic of wit expertly manoeuvre   15
And keep us, all devotion, at your knees.

Forgetting your coffee spreading on our flannel,
Your lipstick grinning on our coat,
So gayly in love's unbreakable heaven
Our souls on glory of spilt bourbon float.   20

Be with me, darling, early and late. Smash glasses—
I will study wry music for your sake.
For should your hands drop white and empty
All the toys of the world would break.

                    John Frederick Nims (b. 1914)

To Be in Love

              To be in love
Is to touch things with a lighter hand.

In yourself you stretch, you are well.

You look at things
Through his eyes.   5
              A Cardinal is red.
              A sky is blue.
Suddenly you know he knows too.
He is not there but
You know you are tasting together   10
The winter, or light spring weather.

His hand to take your hand is overmuch.
Too much to bear.

You cannot look in his eyes
Because your pulse must not say   15
What must not be said.

When he
Shuts a door—

Is not there—
Your arms are water.   20

And you are free
With a ghastly freedom.

You are the beautiful half
Of a golden hurt.

You remember and covet his mouth,   25
To touch, to whisper on.

Oh when to declare
Is certain Death!

Oh when to apprize
Is to mesmerize,   30

To see fall down, the Column of Gold,
Into the commonest ash.

Gwendolyn Brooks (b. 1917)

Complaint

She's gone. She was my love, my moon or more.
She chased the chickens out and swept the floor,
Emptied the bones and nut-shells after feasts,
And smacked the kids for leaping up like beasts.
Now morbid boys have grown past awkwardness;   5
The girls let stitches out, dress after dress,
To free some swinging body's riding space
And form the new child's unimagined face.
Yet, while vague nephews, spitting on their curls,
Amble to pester winds and blowsy girls,   10
What arm will sweep the room, what hand will hold
New snow against the milk to keep it cold?
And who will dump the garbage, feed the hogs,
And pitch the chickens' heads to hungry dogs?
Not my lost hag who dumbly bore such pain: 15
Childbirth and midnight sassafras and rain.
New snow against her face and hands she bore,
And now lies down, who was my moon or more.

James Wright (b. 1927)

The Family

To His Son

Three things there be that prosper all apace
And flourish, while they are asunder far;
But on a day they meet all in a place,
And when they meet, they one another mar.
And they be these: the wood, the weed, the wag.   5
The wood is that that makes the gallows tree;
The weed is that that strings the hangman's bag;
The wag, my pretty knave, betokens thee.
Now mark, dear boy: while these assemble not,
Green springs the tree, hemp grows, the wag is wild;   10
But when they meet, it makes the timber rot,
It frets the halter, and it chokes the child.
    God bless the child!

Sir Walter Ralegh (1552?–1618)

On My First Son

Farewell, thou child of my right hand, and joy;
   My sin was too much hope of thee, lov'd boy,
Seven years tho' wert lent to me, and I thee pay,
   Exacted by thy fate, on the just day.
O, could I lose all father, now. For why   5
   Will man lament the state he should envy?
To have so soon scap'd world's, and flesh's rage,
   And, if no other misery, yet age?
Rest in soft peace, and, ask'd, say here doth lie
   BEN JONSON his best piece of *poetry*.   10

For whose sake, henceforth, all his vows be such,
As what he loves may never like too much.
                                   Ben Jonson (1573?–1637)

A Prayer for My Daughter

Once more the storm is howling, and half hid
Under this cradle-hood and coverlid
My child sleeps on. There is no obstacle
But Gregory's wood and one bare hill
Whereby the haystack- and roof-levelling wind,   5
Bred on the Atlantic, can be stayed;
And for an hour I have walked and prayed
Because of the great gloom that is in my mind.

I have walked and prayed for this young child an hour
And heard the sea-wind scream upon the tower,   10
And under the arches of the bridge, and scream
In the elms above the flooded stream;
Imagining in excited reverie
That the future years had come,
Dancing to a frenzied drum,   15
Out of the murderous innocence of the sea.

May she be granted beauty and yet not
Beauty to make a stranger's eye distraught,
Or hers before a looking-glass, for such,
Being made beautiful overmuch,   20
Consider beauty a sufficient end,
Lose natural kindness and maybe
The heart-revealing intimacy
That chooses right, and never find a friend.

Helen being chosen found life flat and dull   25
And later had much trouble from a fool,
While that great Queen, that rose out of the spray,
Being fatherless could have her way
Yet chose a bandy-leggèd smith for man.
It's certain that fine women eat   30
A crazy salad with their meat
Whereby the Horn of Plenty is undone.

In courtesy I'd have her chiefly learned;
Hearts are not had as a gift but hearts are earned
By those that are not entirely beautiful;   35

Yet many, that have played the fool
For beauty's very self, has charm made wise,
And many a poor man that has roved,
Loved and thought himself beloved,
From a glad kindness cannot take his eyes.   40

May she become a flourishing hidden tree
That all her thoughts may like the linnet be,
And have no business but dispensing round
Their magnanimities of sound,
Nor but in merriment begin a chase,   45
Nor but in merriment a quarrel.
O may she live like some green laurel
Rooted in one dear perpetual place.

My mind, because the minds that I have loved,
The sort of beauty that I have approved,   50
Prosper but little, has dried up of late,
Yet knows that to be choked with hate
May well be of all evil chances chief.
If there's no hatred in a mind
Assault and battery of the wind   55
Can never tear the linnet from the leaf.

An intellectual hatred is the worst,
So let her think opinions are accursed.
Have I not seen the loveliest woman born
Out of the mouth of Plenty's horn,   60
Because of her opinionated mind
Barter that horn and every good
By quiet natures understood
For an old bellows full of angry wind?

Considering that, all hatred driven hence,   65
The soul recovers radical innocence
And learns at last that it is self-delighting,
Self-appeasing, self-affrighting,
And that its own sweet will is Heaven's will;
She can, though every face should scowl   70
And every windy quarter howl
Or every bellows burst, be happy still.

And may her bridegroom bring her to a house
Where all's accustomed, ceremonious;
For arrogance and hatred are the wares   75
Peddled in the thoroughfares.

How but in custom and in ceremony
Are innocence and beauty born?
Ceremony's a name for the rich horn,
And custom for the spreading laurel tree.   80

William Butler Yeats (1865–1939)

NOTES AND QUESTIONS

1. The poem is called a prayer though there is no reference to God
   and no explicitly religious imagery. What, if anything, justifies the
   word "prayer"?
2. The storm described in the first stanza provides a source of imagery
   for the entire poem. Consider each of the storm images—for ex-
   ample, the "old bellows full of angry wind" in line 64—and observe
   how they contribute to the ideas Yeats is developing.
3. Stated in plain language, Yeats' hopes for his young daughter are
   rather disappointing: he wants her to be moderately beautiful,
   courteous, quiet, and unopinionated. How does the language of the
   poem endow these ordinary virtues with exciting and heroic quali-
   ties? In particular, which lines do you remember after putting the
   poem aside?
4. In stanza four there are references to two women of Greek mythol-
   ogy. Helen, of course, is Helen of Troy, and the "fool" from whom
   she had much trouble, after leaving her husband, is Paris; the
   "great Queen" is Aphrodite, whose husband is the lame black-
   smith of Olympus, Hephaestus. In stanza eight Yeats refers to a
   real woman, Maud Gonne, the Irish political activist whom he
   loved in vain for many years. The examples support an opinion
   about great beauty. What is that opinion?
5. The last lines equate two abstract virtues, ceremony and custom,
   with two specific images, the Horn of Plenty and the laurel tree,
   which thereby become fully-defined symbols. Trace the growth of
   these symbols from the beginning, from the first mention of Horn
   and laurel. Note also how certain images—the linnet, for example
   —contribute to the development of the symbolism.

Who's Who

A shilling life will give you all the facts:
How Father beat him, how he ran away,
What were the struggles of his youth, what acts
Made him the greatest figure of his day:

Of how he fought, fished, hunted, worked all night,   5
Though giddy, climbed new mountains; named a sea:
Some of the last researchers even write
Love made him weep his pints like you and me.

With all his honours on, he sighed for one
Who, say astonished critics, lived at home;   10
Did little jobs about the house with skill
And nothing else; could whistle; would sit still
Or potter round the garden; answered some
Of his long marvellous letters but kept none.

W. H. Auden (1907–1973)

My Papa's Waltz

The whiskey on your breath
Could make a small boy dizzy;
But I hung on like death:
Such waltzing was not easy.

We romped until the pans   5
Slid from the kitchen shelf;
My mother's countenance
Could not unfrown itself.

The hand that held my wrist
Was battered on one knuckle;   10
At every step you missed
My right ear scraped a buckle.

You beat time on my head
With a palm caked hard by dirt,
Then waltzed me off to bed   15
Still clinging to your shirt.

Theodore Roethke (1908–1963)

Father and Son

Now in the suburbs and the falling light
I followed him, and now down sandy road
Whiter than bone-dust, through the sweet
Curdle of fields, where the plums
Dropped with their load of ripeness, one by one.   5
Mile after mile I followed, with skimming feet,

After the secret master of my blood,
Him, steeped in the odor of ponds, whose indomitable love
Kept me in chains. Strode years; stretched into bird;
Raced through the sleeping country where I was young,   10
The silence unrolling before me as I came,
The night nailed like an orange to my brow.

How should I tell him my fable and the fears,
How bridge the chasm in a casual tone,
Saying, "The house, the stucco one you built,   15
We lost. Sister married and went from home,
And nothing comes back, it's strange, from where she goes.
I lived on a hill that had too many rooms:
Light we could make, but not enough of warmth,
And when the light failed, I climbed under the hill.   20
The papers are delivered every day;
I am alone and never shed a tear."

At the water's edge, where the smothering ferns lifted
Their arms, "Father!" I cried, "Return! You know
The way. I'll wipe the mudstains from your clothes;   25
No trace, I promise, will remain. Instruct
Your son, whirling between two wars,
In the Gemara of your gentleness,
For I would be a child to those who mourn
And brother to the foundlings of the field   30
And friend of innocence and all bright eyes.
O teach me how to work and keep me kind."

Among the turtles and the lilies he turned to me
The white ignorant hollow of his face.

Stanley Kunitz (b. 1905)

NOTE

Gemara (28): a commentary on the Talmud.

Those Winter Sundays

Sundays too my father got up early
and put his clothes on in the blueblack cold,
then with cracked hands that ached
from labor in the weekday weather made
banked fires blaze. No one ever thanked him.   5

I'd wake and hear the cold splintering, breaking.
When the rooms were warm, he'd call,
and slowly I would rise and dress,
fearing the chronic angers of that house,

Speaking indifferently to him,   10
who had driven out the cold
and polished my good shoes as well.
What did I know, what did I know
of love's austere and lonely offices?

Robert Hayden (b. 1913)

The Celebration

All wheels; a man breathed fire,
Exhaling like a blowtorch down the road
And burnt the stripper's gown
Above her moving-barely feet.
A condemned train climbed from the earth   5
Up stilted nightlights zooming in a track.
I ambled along in that crowd

Between the gambling wheels
At carnival time with the others
Where the dodgem cars shuddered, sparking   10
On grillwire, each in his vehicle half
In control, half helplessly power-mad
As he was in the traffic that brought him.
No one blazed at me; then I saw

NOTE

Comment by James Dickey[1]:
     "The Celebration" is another poem that is pretty much auto-
biographical. In high school I went to a carnival at Lakewood
Park near Atlanta. I was just walking along in the crowd among
the gambling wheels, strip teasers, and carney games, when I
looked up and saw a man and a woman. She had on an old fur
coat, and he had a walking stick and a Stetson hat. I thought, "If
I didn't know it was so impossible, that would look very much like
my mother and father." I looked at the couple again, and that's
who it was! I couldn't have been more surprised if it had been
Jesus Christ and John the Baptist. They were walking there like

[1] From James Dickey, *Self Interviews* (New York: Doubleday &
Company, 1970), pp. 143–44.

My mother and my father, he leaning   15
On a dog-chewed cane, she wrapped to the nose
In the fur of exhausted weasels.
I believed them buried miles back
In the country, in the faint sleep
Of the old, and had not thought to be   20
On this of all nights compelled

To follow where they led, not losing
Sight, with my heart enlarging whenever
I saw his crippled Stetson bob, saw her
With the teddy bear won on the waning   25
Whip of his right arm. They laughed;
She clung to him: then suddenly
The Wheel of wheels was turning

The colored night around.
They climbed aboard. My God, they rose   30
Above me, stopped themselves and swayed
Fifty feet up; he pointed

---

fifty-year-old lovers. My father was swaggering a bit and my mother was holding onto his arm. It was the sweetest thing, I swear to God, I ever saw in my life! I wondered what in the world was going on. They had never been particularly demonstrative or affectionate with each other. I decided to follow them around to see what they would do. They went on the Tunnel of Love, and he won a teddy bear for her throwing baseballs at milk bottles. Then they went on the Ferris wheel. I just stood there watching my mother and father go around and around in the air. They never did know I was within miles of the place.

There's an absolute strangeness of a situation in which you see people you thought you knew so well acting like complete strangers—and you thought you could never find out anything new about them! I guess there's nobody more familiar to most people than their mother and father. But the experience I had made me feel an enormous kinship to them, based partly on the fact that they hadn't revealed everything to me and I had by accident discovered not only something about them but something about myself that I hadn't sufficiently reckoned with.

By the way, the local reference about the condemned train climbing up a track is an actual reference to the Lakewood Amusement Park. They used to have a roller-coaster there called "The Greyhound." It's been condemned since 1910, so naturally everybody wants to ride it. And everything at the carnival is in some way circular. The gambling wheels, or the carney Come On In are all circular, and all the rides end where they begin; and of course, the Wheel of wheels is the Ferris wheel. You can see it from all over the fair, the lights going around like Ezekiel's wheel in the middle of the air. All carnivals and midways are circular and wheel-like, in one way or another.

With his toothed cane, and took in
The whole Midway till they dropped,
Came down, went from me, came and went   35

Faster and faster, going up backward,
Cresting, out-topping, falling roundly.
From the crowd I watched them,
Their gold teeth flashing,
Until my eyes blurred with their riding   40
Lights, and I turned from the standing
To the moving mob, and went on:

Stepped upon sparking shocks
Of recognition when I saw my feet
Among the others, knowing them given,   45
Understanding the whirling impulse
From which I had been born,
The great gift of shaken lights,
The being wholly lifted with another,

All this having all and nothing   50
To do with me. Believers, I have seen
The wheel in the middle of the air
Where old age rises and laughs,
And on Lakewood Midway became
In five strides a kind of loving,   55
A mortal, a dutiful son.

James Dickey (b. 1923)

Rainbow

After the shot the driven feathers rock
In the air and are by sunlight trapped.
Their moment of descent is eloquent.
It is the rainbow echo of a bird
Whose thunder, stopped, puts in my daughter's eyes   5
A question mark. She does not see the rainbow,
And the folding bird-fall was for her too quick.
It is about the stillness of the bird
Her eyes are asking. She is three years old;
Has cut her fingers; found blood tastes of salt;   10
But she has never witnessed quiet blood,
Nor ever seen before the peace of death.

I say: "The feathers—Look!" but she is torn
And wretched and draws back. And I am glad
That I have wounded her, have winged her heart,   15
And that she goes beyond my fathering.

Robert Huff (b. 1924)

Ten Days Leave

He steps down from the dark train, blinking; stares
At trees like miracles. He will play games
With boys or sit up all night touching chairs.
Talking with friends, he can recall their names.

Noon burns against his eyelids, but he lies   5
Hunched in his blankets; he is half awake
But still lacks nerve to open up his eyes;
Supposing it were just his old mistake?

But no; it seems just like it seemed. His folks
Pursue their lives like toy trains on a track.   10
He can foresee each of his father's jokes
Like words in some old movie that's come back.

He is like days when you've gone some place new
To deal with certain strangers, though you never
Escape the sense in everything you do,   15
"We've done this all once. Have I been here, ever?"

But no; he thinks it must recall some old film, lit
By lives you want to touch; as if he'd slept
And must have dreamed this setting, peopled it,
And wakened out of it. But someone's kept   20

His dream asleep here like a small homestead
Preserved long past its time in memory
Of some great man who lived here and is dead.
They have restored his landscape faithfully:

The hills, the little houses, the costumes: 25
How real it seems! But he comes, wide awake,
A tourist whispering through the priceless rooms
Who must not touch things or his hand might break

Their sleep and black them out. He wonders when
He'll grow into his sleep so sound again.   30

W. D. Snodgrass (b. 1926)

Big Bessie Throws Her Son into the Street

A day of sunny face and temper.
The winter trees
Are musical.

Bright lameness from my beautiful disease,
You have your destiny to chip and eat.   5

Be precise.
With something better than candles in the eyes.
(Candles are not enough.)

At the root of the will, a wild inflammable stuff.

New pioneer of days and ways, be gone.   10
Hunt out your own or make your own alone.

Go down the street.

Gwendolyn Brooks (b. 1917)

NOTES AND QUESTIONS

1. *chip and eat* (5): a reference to children chipping and eating lead-based paint, which is poisonous. What other images involving destiny are in the poem?
2. *candles* (7–8): church candles? Why is candlelight not enough?

Nikki-Rosa

childhood rememberances are always a drag
if you're Black
you always remember things like living in Woodlawn
with no inside toilet
and if you become famous or something   5
they never talk about how happy you were to have your mother
all to yourself and
how good the water felt when you got your bath from one of those
big tubs that folk in chicago barbecue in
and somehow when you talk about home   10
it never gets across how much you
understood their feelings
as the whole family attended meetings about Hollydale
and even though you remember
your biographers never understand   15

your father's pain as he sells his stock
and another dream goes
and though you're poor it isn't poverty that
concerns you
and though they fought a lot   20
it isn't your father's drinking that makes any difference
but only that everybody is together and you
and your sister have happy birthdays and very good christmasses
and I really hope no white person ever has cause to write about me
because they never understand Black love is Black wealth
        and they'll   25
probably talk about my hard childhood and never understand that
all the while I was quite happy

                              Nikki Giovanni (b. 1943)

My Grandmother's Love Letters

There are no stars to-night
But those of memory.
Yet how much room for memory there is
In the loose girdle of soft rain.

There is even room enough   5
For the letters of my mother's mother,
Elizabeth,
That have been pressed so long
Into a corner of the roof
That they are brown and soft,   10
And liable to melt as snow.

Over the greatness of such space
Steps must be gentle.
It is all hung by an invisible white hair.
It trembles as birch limbs webbing the air.   15

And I ask myself:

"Are your fingers long enough to play
Old keys that are but echoes:
Is the silence strong enough
To carry back the music to its source   20
And back to you again
As though to her?"

Yet I would lead my grandmother by the hand
Through much of what she would not understand;
And so I stumble. And the rain continues on the roof   25
With such a sound of gently pitying laughter.

Hart Crane (1899–1933)

My Grandmother

My grandmother moves to my mind in context of sorrow
And, as if apprehensive of near death, in black;
Whether erect in chair, her dry and corded throat harangued by grief,
Or at ragged book bent in Hebrew prayer,
Or gentle, submissive, and in tears to strangers;   5
Whether in sunny parlor or back of drawn blinds.

Though time and tongue made any love disparate,
On daguerreotype with classic perspective
Beauty I sigh and soften at is hers.
I pity her life of deaths, the agony of her own,   10
But most that history moved her through
Stranger lands and many houses,
Taking her exile for granted, confusing
The tongues and tasks of her children's children.

Karl Shapiro (b. 1913)

Grandparents

They're altogether otherworldly now,
those adults champing for their ritual Friday spin
to pharmacist and five-and-ten in Brockton.
Back in my throw-away and shaggy span
of adolescence, Grandpa still waves his stick   5
like a policeman;
Grandmother, like a Mohammedan, still wears her thick
lavender mourning and touring veil;
the Pierce Arrow clears its throat in a horse-stall.
Then the dry road dust rises to whiten   10
the fatigued elm leaves—
the nineteenth century, tired of children, is gone.
They're all gone into a world of light; the farm's my own.

The farm's my own!
Back there alone,   15
I keep indoors, and spoil another season.
I hear the rattley little country gramophone
racking its five foot horn:
"O Summer Time!"
Even at noon here the formidable   20
Ancien Regime still keeps nature at a distance. Five
green shaded light bulbs spider the billiards-table;
no field is greener than its cloth,
where Grandpa, dipping sugar for us both,
once spilled his demitasse.   25
His favorite ball, the number three,
still hides the coffee stain.

Never again
to walk there, chalk our cues,
insist on shooting for us both.   30
Grandpa! Have me, hold me, cherish me!
Tears smut my fingers. There
half my life-lease later,
I hold an *Illustrated London News*—;
disloyal still,   35
I doodle handlebar
mustaches on the last Russian Czar.

Robert Lowell (b. 1917)

NOTE

Ancien Regime (21): the royal regime in France just before the Revolution, now an archetype of repressive aristocracy.

Grandmother Watching at Her Window

There was always the river or the train
Right past the door, and someone might be gone
Come morning. When I was a child I mind
Being held up at a gate to wave
Good-bye, good-bye to I didn't know who,   5
Gone to the War, and how I cried after.
When I married I did what was right
But I knew even that first night
That he would go. And so shut my soul tight

Behind my mouth, so he could not steal it   10
When he went. I brought the children up clean
With my needle, taught them that stealing
Is the worst sin; knew if I loved them
They would be taken away, and did my best
But must have loved them anyway   15
For they slipped through my fingers like stitches.
Because God loves us always, whatever
We do. You can sit all your life in churches
And teach your hands to clutch when you pray
And never weaken, but God loves you so dearly   20
Just as you are, that nothing you are can stay,
But all the time you keep going away, away.

W. S. Merwin (b. 1927)

Guilt and Responsibility

Personal

Edward

"Why does your brand° sae drop wi' blude,   sword
  Edward, Edward?
Why does your brand sae drop wi' blude,
  And why sae sad gang ye, O?"—
"O I hae kill'd my hawk sae gude,   5
  Mither, mither;
O I hae kill'd my hawk sae gude,
  And I had nae mair but he, O."

"Your hawk's blude was never sae red,
  Edward, Edward;   10
Your hawk's blude was never sae red,
  My dear son, I tell thee, O."—
"O I hae kill'd my red-roan steed,
  Mither, mither;
O I hae kill'd my red-roan steed,   15
  That earst° was sae fair and free, O."   earlier

"Your steed was auld, and ye hae got mair,°   more
  Edward, Edward;
Your steed was auld, and ye hae got mair;
  Some other dule° ye dree,° O."   20   grief, suffer

271

"O I hae kill'd my father dear,
　Mither, mither;
O I hae kill'd my father dear,
　Alas, and wae is me, O!"

"And whatten penance will ye dree° for that,　　25　undergo
　Edward, Edward?
Whatten penance will ye dree for that?
　My dear son, now tell me, O."—
"I'll set my feet in yonder boat,
　Mither, mither;　30
I'll set my feet in yonder boat,
　And I'll fare over the sea, O."

"And what will ye do wi' your tow'rs and your ha',°　　hall
　Edward, Edward?
And what will ye do wi' your tow'rs and your ha',　　35
　That were sae fair to see, O?"
"I'll let them stand till they doun fa',°　　fall
　Mither, mither;
I'll let them stand till they doun fa',
　For here never mair maun° I be, O."　　40　　must

"And what will ye leave to your bairns° and your wife,　children
　Edward, Edward?
And what will ye leave to your bairns and your wife,
　When ye gang owre the sea, O?"—
"The warld's room: let them beg through life,　　45
　Mither, mither;
The warld's room: let them beg through life;
　For them never mair will I see, O."

"And what will ye leave to your ain mither dear,
　Edward, Edward?　　50
And what will ye leave to your ain mither dear,
　My dear son, now tell me, O?"—
"The curse of hell frae me sall ye bear,
　Mither, mither;
The curse of hell frae me sall ye bear:　　55
　Sic° counsels ye gave to me, O!"　　such

Anonymous

A Poison Tree

I was angry with my friend:
I told my wrath, my wrath did end.
I was angry with my foe:
I told it not, my wrath did grow.

And I water'd it in fears,   5
Night and morning with my tears;
And I sunnèd it with smiles,
And with soft deceitful wiles.

And it grew both day and night,
Till it bore an apple bright;   10
And my foe beheld it shine,
And he knew that it was mine,

And into my garden stole
When the night had veil'd the pole:
In the morning glad I see   15
My foe outstretch'd beneath the tree.

William Blake (1757–1827)

In Memory of Sigmund Freud

(d. Sept. 1939)

When there are so many we shall have to mourn,
when grief has been made so public, and exposed
     to the critique of a whole epoch
     the frailty of our conscience and anguish,

of whom shall we speak? For every day they die   5
among us, those who were doing us some good,
     who knew it was never enough but
     hoped to improve a little by living.

Such was this doctor: still at eighty he wished
to think of our life from whose unruliness   10
     so many plausible young futures
     with threats or flattery ask obedience,

but his wish was denied him: he closed his eyes
upon that last picture, common to us all,
     of problems like relatives gathered   15
     puzzled and jealous about our dying.

For about him till the very end were still
those he had studied, the fauna of the night,
    and shades that still waited to enter
    the bright circle of his recognition   20

turned elsewhere with their disappointment as he
was taken away from his life interest
    to go back to the earth in London,
    an important Jew who died in exile.

Only Hate was happy, hoping to augment   25
his practice now, and his dingy clientele
    who think they can be cured by killing
    and covering the gardens with ashes.

They are still alive, but in a world he changed
simply by looking back with no false regrets;   30
    all he did was to remember
    like the old and be honest like children.

He wasn't clever at all: he merely told
the unhappy Present to recite the Past
    like a poetry lesson till sooner   35
    or later it faltered at the line where

long ago the accusations had begun,
and suddenly knew by whom it had been judged,
    how rich life had been and how silly,
    and was life-forgiven and more humble,   40

able to approach the Future as a friend
without a wardrobe of excuses, without
    a set mask of rectitude or an
    embarrassing over-familiar gesture.

No wonder the ancient cultures of conceit   45
in his technique of unsettlement foresaw
    the fall of princes, the collapse of
    their lucrative patterns of frustration:

if he succeeded, why, the Generalised Life
would become impossible, the monolith   50
    of State be broken and prevented
    the co-operation of avengers.

Of course they called on God, but he went his way
down among the lost people like Dante, down
    to the stinking fosse where the injured   55
    lead the ugly life of the rejected,

and showed us what evil is, not, as we thought,
deeds that must be punished, but our lack of faith,
    our dishonest mood of denial,
    the concupiscence of the oppressor.   60

If some traces of the autocratic pose,
the paternal strictness he distrusted, still
    clung to his utterance and features,
    it was a protective coloration

for one who'd lived among enemies so long: 65
if often he was wrong and, at times, absurd,
    to us he is no more a person
    now but a whole climate of opinion

under whom we conduct our different lives:
Like weather he can only hinder or help,   70
    the proud can still be proud but find it
    a little harder, the tyrant tries to

make do with him but doesn't care for him much:
he quietly surrounds all our habits of growth
    and extends, till the tired in even   75
    the remotest miserable duchy

have felt the change in their bones and are cheered,
till the child, unlucky in his little State,
    some hearth where freedom is excluded,
    a hive whose honey is fear and worry,   80

feels calmer now and somehow assured of escape,
while, as they lie in the grass of our neglect,
    so many long-forgotten objects
    revealed by his undiscouraged shining

are returned to us and made precious again;   85
games we had thought we must drop as we grew up,
    little noises we dared not laugh at,
    faces we made when no one was looking.

But he wishes us more than this. To be free
is often to be lonely. He would unite   90
    the unequal moieties fractured
    by our own well-meaning sense of justice,

would restore to the larger the wit and will
the smaller possesses but can only use
    for arid disputes, would give back to   95
    the son the mother's richness of feeling:

but he would have us remember most of all
to be enthusiastic over the night
    not only for the sense of wonder
  it alone has to offer, but also   100

because it needs our love. With large sad eyes
its delectable creatures look up and beg
    us dumbly to ask them to follow:
  they are exiles who long for the future

that lies in our power, they too would rejoice   105
if allowed to serve enlightenment like him,
    even to bear our cry of "Judas,"
  as he did and all must bear who serve it.

One rational voice is dumb. Over his grave
the household of Impulse mourns one dearly loved: 110
    sad is Eros, builder of cities,
  and weeping anarchic Aphrodite.

                      W. H. Auden (1907–1973)

Catamount

    Crouched in the center of my sight
    The cougar treed at Crawford Springs
    Still whips his dogged tail down and waits for me.
    Light moves like leaves along his side,
    His eyes among the shadows hide,   5
    The beast controls the swinging of his tail.

    I dragged the hounds home years ago,
    Thinking myself most righteous then,
    But I was running nearly all the way,
    That Hades-heavy half of man   10
    Astride me all the time I ran,
    Lashing the air behind me with his tail.

                      Robert Huff (b. 1924)

Dream Song 29

    There sat down, once, a thing on Henry's heart
    só heavy, if he had a hundred years
    & more, & weeping, sleepless, in all them time
    Henry could not make good.
    Starts again always in Henry's ears   5
    the little cough somewhere, an odour, a chime.

And here is another thing he has in mind
like a grave Sienese face a thousand years
would fail to blur the still profiled reproach of. Ghastly,
with open eyes, he attends, blind.   10
All the bells say: too late. This is not for tears;
thinking.

But never did Henry, as he thought he did,
end anyone and hacks her body up
and hide the pieces, where they may be found.   15
He knows: he went over everyone, & nobody's missing.
Often he reckons, in the dawn, them up.
Nobody is ever missing.

John Berryman (1914–1972)

Fly

I have been cruel to a fat pigeon
Because he would not fly
All he wanted was to live like a friendly old man

He had let himself become a wreck filthy and confiding
Wild for his food beating the cat off the garbage   5
Ignoring his mate perpetually snotty at the beak
Smelling waddling having to be
Carried up the ladder at night content

Fly I said throwing him into the air
But he would drop and run back expecting to be fed   10
I said it again and again throwing him up
As he got worse
He let himself be picked up every time
Until I found him in the dovecote dead
Of the needless efforts   15

So that is what I am

Pondering his eye that could not
Conceive that I was a creature to run from

I who have always believed too much in words

W. S. Merwin (b. 1927)

QUESTIONS

1. That the speaker "was a creature to run from" supports the judgment of the first line that he had been "cruel to a fat pigeon." But the reader has misgivings. After all, the speaker carried the pigeon up a ladder every night, and the reader must ask himself whether he would have taken so much trouble—over a pigeon! The speaker does feel guilty. How do you feel about his attitude?

2. How does the poet expect the reader to react to the speaker's disgust reflected in words like "filthy," "confiding," "snotty," and "waddling"? By discrediting the pigeon, is the speaker attempting to absolve himself from guilt?

3. What is the poem about—pigeons, cruelty toward animals, guilt, or words? What is the relationship between cruelty and believing too much in words? Can words be used to hide cruelty? Can guilt be hidden by words?

4. Why does the speaker compare the bird to a friendly old man? Is the analogy valid?

5. "Fly" is developed in four parts: an opening statement of the speaker's attitude, a dramatic presentation (in parts two and three) where the relationship is shown to the reader, and a final four lines that make clear assertions. Explain the effects gained by this organization. What other methods of organization might have been possible?

6. Explain what the poet has done to overcome the difficulties created by the lack of punctuation. Why did Merwin decide not to use punctuation?

The Abortion

Somebody who should have been born
is gone.

Just as the earth puckered its mouth,
each bud puffing out from its knot,
I changed my shoes, and then drove south.   5

Up past the Blue Mountains, where
Pennsylvania humps on endlessly,
wearing, like a crayoned cat, its green hair,

its roads sunken in like a gray washboard;
where, in truth, the ground cracks evilly,   10
a dark socket from which the coal has poured,

Somebody who should have been born
is gone.

the grass as bristly and stout as chives,
and me wondering when the ground would break,   15
and me wondering how anything fragile survives;

up in Pennsylvania, I met a little man,
not Rumpelstiltskin, at all, at all . . .
he took the fullness that love began.

Returning north, even the sky grew thin   20
like a high window looking nowhere.
The road was as flat as a sheet of tin.

Somebody who should have been born
is gone.

Yes, woman, such logic will lead   25
to loss without death. Or say what you meant,
you coward . . . this baby that I bleed.

Anne Sexton (1928–1974)

NOTE

Rumpelstiltskin (18): a dwarf in German folklore who bargained with a young bride to spin a great quantity of flax into gold, required by an unreasonable king. The bargain required that unless she guessed the dwarf's first name she would have to give him her first child. She guessed the name, with magical help, and the dwarf disappeared.

Social

The Lie

Go, soul, the body's guest,
    Upon a thankless errand:
Fear not to touch the best;
    The truth shall be thy warrant.
        Go, since I needs must die,   5
        And give the world the lie.

Say to the court, it glows
   And shines like rotten wood;
Say to the church, it shows
   What's good, and doth no good: 10
      If church and court reply,
      Then give them both the lie.

Tell potentates, they live
   Acting by others' action,
Not loved unless they give,   15
   Not strong but by a faction:
      If potentates reply,
      Give potentates the lie.

Tell men of high condition
   That manage the estate,   20
Their purpose is ambition,
   Their practice only hate:
      And if they once reply,
      Then give them all the lie.

Tell them that brave it most,   25
   They beg for more by spending,
Who, in their greatest cost,
   Seek nothing but commending:
      And if they make reply,
      Then give them all the lie.   30

Tell zeal it wants devotion;
   Tell love it is but lust;
Tell time it is but motion;
   Tell flesh it is but dust:
      And wish them not reply,   35
      For thou must give the lie.

Tell age it daily wasteth;
   Tell honor how it alters;
Tell beauty how she blasteth;
   Tell favor how it falters: 40
      And as they shall reply,
      Give every one the lie.

Tell wit how much it wrangles
   In tickle points of niceness;
Tell wisdom she entangles   45
   Herself in over-wiseness:
      And when they do reply,
      Straight give them both the lie.

Tell physic of her boldness;
   Tell skill it is prevention;   50
Tell charity of coldness;
   Tell law it is contention:
     And as they do reply,
     So give them still the lie.

Tell fortune of her blindness;   55
   Tell nature of decay;
Tell friendship of unkindness;
   Tell justice of delay:
     And if they will reply,
     Then give them all the lie.   60

Tell arts they have no soundness,
   But vary by esteeming;
Tell schools they want profoundness,
   And stand too much on seeming:
     If arts and schools reply,   65
     Give arts and schools the lie.

Tell faith it's fled the city;
   Tell how the country erreth;
Tell, manhood shakes off pity;
   Tell, virtue least preferreth: 70
     And if they do reply
     Spare not to give the lie.

So when thou hast, as I
   Commanded thee, done blabbing,
Because to give the lie   75
   Deserves no less than stabbing,
     Stab at thee he that will,
     No stab the soul can kill.
               Sir Walter Ralegh (1552?–1618)

A Description of the Morning

Now hardly here and there an hackney-coach
Appearing, showed the ruddy morn's approach.
Now Betty from her master's bed had flown,
And softly stole to discompose her own;
The slip-shod 'prentice from his master's door   5
Had pared the dirt, and sprinkled round the floor.
Now Moll had whirled her mop with dexterous airs,

Prepared to scrub the entry and the stairs.
The youth with broomy stumps began to trace
The kennel-edge, where wheels had worn the place.   10
The small-coal man was heard with cadence deep,
Till drowned in shriller notes of chimney-sweep:
Duns at his lordship's gate began to meet;
And brickdust Moll had screamed through half the street.
The turnkey now his flock returning sees,   15
Duly let out a-nights to steal for fees:
The watchful bailiffs take their silent stands,
And schoolboys lag with satchels in their hands.

                                         Jonathan Swift (1667–1745)

The Chimney Sweeper

When my mother died I was very young,
And my father sold me while yet my tongue
Could scarcely cry " 'weep! 'weep! 'weep!"
So your chimneys I sweep, & in soot I sleep.

There's little Tom Dacre, who cried when his head,   5
That curl'd like a lamb's back, was shav'd: so I said
"Hush, Tom! never mind it, for when your head's bare
You know that the soot cannot spoil your white hair."

And so he was quiet, & that very night,
As Tom was a-sleeping, he had such a sight!   10
That thousands of sweepers, Dick, Joe, Ned, & Jack,
Were all of them lock'd up in coffins of black.

And by came an Angel who had a bright key,
And he open'd the coffins & set them all free;
Then down a green plain leaping, laughing, they run,   15
And wash in a river, and shine in the Sun.

Then naked & white, all their bags left behind,
They rise upon clouds and sport in the wind;
And the Angel told Tom, if he'd be a good boy,
He'd have God for his father, & never want joy.   20

And so Tom awoke; and we rose in the dark,
And got with our bags & our brushes to work.
Tho' the morning was cold, Tom was happy & warm;
So if all do their duty they need not fear harm.

                                         William Blake (1757–1827)

On Moonlit Heath and Lonesome Bank

On moonlit heath and lonesome bank
   The sheep beside me graze;
And yon the gallows used to clank
   Fast by the four cross ways.

A careless shepherd once would keep   5
   The flocks by moonlight there,
And high amongst the glimmering sheep
   The dead man stood on air.

They hang us now in Shrewsbury jail:
   The whistles blow forlorn,   10
And trains all night groan on the rail
   To men that die at morn.

There sleeps in Shrewsbury jail to-night,
   Or wakes, as may betide,
A better lad, if things went right,   15
   Than most that sleep outside.

And naked to the hangman's noose
   The morning clocks will ring
A neck God made for other use
   Than strangling in a string.   20

And sharp the link of life will snap,
   And dead on air will stand
Heels that held up as straight a chap
   As treads upon the land.

So here I'll watch the night and wait   25
   To see the morning shine,
When he will hear the stroke of eight
   And not the stroke of nine;

And wish my friend as sound a sleep
   As lads' I did not know,   30
That shepherded the moonlit sheep
   A hundred years ago.

                A. E. Housman (1859–1936)

NOTES AND QUESTIONS

1. Housman's note to line 6: "Hanging in chains was called keeping sheep by moonlight." Why was hanging once so called?
2. The situation is complex and can be visualized in four images, one in the past, two in the present, and one in the future. What are these four situations? Describe the sketches you might draw to depict them.
3. Is the central concern of the speaker hanging or something else?

To an Unborn Pauper Child

I

Breathe not, hid Heart: cease silently,
And though thy birth-hour beckons thee,
   Sleep the long sleep:
   The Doomsters heap
Travails and teens around us here,   5
And Time-wraiths turn our songsingings to fear.

II

Hark, how the peoples surge and sigh,
And laughters fail, and greetings die:
   Hopes dwindle; yea,
   Faiths waste away,   10
Affections and enthusiasms numb;
Thou canst not mend these things if thou dost come.

III

Had I the ear of wombèd souls
Ere their terrestrial chart unrolls,
   And thou wert free   15
   To cease, or be,
Then would I tell thee all I know,
And put it to thee: Wilt thou take Life so?

IV

Vain vow! No hint of mine may hence
To theeward fly: to thy locked sense   20

NOTES

teens (5): troubles. *wraiths* (6): specters.

Explain none can
Life's pending plan:
Thou wilt thy ignorant entry make
Though skies spout fire and blood and nations quake.

V

Fain would I, dear, find some shut plot   25
Of earth's wide wold for thee, where not
    One tear, one qualm,
    Should break the calm.
But I am weak as thou and bare;
No man can change the common lot to rare.   30

VI

Must come and bide. And such are we—
Unreasoning, sanguine, visionary—
    That I can hope
    Health, love, friends, scope
In full for thee; can dream thou wilt find   35
Joys seldom yet attained by humankind!

Thomas Hardy (1840–1928)

Southern Mansion

Poplars are standing there still as death
And ghosts of dead men
Meet their ladies walking
Two by two beneath the shade
And standing on the marble steps.   5

There is a sound of music echoing
Through the open door
And in the field there is
Another sound tinkling in the cotton:
Chains of bondmen dragging on the ground.   10

The years go back with an iron clank,
A hand is on the gate,
A dry leaf trembles on the wall.
Ghosts are walking.
They have broken roses down   15
And poplars stand there still as death.

Arna Bontemps (1902–1973)

National

The Battle of Blenheim

It was a summer evening,
  Old Kaspar's work was done,
And he before his cottage door
  Was sitting in the sun,
And by him sported on the green   5
His little grandchild Wilhelmine.

She saw her brother Peterkin
  Roll something large and round,
Which he beside the rivulet
  In playing there had found;   10
He came to ask what he had found,
That was so large, and smooth, and round.

Old Kaspar took it from the boy,
  Who stood expectant by;
And then the old man shook his head,   15
  And, with a natural sigh,
" 'Tis some poor fellow's skull," said he,
"Who fell in the great victory.

"I find them in the garden,
  For there's many here about;   20
And often when I go to plough,
  The ploughshare turns them out!
For many a thousand men," said he,
"Were slain in that great victory."

"Now tell us what 'twas all about,"   25
  Young Peterkin, he cries;
And little Wilhelmine looks up
  With wonder-waiting eyes;
"Now tell us all about the war,
And what they fought each other for."   30

NOTE

Blenheim (title): in Bavaria, the scene of the battle (1704) where the French were defeated by the combined armies of England, Austria, and the Netherlands under the command of the Duke of Marlborough and Prince Eugene of Austria.

"It was the English," Kaspar cried,
  "Who put the French to rout;
But what they fought each other for,
  I could not well make out;
But everybody said," quoth he,   35
"That 'twas a famous victory.

"My father lived at Blenheim then,
  Yon little stream hard by;
They burnt his dwelling to the ground,
  And he was forced to fly;   40
So with his wife and child he fled,
Nor had he where to rest his head.

"With fire and sword the country round
  Was wasted far and wide,
And many a childing mother then,   45
  And new-born baby died;
But things like that, you know, must be
At every famous victory.

"They say it was a shocking sight
  After the field was won;   50
For many thousand bodies here
  Lay rotting in the sun;
But things like that, you know, must be
After a famous victory.

"Great praise the Duke of Marlbro' won,   55
  And our good Prince Eugene."
"Why 'twas a very wicked thing!"
  Said little Wilhelmine.
"Nay, nay, my little girl," quoth he,
"It was a famous victory.   60

"And everybody praised the Duke
  Who this great fight did win."
"But what good came of it at last?"
  Quoth little Peterkin.
"Why that I cannot tell," said he,   65
"But 'twas a famous victory."

                    Robert Southey (1774–1843)

Shiloh

A Requiem

Skimming lightly, wheeling still,
  The swallows fly low
Over the field in clouded days,
  The forest-field of Shiloh—
Over the field where April rain   5
Solaced the parched one stretched in pain
Through the pause of night
That followed the Sunday fight
  Around the church of Shiloh—
The church so lone, the log-built one,   10
That echoed to many a parting groan
    And natural prayer
Of dying foemen mingled there—
Foemen at morn, but friends at eve—
  Fame or country least their care: 15
(What like a bullet can undeceive!)
  But now they lie low,
While over them the swallows skim
And all is hushed at Shiloh.

> Herman Melville (1819–1891)

Beat! Beat! Drums!

Beat! beat! drums!—blow! bugles! blow!
Through the windows—through doors—burst like a ruthless force,
Into the solemn church, and scatter the congregation,
Into the school where the scholar is studying;
Leave not the bridegroom quiet—no happiness must he have now with
    his bride,   5
Nor the peaceful farmer any peace, ploughing his field or gathering
    his grain,
So fierce you whirr and pound you drums—so shrill you bugles blow.

Beat! beat! drums!—blow! bugles! blow!
Over the traffic of cities—over the rumble of wheels in the streets;
Are beds prepared for sleepers at night in the houses? no sleepers must
    sleep in those beds,   10
No bargainers' bargains by day—no brokers or speculators—would
    they continue?

Would the talkers be talking? would the singer attempt to sing?
Would the lawyer rise in the court to state his case before the judge?
Then rattle quicker, heavier drums—you bugles wilder blow.

Beat! beat! drums!—blow! bugles! blow! 15
Make no parley—stop for no expostulation,
Mind not the timid—mind not the weeper or prayer,
Mind not the old man beseeching the young man,
Let not the child's voice be heard, nor the mother's entreaties,
Make even the trestles to shake the dead where they lie awaiting the
    hearses, 20
So strong you thump O terrible drums—so loud you bugles blow.

                                        Walt Whitman (1819–1892)

The Man He Killed

"Had he and I but met
    By some old ancient inn,
We should have sat us down to wet
    Right many a nipperkin!

"But ranged as infantry, 5
    And staring face to face,
I shot at him as he at me,
    And killed him in his place.

"I shot him dead because—
    Because he was my foe, 10
Just so: my foe of course he was;
    That's clear enough; although

"He thought he'd 'list, perhaps,
    Off-hand like—just as I—
Was out of work—had sold his traps— 15
    No other reason why.

"Yes; quaint and curious war is!
    You shoot a fellow down
You'd treat if met where any bar is,
    Or help to half-a-crown." 20

                    Thomas Hardy (1840–1928)

Dulce et Decorum Est

Bent double, like old beggars under sacks,
Knock-kneed, coughing like hags, we cursed through sludge,
Till on the haunting flares we turned our backs
And towards our distant rest began to trudge.
Men marched asleep. Many had lost their boots   5
But limped on, blood-shod. All went lame; all blind;
Drunk with fatigue; deaf even to the hoots
Of tired, outstripped Five-Nines that dropped behind.

Gas! GAS! Quick, boys!—An ecstasy of fumbling,
Fitting the clumsy helmets just in time;   10
But someone still was yelling out and stumbling
And flound'ring like a man in fire or lime . . .
Dim, through the misty panes and thick green light,
As under a green sea, I saw him drowning.

In all my dreams, before my helpless sight,   15
He plunges at me, guttering, choking, drowning.

If in some smothering dreams you too could pace
Behind the wagon that we flung him in,
And watch the white eyes writhing in his face,
His hanging face, like a devil's sick of sin;   20
If you could hear, at every jolt, the blood
Come gargling from the froth-corrupted lungs,
Obscene as cancer, bitter as the cud
Of vile, incurable sores on innocent tongues,—
My friend, you would not tell with such high zest   25
To children ardent for some desperate glory,
The old Lie: Dulce et decorum est
Pro patria mori.

                    Wilfred Owen (1893–1918)

NOTE

Dulce . . . mori (27–28): It is sweet and honorable to die for one's country. (Horace)

from *Hugh Selwyn Mauberley*, IV, V

IV

These fought in any case,
and some believing,
                    pro domo, in any case . . .

Some quick to arm,
some for adventure,   5
some from fear of weakness,
some from fear of censure,
some for love of slaughter, in imagination,
learning later . . .
some in fear, learning love of slaughter;   10

Died some, pro patria,
                    non "dulce" non "et decor" . . .
walked eye-deep in hell
believing in old men's lies, then unbelieving
came home, home to a lie,   15
home to many deceits,
home to old lies and new infamy;
usury age-old and age-thick
and liars in public places.

Daring as never before, wastage as never before.   20
Young blood and high blood,
fair cheeks, and fine bodies;

fortitude as never before

frankness as never before,
disillusions as never told in the old days,   25
hysterias, trench confessions,
laughter out of dead bellies.

V

There died a myriad,
And of the best, among them,
For an old bitch gone in the teeth,
For a botched civilization,

Charm, smiling at the good mouth,   5
Quick eyes gone under earth's lid,

For two gross of broken statues,
For a few thousand battered books.

Ezra Pound (1885–1972)

In Distrust of Merits

Strengthened to live, strengthened to die for
   medals and positioned victories?
They're fighting, fighting, fighting the blind
   man who thinks he sees—
who cannot see that the enslaver is   5
enslaved; the hater, harmed. O shining O
     firm star, O tumultuous
       ocean lashed till small things go
     as they will, the mountainous
       wave makes us who look, know   10

depth. Lost at sea before they fought! O
   star of David, star of Bethlehem,
O black imperial lion
   of the Lord—emblem
of a risen world—be joined at last, be   15
joined. There is hate's crown beneath which all is
     death; there's love's without which none
       is king; the blessed deeds bless
     the halo. As contagion
       of sickness makes sickness,   20

contagion of trust can make trust. They're
   fighting in deserts and caves, one by
one, in battalions and squadrons;
   they're fighting that I
may yet recover from the disease, My   25
Self; some have it lightly; some will die. "Man's
     wolf to man" and we devour
       ourselves. The enemy could not
     have made a greater breach in our
       defenses. One pilot-   30

ing a blind man can escape him, but
   Job disheartened by false comfort knew
that nothing can be so defeating
   as a blind man who
can see. O alive who are dead, who are   35
proud not to see, O small dust of the earth
     that walks so arrogantly,
       trust begets power and faith is
     an affectionate thing. We
       vow, we make this promise   40

to the fighting—it's a promise—"We'll
  never hate black, white, red, yellow, Jew,
Gentile, Untouchable." We are
  not competent to
make our vows. With set jaw they are fighting,   45
fighting, fighting—some we love whom we know,
    some we love but know not—that
      hearts may feel and not be numb.
    It cures me; or am I what
      I can't believe in? Some   50

in snow, some on crags, some in quicksands,
  little by little, much by much, they
are fighting fighting fighting that where
  there was death there may
be life. "When a man is prey to anger,   55
he is moved by outside things; when he holds
    his ground in patience patience
      patience, that is action or
    beauty," the soldier's defense
      and hardest armor for   60

the fight. The world's an orphans' home. Shall
  we never have peace without sorrow?
without pleas of the dying for
  help that won't come? O
quiet form upon the dust, I cannot   65
look and yet I must. If these great patient
    dyings—all these agonies
      and wound-bearings and bloodshed—
    can teach us how to live, these
      dyings were not wasted.   70

Hate-hardened heart, O heart of iron,
  iron is iron till it is rust.
There never was a war that was
  not inward; I must
fight till I have conquered in myself what   75
causes war, but I would not believe it.
    I inwardly did nothing.
      O Iscariot-like crime!
    Beauty is everlasting
      and dust is for a time.   80

              Marianne Moore (1887–1972)

Identity

His Creed

I do believe that die I must,
And be return'd from out my dust:
I do believe that when I rise,
Christ I shall see, with these same eyes:
I do believe that I must come,   5
With others, to the dreadful Doom:
I do believe the bad must go
From thence, to everlasting woe:
I do believe the good, and I,
Shall live with Him eternally: 10
I do believe I shall inherit
Heaven, by Christ's mercies, not my merit:
I do believe the One in Three,
and Three in perfect Unity:
Lastly, that JESUS is a Deed   15
Of Gift from God: *And here's my Creed.*

Robert Herrick (1591–1674)

The Collar

I struck the board and cried, No more!
     I will abroad.
What? shall I ever sigh and pine?
My lines and life are free, free as the road,
Loose as the wind, and large as store.   5

Shall I be still in suit?
Have I no harvest but a thorn
To let me blood, and not restore
What I have lost with cordial fruit?
    Sure there was wine   10
Before my sighs did dry it; there was corn
  Before my tears did drown it.
Is the year only lost to me?
  Have I no bays to crown it?
No flowers, no garlands gay? all blasted?   15
    All wasted?
Not so, my heart: but there is fruit,
    And thou hast hands.
Recover all thy sigh-blown age
On double pleasures: leave thy cold dispute   20
Of what is fit and not; forsake thy cage,
    Thy rope of sands,
Which petty thoughts have made, and made to thee
  Good cable, to enforce and draw,
    And be thy law,   25
While thou didst wink and wouldst not see.
    Away! Take heed!
    I will abroad.
Call in thy death's-head there; tie up thy fears.
    He that forbears   30
  To suit and serve his need,
    Deserves his load.
But as I raved and grew more fierce and wild
    At every word,
Methought I heard one calling, *Child!*   35
  And I replied, *My Lord.*

George Herbert (1593–1633)

NOTES

in suit (6): as a suitor to the king. *cordial* (9): used as a heart stimulant.
death's-head (29): a skull kept as a reminder of death.

Sonnet: When I consider how my light is spent

When I consider how my light is spent
   Ere half my days in this dark world and wide,
   And that one talent which is death to hide
   Lodged with me useless, though my soul more bent
To serve therewith my Maker, and present   5
   My true account, lest He returning chide;
   "Doth God exact day-labor, light denied?"
   I fondly ask. But Patience, to prevent
That murmur, soon replies, "God doth not need
   Either man's work or His own gifts. Who best   10
   Bear His mild yoke, they serve Him best. His state
Is kingly: Thousands at His bidding speed,
   And post o'er land and ocean without rest;
   They also serve who only stand and wait."

                            John Milton (1608–1674)

NOTE

talent (3): see "Parable of the Talents," Matthew 25:14–30.

from Song of Myself, 24

I speak the pass-word primeval, I give the sign of democracy,
By God! I will accept nothing which all cannot have their counterpart
   of on the same terms.

Through me many long dumb voices,
Voices of the interminable generations of prisoners and slaves,
Voices of the diseas'd and despairing and of thieves and
   dwarfs,   5
Voices of cycles of preparation and accretion,
And of the threads that connect the stars, and of wombs and of the
   fatherstuff,
And of the rights of them the others are down upon,
Of the deform'd, trivial, flat, foolish, despised,
Fog in the air, beetles rolling balls of dung.   10

Through me forbidden voices,
Voices of sexes and lusts, voices veil'd and I remove the veil,
Voices indecent by me clarified and transfigur'd.

I do not press my fingers across my mouth,
I keep as delicate around the bowels as around the head and
    heart,   15
Copulation is no more rank to me than death is.

I believe in the flesh and the appetites,
Seeing, hearing, feeling, are miracles, and each part and tag of me is
    a miracle.

Walt Whitman (1819–1892)

I died for Beauty—but was scarce

I died for Beauty—but was scarce
Adjusted in the Tomb
When One who died for Truth, was lain
In an adjoining Room—

He questioned softly "Why I failed?"   5
"For Beauty," I replied—
"And I—for Truth—Themself are One—
We Bretheren, are," He said—

And so, as Kinsmen, met a Night—
We talked between the Rooms—   10
Until the Moss had reached our lips—
And covered up—our names—

Emily Dickinson (1830–1886)

Revelation

We make ourselves a place apart
    Behind light words that tease and flout,
But oh, the agitated heart
    Till someone really find us out.

'Tis pity if the case require   5
    (Or so we say) that in the end
We speak the literal to inspire
    The understanding of a friend.

But so with all, from babes that play
    At hide-and-seek to God afar,   10
So all who hide too well away
    Must speak and tell us where they are.

Robert Frost (1874–1963)

A Sort of a Song

Let the snake wait under
his weed
and the writing
be of words, slow and quick, sharp
to strike, quiet to wait,   5
sleepless.

—through metaphor to reconcile
the people and the stones.
Compose. (No ideas
but in things) Invent!   10
Saxifrage is my flower that splits
the rocks.

William Carlos Williams (1883–1963)

Nevertheless

you've seen a strawberry
    that's had a struggle; yet
    was, where the fragments met,

a hedgehog or a star-
    fish for the multitude   5
    of seeds. What better food

than apple seeds—the fruit
    within the fruit—locked in
    like counter-curved twin

hazelnuts? Frost that kills   10
    the little rubber-plant-
    leaves of *kok-saghyz*-stalks, can't

harm the roots; they still grow
    in frozen ground. Once where
    there was a prickly-pear-   15

leaf clinging to barbed wire,
    a root shot down to grow
    in earth two feet below;

as carrots form mandrakes
    or a ram's-horn root some-   20
    times. Victory won't come

          to me unless I go
                to it; a grape tendril
                ties a knot in knots till

          knotted thirty times—so   25
                the bound twig that's under-
                gone and over-gone, can't stir.

          The weak overcomes its
                menace, the strong over-
                comes itself. What is there   30

          like fortitude! What sap
                went through that little thread
                to make the cherry red!
                          Marianne Moore (1887–1972)

The Love Song of J. Alfred Prufrock

S'io credessi che mia risposta fosse
a persona che mai tornasse al mondo,
questa fiamma staria senza più scosse.
Ma per ciò che giammai di questo fondo
non tornò vivo alcun, s'i'odo il vero,
senza tema d'infamia ti rispondo.

Let us go then, you and I,
When the evening is spread out against the sky
Like a patient etherised upon a table;
Let us go, through certain half-deserted streets,
The muttering retreats   5
Of restless nights in one-night cheap hotels
And sawdust restaurants with oyster-shells:
Streets that follow like a tedious argument
Of insidious intent
To lead you to an overwhelming question . . .   10
Oh, do not ask, "What is it?"
Let us go and make our visit.

In the room the women come and go
Talking of Michelangelo.

The yellow fog that rubs its back upon the window-panes,   15
The yellow smoke that rubs its muzzle on the window-panes,
Licked its tongue into the corners of the evening,

Lingered upon the pools that stand in drains,
Let fall upon its back the soot that falls from chimneys,
Slipped by the terrace, made a sudden leap,   20
And seeing that it was a soft October night,
Curled once about the house, and fell asleep.

And indeed there will be time
For the yellow smoke that slides along the street
Rubbing its back upon the window-panes;   25
There will be time, there will be time
To prepare a face to meet the faces that you meet;
There will be time to murder and create,
And time for all the works and days of hands
That lift and drop a question on your plate;   30
Time for you and time for me,
And time yet for a hundred indecisions,
And for a hundred visions and revisions,
Before the taking of a toast and tea.

In the room the women come and go   35
Talking of Michelangelo.

And indeed there will be time
To wonder, "Do I dare?" and, "Do I dare?"
Time to turn back and descend the stair,
With a bald spot in the middle of my hair—   40
(They will say: "How his hair is growing thin!")
My morning coat, my collar mounting firmly to the chin,
My necktie rich and modest, but asserted by a simple pin—
(They will say: "But how his arms and legs are thin!")
Do I dare   45
Disturb the universe?
In a minute there is time
For decisions and revisions which a minute will reverse.

For I have known them all already, known them all—
Have known the evenings, mornings, afternoons,   50
I have measured out my life with coffee spoons;
I know the voices dying with a dying fall
Beneath the music from a farther room.
     So how should I presume?

And I have known the eyes already, known them all—   55
The eyes that fix you in a formulated phrase,
And when I am formulated, sprawling on a pin,
When I am pinned and wriggling on the wall,

Then how should I begin
To spit out all the butt-ends of my days and ways?   60
   And how should I presume?

And I have known the arms already, known them all—
Arms that are braceleted and white and bare
(But in the lamplight, downed with light brown hair!)
Is it perfume from a dress   65
That makes me so digress?
Arms that lie along a table, or wrap about a shawl.
   And should I then presume?
   And how should I begin?
   . . . . .

Shall I say, I have gone at dusk through narrow streets   70
And watched the smoke that rises from the pipes
Of lonely men in shirt-sleeves, leaning out of windows? . . .

I should have been a pair of ragged claws
Scuttling across the floors of silent seas.
   . . . . .

And the afternoon, the evening, sleeps so peacefully!   75
Smoothed by long fingers,
Asleep . . . tired . . . or it malingers,
Stretched on the floor, here beside you and me.
Should I, after tea and cakes and ices,
Have the strength to force the moment to its crisis?   80
But though I have wept and fasted, wept and prayed,
Though I have seen my head (grown slightly bald) brought in upon
   a platter,
I am no prophet—and here's no great matter;
I have seen the moment of my greatness flicker,
And I have seen the eternal Footman hold my coat, and
   snicker,   85
And in short, I was afraid.

And would it have been worth it, after all,
After the cups, the marmalade, the tea,
Among the porcelain, among some talk of you and me,
Would it have been worth while,   90
To have bitten off the matter with a smile,
To have squeezed the universe into a ball
To roll it towards some overwhelming question,
To say: "I am Lazarus, come from the dead,

Come back to tell you all, I shall tell you all"—   95
If one, settling a pillow by her head,
   Should say: "That is not what I meant at all.
   That is not it, at all."

And would it have been worth it, after all,
Would it have been worth while,   100
After the sunsets and the dooryards and the sprinkled streets,
After the novels, after the teacups, after the skirts that trail along
   the floor—
And this, and so much more?—
It is impossible to say just what I mean!
But as if a magic lantern threw the nerves in patterns on a
   screen: 105
Would it have been worth while
If one, settling a pillow or throwing off a shawl,
And turning toward the window, should say:
   "That is not it at all,
   That is not what I meant, at all."   110
   . . . . .

No! I am not Prince Hamlet, nor was meant to be;
Am an attendant lord, one that will do
To swell a progress, start a scene or two,
Advise the prince; no doubt, an easy tool,
Deferential, glad to be of use,   115
Politic, cautious, and meticulous;
Full of high sentence, but a bit obtuse;
At times, indeed, almost ridiculous—
Almost, at times, the Fool.

I grow old . . . I grow old . . .   120
I shall wear the bottoms of my trousers rolled.

Shall I part my hair behind? Do I dare to eat a peach?
I shall wear white flannel trousers, and walk upon the beach.
I have heard the mermaids singing, each to each.

I do not think that they will sing to me.   125

I have seen them riding seaward on the waves
Combing the white hair of the waves blown back
When the wind blows the water white and black.

We have lingered in the chambers of the sea
By sea-girls wreathed with seaweed red and brown   130
Till human voices wake us, and we drown.

                             T. S. Eliot (1888–1965)

NOTES AND QUESTIONS

1. Eliot's poem, though a dramatic monologue, is called a "love song."
   How does it differ from traditional courtly and pastoral love songs?
   How does Prufrock differ from the traditional lover?
2. *S'io credessi . . . rispondo* (epigraph): The poem is full of literary
   and historical references, beginning with the epigraph, which is
   from Canto XXVII of Dante's *Inferno*. Dante is walking through
   hell conversing with the souls of the damned, and the speaker of
   these lines is Guido da Montefeltro. Because his sin was fraud, a
   sin of the tongue, Guido must speak through the tongue of the
   flame that envelops him:

   > If I believed my answer were
   > to one who might return to earth
   > this flame would shake no longer.
   > But since, if what I hear is true,
   > no man goes living from this pit,
   > I answer without fear of infamy.

   How can the lines be said to apply to Prufrock? Conversely, how
   is the world of Eliot's poem different from the image created by
   Dante?
3. *Michelangelo* (14): Prufrock's walk has taken him to a party where
   intellectual women talk about art. But why do they talk about
   Michelangelo? How would the effect of the lines be changed if
   Eliot had rhymed "go" with the name of a less titanic artist—Cara-
   vaggio or Fra Angelico?
4. *I am no prophet* (83): The "head . . . brought in upon a platter"
   in the previous line is that of the prophet John the Baptist (Mat-
   thew 14:3–11). When he envisions his own head on a platter,
   Prufrock establishes a connection between his own situation and
   that of the Baptist—though, as he himself says, he is no prophet.
   Does Matthew's account of the Baptist's martyrdom suggest what
   the connection is?
5. *"I am Lazarus"* (94): Here again Prufrock compares and contrasts
   himself with a New Testament figure; this time it is the man
   Christ raised from the dead in John 11:1–44. Why is it that
   Prufrock can define his own identity only by considering himself
   in relation to others?
6. *magic lantern* (105): A forerunner of the modern slide projector,
   which threw onto a screen a magnified image of a drawing or
   photograph. The magic lantern was popular at sophisticated get-
   togethers during the period described in the poem. What other
   period furnishings does Prufrock mention, and what is their pur-
   pose in the poem?

7. *No! I am not Prince Hamlet* (111): Prufrock, in his effort to determine who and what he is, now makes the last of his several references to the great figures of history and literature. He tries to place himself within the context of Shakespearean tragedy, with its tragic heroes, attendant lords, and fools. He realizes he may be the fool, but the Shakespearean fool is often a wise man who uses the role of fool to speak truths that the other persons in the play dare not speak. Does the poem suggest that Prufrock may be this sort of philosophic fool? Considering the word in its everyday, non-Shakespearean sense, is Prufrock a fool?
8. In the last lines of the poem the scene shifts from the drawing room to the seaside, and the langorous chit-chat of the intellectual ladies is replaced by vivid images of mermaids on the rolling waves. Here, in his imagination, Prufrock has known happiness— a happiness disrupted by "human voices," presumably those of the drawing room. At the same time, the personal pronouns change from "I" and "me" to "we" and "us." Is this change effective? In what sense is Prufrock representative of us all?

I Think Continually of Those Who Were Truly Great

I think continually of those who were truly great.
Who, from the womb, remembered the soul's history
Through corridors of light where the hours are suns,
Endless and singing. Whose lovely ambition
Was that their lips, still touched with fire, 5
Should tell of the Spirit, clothed from head to foot in song.
And who hoarded from the Spring branches
The desires falling across their bodies like blossoms.

What is precious, is never to forget
The essential delight of the blood drawn from ageless springs 10
Breaking through rocks in worlds before our earth.
Never to deny its pleasure in the morning simple light
Nor its grave evening demand for love.
Never to allow gradually the traffic to smother
With noise and fog, the flowering of the Spirit. 15

Near the snow, near the sun, in the highest fields,
See how these names are fêted by the waving grass
And by the streamers of white cloud
And whispers of wind in the listening sky.

The names of those who in their lives fought for life,   20
Who wore at their hearts the fire's centre.
Born of the sun, they travelled a short while toward the sun,
And left the vivid air signed with their honour.

Stephen Spender (b. 1909)

Walter Llywarch

I am, as you know, Walter Llywarch,
Born in Wales of approved parents,
Well goitred, round in the bum,
Sure prey of the slow virus
Bred in quarries of grey rain.   5

Born in autumn at the right time
For hearing stories from the cracked lips
Of old folk dreaming of summer,
I piled them on to the bare hearth
Of my own fancy to make a blaze   10
To warm myself, but achieved only
The smoke's acid that brings the smart
Of false tears into the eyes.

Months of fog, months of drizzle;
Thought wrapped in the grey cocoon   15
Of race, of place, awaiting the sun's
Coming, but when the sun came,
Touching the hills with a hot hand,
Wings were spread only to fly
Round and round in a cramped cage   20
Or beat in vain at the sky's window.

School in the week, on Sunday chapel:
Tales of a land fairer than this
Were not so tall, for others had proved it
Without the grave's passport, they sent   25
The fruit home for ourselves to taste.

Walter Llywarch—the words were a name
On a lost letter that never came
For one who waited in the long queue
Of life that wound through a Welsh valley.   30
I took instead, as others had done
Before, a wife from the back pews

In chapel, rather to share the rain
Of winter evenings, than to intrude
On her pale body; and yet we lay   35
For warmth together and laughed to hear
Each new child's cry of despair.

R. S. Thomas (b. 1913)

The Woman at the Washington Zoo

The saris go by me from the embassies.

Cloth from the moon. Cloth from another planet.
They look back at the leopard like the leopard.

And I. . . .
               this print of mine, that has kept its color   5
Alive through so many cleanings; this dull null
Navy I wear to work, and wear from work, and so
To my bed, so to my grave, with no
Complaints, no comment: neither from my chief,
The Deputy Chief Assistant, nor his chief—   10
Only I complain. . . . this serviceable
Body that no sunlight dyes, no hand suffuses
But, dome-shadowed, withering among columns,
Wavy beneath fountains—small, far-off, shining
In the eyes of animals, these beings trapped   15
As I am trapped but not, themselves, the trap,
Aging, but without knowledge of their age,
Kept safe here, knowing not of death, for death—
Oh, bars of my own body, open, open!

The world goes by my cage and never sees me.   20
And there come not to me, as come to these,
The wild beasts, sparrows pecking the llamas' grain,
Pigeons settling on the bears' bread, buzzards
Tearing the meat the flies have clouded. . . .
                        Vulture,   25

When you come for the white rat that the foxes left,
Take off the red helmet of your head, the black
Wings that have shadowed me, and step to me as man:
The wild brother at whose feet the white wolves fawn,

To whose hand of power the great lioness   30
Stalks, purring. . . .
                    You know what I was,
You see what I am: change me, change me!

                                    Randall Jarrell (1914–1965)

The Liar

What I thought was love
in me, I find a thousand instances
as fear. (Of the tree's shadow
winding around the chair, a distant music
of frozen birds rattling   5
in the cold.)
                    Where ever I go to claim
my flesh, there are entrances
of spirit. And even its comforts
are hideous uses I strain
to understand.
                    Though I am a man   10
who is loud
on the birth
of his ways. Publicly redefining
each change in my soul, as if I had predicted
them,
            and profited, biblically, even tho   15
            their chanting weight,
                                erased familiarity
                                from my face.
                                A question I think,
an answer; whatever sits
counting the minutes
till you die.   20

            When they say, "It is Roi
            who is dead?" I wonder
            who will they mean?

            Imamu Amiri Baraka (LeRoi Jones, b. 1934)

Meditation on Identity

Arrangements of molecules held together by
Reactions of laws and forces
Have produced and have preserved this identity—

That is, what remembers, acts, is acted on, fears,
And being moved by, endorses   5
What it is part of: earth's, air's, and water's

Creation by that hypostasis up in the sky
Or whatever wherever houses
The imagination of the illusory.

Ephemeral substance of the body! Even   10
Its bone is transient, changes;
What rag is left of flesh the womb first clad us in?

Creation's matter flows through us like a river.
We have the loan of it, nothing's ours.
Man, plant, animal, everyone a borrower.   15

This one can understand, but not what makes up "I"
As a fountain rehearses
Water, to wield a shape from volatility.

David Wright (b. 1920)

Aztec Angel

I

I am an Aztec angel
        criminal
            of a scholarly
                society
        I do favors   5
            for whimsical
                magicians
        where I pawn
            my heart
                for truth   10
            and find
                my way
        through obscure
            streets
                of soft spoken   15
                    hara-kiris

II

I am an Aztec angel
  forlorn passenger
    on a train
  of chicken farmers   20
    and happy children

III

I am the Aztec angel
  fraternal partner
    of an orthodox
      society   25
  where pachuco children
    hurl stones
  through poetry rooms
and end up in a cop car
    their bones itching   30
    and their hearts
busted from malnutrition

IV

I am the Aztec angel
  who frequents bars
  spends evenings   35
    with literary circles
  and socializes
    with spiks
  niggers and wops
    and collapses on his way   40
    to funerals

V

Drunk
  lonely
    bespectacled
  the sky   45
    opens my veins
    like rain
    clouds go berserk
    around me
    my Mexican ancestors   50
      chew my fingernails

I am an Aztec angel
   offspring
   of a woman
     who was beautiful   55

        Luis Omar Salinas (b. 1937)

My Name Is Jesús

My name is Jesús.
The last one I don't know.
Does that make a difference?
My last one I don't know;
My first one was a gift.   5
I didn't earn either one.

My name is foreign,
Yet I was home born.
I am not an abortion.
Nor am I a prince,   10
   or a juggler of balls.
I am a little world.

The Universe is my eyes.
The planets are my arms and legs.
My Sun is my love.   15
The cold and the hate that
   cling to the ship of hope are
   supplied by you.

But what do I say?
That I talk with an accent?   20
You listen to my voice, yes,
   but not to my words.
For each man must say something
   in protest of the cold.

My name is man.   25
My skin is brown;
   but is yours warm?
And that makes a difference.
We're all here.
My name is Jesús.   30

And what is yours?
Is it in the phone book?
I'll bet you live someplace.
But then, someone lives in Tasmania.
Are you vaccinated against love?   35
Or have you developed an antidote.

I suppose you've volunteered for heaven.
Made arrangements for your cloud.
Will you look for your neighbor?
You might have to look hard.   40
Only your name will get you there,
And my name is Jesús.

                    Jesús Ascension Arreola, Jr.

Mutability

The Naturalistic Perspective

The Glories of Our Blood and State

The glories of our blood and state,
   Are shadows, not substantial things,
There is no armour against fate,
   Death lays his icy hand on Kings,
      Scepter and Crown,   5
      Must tumble down,
And in the dust be equal made,
With the poor crooked sithe and spade.

Some men with swords may reap the field,
   And plant fresh laurels where they kill,   10
But their strong nerves at last must yield,
   They tame but one another still;
      Early or late,
      They stoop to fate,
And must give up the murmuring breath,   15
When they pale Captives creep to death.

The Garlands wither on your brow,
   Then boast no more your mighty deeds,
Upon Death's purple Altar now,
   See where the Victor-victim bleeds,   20
      Your heads must come,
      To the cold Tomb;
Only the actions of the just
Smell sweet, and blossom in their dust.

                James Shirley (1596–1666)

The Chestnut Casts His Flambeaux

The chestnut casts his flambeaux, and the flowers
   Stream from the hawthorn on the wind away,
The doors clap to, the pane is blind with showers.
   Pass me the can, lad; there's an end of May.

There's one spoilt spring to scant our mortal lot,   5
   One season ruined of our little store.
May will be fine next year as like as not:
   Oh ay, but then we shall be twenty-four.

We for a certainty are not the first
   Have sat in taverns while the tempest hurled   10
Their hopeful plans to emptiness, and cursed
   Whatever brute and blackguard made the world.

It is in truth iniquity on high
   To cheat our sentenced souls of aught they crave,
And mar the merriment as you and I   15
   Fare on our long fool's-errand to the grave.

Iniquity it is; but pass the can.
   My lad, no pair of kings our mothers bore;
Our only portion is the estate of man:
   We want the moon, but we shall get no more.   20

If here to-day the cloud of thunder lours
   To-morrow it will hie on far behests;
The flesh will grieve on other bones than ours
   Soon, and the soul will mourn in other breasts.

The troubles of our proud and angry dust   25
   Are from eternity, and shall not fail.
Bear them we can, and if we can we must.
   Shoulder the sky, my lad, and drink your ale.

                     A. E. Housman (1859–1936)

During Wind and Rain

   They sing their dearest songs—
   He, she, all of them—yea,
   Treble and tenor and bass,
     And one to play;

With the candles mooning each face. . . .   5
  Ah, no; the years O!
How the sick leaves reel down in throngs!

They clear the creeping moss—
Elders and juniors—aye,
Making the pathways neat   10
  And the garden gay;
And they build a shady seat. . . .
  Ah, no; the years, the years;
See, the white storm-birds wing across!

They are blithely breakfasting all—   15
Men and maidens—yea,
Under the summer tree,
  With a glimpse of the bay,
While pet fowl come to the knee. . . .
  Ah, no; the years O!   20
And the rotten rose it ript from the wall.

They change to a high new house,
He, she, all of them—aye,
Clocks and carpets and chairs
  On the lawn all day,   25
And brightest things that are theirs. . . .
  Ah, no; the years, the years;
Down their carved names the rain-drop ploughs.

          Thomas Hardy (1840–1928)

The Snow Man

One must have a mind of winter
To regard the frost and the boughs
Of the pine-trees crusted with snow;

And have been cold a long time
To behold the junipers shagged with ice,   5
The spruces rough in the distant glitter

Of the January sun; and not to think
Of any misery in the sound of the wind,
In the sound of a few leaves,

Which is the sound of the land   10
Full of the same wind
That is blowing in the same bare place

For the listener, who listens in the snow,
And, nothing himself, beholds
Nothing that is not there and the nothing that is.   15

Wallace Stevens (1879–1955)

Spring and All

By the road to the contagious hospital
under the surge of the blue
mottled clouds driven from the
northeast—a cold wind. Beyond, the
waste of broad, muddy fields   5
brown with dried weeds, standing and fallen

patches of standing water
the scattering of tall trees

All along the road the reddish
purplish, forked, upstanding, twiggy   10
stuff of bushes and small trees
with dead, brown leaves under them
leafless vines—

Lifeless in appearance, sluggish
dazed spring approaches—   15

They enter the new world naked,
cold, uncertain of all
save that they enter. All about them
the cold, familiar wind—

Now the grass, tomorrow   20
the stiff curl of wildcarrot leaf
One by one objects are defined—
It quickens: clarity, outline of leaf

But now the stark dignity of
entrance—Still, the profound change   25
has come upon them: rooted, they
grip down and begin to awaken

William Carlos Williams (1883–1963)

The Lovers' Resolution

Sonnet: When I consider everything that grows

When I consider everything that grows
Holds in perfection but a little moment,
That this huge stage presenteth naught but shows
Whereon the stars in secret influence comment;
When I perceive that men as plants increase,   5
Cheered and checked even by the selfsame sky,
Vaunt in their youthful sap, at height decrease,
And wear their brave state out of memory—
Then the conceit of this inconstant stay
Sets you most rich in youth before my sight,   10
Where wasteful Time debateth with Decay,
To change your day of youth to sullied night.
And all in war with Time for love of you,
As he takes from you, I engraft you new.

William Shakespeare (1564–1616)

The Good-Morrow

I wonder, by my troth, what thou and I
Did, till we loved? were we not weaned till then?
But sucked on country pleasures, childishly?
Or snorted we in the Seven Sleepers' den?
'Twas so; but this, all pleasures fancies be.   5
If ever any beauty I did see,
Which I desired, and got, 'twas but a dream of thee.

And now good-morrow to our waking souls,
Which watch not one another out of fear;
For love, all love of other sights controls,   10
And makes one little room an everywhere.
Let sea-discoverers to new worlds have gone,
Let maps to others, worlds on worlds have shown,
Let us possess one world, each hath one, and is one.

My face in thine eye, thine in mine appears,   15
And true plain hearts do in the faces rest;
Where can we find two better hemispheres,
Without sharp north, without declining west?

Whatever dies was not mixed equally;
If our two loves be one, or, thou and I   20
Love so alike that none do slacken, none can die.

John Donne (1572?–1631)

To His Coy Mistress

Had we but world enough, and time,
This coyness, lady, were no crime.
We would sit down, and think which way
To walk, and pass our long love's day.
Thou by the Indian Ganges' side   5
Should'st rubies find; I by the tide
Of Humber would complain. I would
Love you ten years before the Flood;
And you should, if you please, refuse
Till the conversion of the Jews.   10
My vegetable love should grow
Vaster than empires, and more slow.
An hundred years should go to praise
Thine eyes, and on thy forehead gaze;
Two hundred to adore each breast;   15
But thirty thousand to the rest:
An age at least to every part,
And the last age should show your heart.
For, lady, you deserve this state,
Nor would I love at lower rate.   20
   But at my back I always hear
Time's wingèd chariot hurrying near;
And yonder all before us lie
Deserts of vast eternity.
Thy beauty shall no more be found,   25
Nor in thy marble vault shall sound
My echoing song; then worms shall try
That long-preserved virginity;
And your quaint honor turn to dust,
And into ashes all my lust.   30
The grave's a fine and private place,
But none, I think, do there embrace.
   Now, therefore, while the youthful hue
Sits on thy skin like morning dew,
And while thy willing soul transpires   35
At every pore with instant fires,

Now let us sport us while we may;
And now, like amorous birds of prey,
Rather at once our time devour,
Than languish in his slow-chapped power.   40
Let us roll all our strength and all
Our sweetness up into one ball;
And tear our pleasures with rough strife
Through the iron gates of life.
Thus, though we cannot make our sun   45
Stand still, yet we will make him run.

Andrew Marvell (1621–1678)

NOTES AND QUESTIONS

1. *Coy* (title): a paradox, rejecting and attracting.
2. *Humber* (7): a river in England, far from the Ganges in India. What verbal figure is employed here and throughout the poem?
3. *complain* (7): an allusion to lovers' writing complaints to distant ladies. The tension between the lovers is a fiction Marvell used to create a poem. What traditions of the love poem are reflected in this poem?
4. *vegetable* (11): a reference to the philosophical distinction between men, who are both rational and sensitive, animals, which have only sense, and vegetables, which merely generate and decay. The assumption of the speaker is that his lady would have him live as a vegetable with neither sensory nor sensual satisfaction. His response is to use his rational faculty. The opening words of each stanza show the logical structure of his argument. What is his line of reasoning?

(ponder,darling,these busted statues

(ponder,darling,these busted statues
of yon motheaten forum be aware
notice what hath remained
—the stone cringes
clinging to the stone,how obsolete   5

lips utter their extant smile . . . .
remark

a few deleted of texture
or meaning monuments and dolls

resist Them Greediest Paws of careful   10
time all of which is extremely
unimportant)whereas Life

matters if or

when the your- and my-
idle vertical worthless   15
self unite in a peculiarly
momentary

partnership(to instigate
constructive
                    Horizontal   20
business . . . . even so,let us make haste
—consider well this ruined aqueduct

lady,
which used to lead something into somewhere)

                    e. e. cummings (1894–1962)

The Equilibrists

Full of her long white arms and milky skin
He had a thousand times remembered sin.
Alone in the press of people traveled he,
Minding her jacinth, and myrrh, and ivory.

Mouth he remembered: the quaint orifice   5
From which came heat that flamed upon the kiss,
Till cold words came down spiral from the head,
Grey doves from the officious tower illsped.

Body: it was a white field ready for love,
On her body's field, with the gaunt tower above,   10
The lilies grew, beseeching him to take,
If he would pluck and wear them, bruise and break.

Eyes talking: Never mind the cruel words,
Embrace my flowers, but not embrace the swords.
But what they said, the doves came straightway flying   15
And unsaid: Honor, Honor, they came crying.

Importunate her doves. Too pure, too wise,
Clambering on his shoulder, saying, Arise,
Leave me now, and never let us meet,
Eternal distance now command thy feet.   20

Predicament indeed, which thus discovers
Honor among thieves, Honor between lovers.
O such a little word is Honor, they feel!
But the grey word is between them cold as steel.

At length I saw these lovers fully were come   25
Into their torture of equilibrium;
Dreadfully had forsworn each other, and yet
They were bound each to each, and they did not forget.

And rigid as two painful stars, and twirled
About the clustered night their prison world,   30
They burned with fierce love always to come near,
But Honor beat them back and kept them clear.

Ah, the strict lovers, they are ruined now!
I cried in anger. But with puddled brow
Devising for those gibbeted and brave   35
Came I descanting: Man, what would you have?

For spin your period out, and draw your breath,
A kinder sæculum begins with Death.
Would you ascend to Heaven and bodiless dwell?
Or take your bodies honorless to Hell?   40

In Heaven you have heard no marriage is,
No white flesh tinder to your lecheries,
Your male and female tissue sweetly shaped
Sublimed away, and furious blood escaped.

Great lovers lie in Hell, the stubborn ones   45
Infatuate of the flesh upon the bones;
Stuprate, they rend each other when they kiss,
The pieces kiss again, no end to this.

But still I watched them spinning, orbited nice.
Their flames were not more radiant than their ice.   50
I dug in the quiet earth and wrought the tomb
And made these lines to memorize their doom:—

EPITAPH

Equilibrists lie here; stranger, tread light;
Close, but untouching in each other's sight;
Mouldered the lips and ashy the tall skull.   55
Let them lie perilous and beautiful.

John Crowe Ransom (1888–1974)

The Aesthetic Resolution

Sapphic Fragment

"Thou shalt be—Nothing."—Omar Khayyam.

"Tombless, with no remembrance."—W. Shakespeare.

Dead shalt thou lie; and nought
Be told of thee or thought,
For thou hast plucked not of the Muses' tree:
And even in Hades' halls
Amidst thy fellow-thralls   5
No friendly shade thy shade shall company!

Sappho (630–552 B.C.)
adapted by Thomas Hardy

Sonnet: Shall I compare thee to a summer's day?

Shall I compare thee to a summer's day?
Thou art more lovely and more temperate.
Rough winds do shake the darling buds of May,
And summer's lease hath all too short a date.
Sometime too hot the eye of heaven shines,   5
And often is his gold complexion dimmed.
And every fair from fair sometime declines,
By chance or nature's changing course untrimmed.
But thy eternal summer shall not fade,
Nor lose possession of that fair thou owest,   10
Nor shall Death brag thou wander'st in his shade
When in eternal lines to time thou grow'st.
So long as men can breathe, or eyes can see,
So long lives this, and this gives life to thee.

William Shakespeare (1564–1616)

On English Verse

Poets may boast, as safely vain,
Their works shall with the world remain;
Both, bound together, live or die,
The verses and the prophecy.

But who can hope his lines should long   5
Last in a daily changing tongue?
While they are new, envy prevails;
And as that dies, our language fails.

When architects have done their part,
The matter may betray their art;   10
Time, if we use ill-chosen stone,
Soon brings a well-built palace down.

Poets that lasting marble seek
Must carve in Latin or in Greek;
We write in sand, our language grows,   15
And, like the tide, our work o'erflows.

Chaucer his sense can only boast,
The glory of his numbers lost!
Years have defaced his matchless strain,
And yet he did not sing in vain.   20

The beauties which adorned that age,
The shining subjects of his rage,
Hoping they should immortal prove,
Rewarded with success his love.

This was the generous poet's scope,   25
And all an English pen can hope,
To make the fair approve his flame,
That can so far extend their fame.

Verse, thus designed, has no ill fate
If it arrive but at the date   30
Of fading beauty; if it prove
But as long-lived as present love.

Edmund Waller (1606–1687)

Ode on a Grecian Urn

I

Thou still unravished bride of quietness,
  Thou foster-child of silence and slow time,
Sylvan historian, who canst thus express
  A flowery tale more sweetly than our rhyme:

NOTE

Sylvan (3): pastoral.

What leaf-fringed legend haunts about thy shape   5
  Of deities or mortals, or of both,
    In Tempe or the dales of Arcady?
What men or gods are these? What maidens loath?
  What mad pursuit? What struggle to escape?
    What pipes and timbrels? What wild ecstasy?   10

II

Heard melodies are sweet, but those unheard
  Are sweeter; therefore, ye soft pipes, play on;
Not to the sensual ear, but, more endeared,
  Pipe to the spirit, ditties of no tone:
Fair youth, beneath the trees, thou canst not leave   15
  Thy song, nor ever can those trees be bare;
    Bold Lover, never, never canst thou kiss,
Though winning near the goal—yet, do not grieve;
  She cannot fade, though thou hast not thy bliss,
    Forever wilt thou love, and she be fair!   20

III

Ah, happy, happy boughs! that cannot shed
  Your leaves, nor ever bid the spring adieu;
And, happy melodist, unwearièd,
  Forever piping songs forever new;
More happy love! more happy, happy love!   25
  Forever warm and still to be enjoyed,
    Forever panting, and forever young;
All breathing human passion far above,
  That leaves a heart high-sorrowful and cloyed,
    A burning forehead, and a parching tongue.   30

IV

Who are these coming to the sacrifice?
  To what green altar, O mysterious priest,
  Lead'st thou that heifer lowing at the skies,
    And all her silken flanks with garlands dressed?
What little town by river or sea shore,   35
  Or mountain-built with peaceful citadel,
    Is emptied of this folk, this pious morn?
And, little town, thy streets forevermore

NOTE

Tempe, Arcady (7): places in Greece, now conventional terms for pastoral settings.

Will silent be; and not a soul to tell
    Why thou are desolate, can e'er return.   40

V

O Attic shape! Fair attitude! with brede
    Of marble men and maidens overwrought,
With forest branches and the trodden weed;
    Thou, silent form, dost tease us out of thought
As doth eternity: Cold Pastoral!   45
    When old age shall this generation waste,
    Thou shalt remain, in midst of other woe
Than ours, a friend to man, to whom thou say'st,
    "Beauty is truth, truth beauty,—that is all
    Ye know on earth, and all ye need to know."   50

John Keats (1795–1821)

NOTE

brede (41): embroidery, design.

Musée des Beaux Arts

About suffering they were never wrong,
The Old Masters: how well they understood
Its human position; how it takes place
While someone else is eating or opening a window or just walking
        dully along;
How, when the aged are reverently, passionately waiting   5
For the miraculous birth, there always must be
Children who did not specially want it to happen, skating
On a pond at the edge of the wood:
They never forgot
That even the dreadful martyrdom must run its course   10
Anyhow in a corner, some untidy spot
Where the dogs go on with their doggy life and the torturer's horse
Scratches its innocent behind on a tree.

In Brueghel's *Icarus*, for instance: how everything turns away
Quite leisurely from the disaster; the ploughman may   15
Have heard the splash, the forsaken cry,
But for him it was not an important failure; the sun shone
As it had to on the white legs disappearing into the green
Water; and the expensive delicate ship that must have seen
Something amazing, a boy falling out of the sky,   20
Had somewhere to get to and sailed calmly on.

W. H. Auden (1907–1973)

The Religious Resolution

Mortification

How soon doth man decay!
When clothes are taken from a chest of sweets
   To swaddle infants, whose young breath
      Scarce knows the way,
   Those clouts are little winding-sheets   5
Which do consign and send them unto death.

   When boys go first to bed,
They step into their voluntary graves;
   Sleep binds them fast; only their breath
      Makes them not dead.   10
   Successive nights, like rolling waves,
Convey them quickly who are bound for death.

   When youth is frank and free,
And calls for music, while his veins do swell,
   All day exchanging mirth and breath   15
      In company,
   That music summons to the knell
Which shall befriend him at the house of death.

   When man grows staid and wise,
Getting a house and home, where he may move   20
   Within the circle of his breath,
      Schooling his eyes,
   That dumb inclosure maketh love
Unto the coffin that attends his death.

   When age grows low and weak,   25
Marking his grave, and thawing ev'ry year,
   Till all do melt and drown his breath
      When he would speak,
   A chair or litter shows the bier
Which shall convey him to the house of death.   30

   Man, ere he is aware,
Hath put together a solemnity,
   And dressed his hearse, while he has breath
      As yet to spare;
   Yet, Lord, instruct us so to die,   35
That all these dyings may be life in death.

                  George Herbert (1593–1633)

Quickness

False life! a foil and no more, when
               Wilt thou be gone?
Thou foul deception of all men
That would not have the true come on.

Thou art a moon-like toil; a blind   5
               Self-posing state;
A dark contest of waves and wind;
A mere tempestuous debate.

Life is a fix'd, discerning light,
               A knowing joy;   10
No chance, or fit: but ever bright,
And calm and full, yet doth not cloy.

'Tis such a blissful thing, that still
               Doth vivify,
And shine and smile, and hath the skill   15
To please without eternity.

Thou art a toilsome mole, or less
               A moving mist.
But life is, what none can express,
A quickness, which my God hath kist.   20

            Henry Vaughan (1621–1693)

NOTE

moon-like toil (5): a reference to the inconstancy of the moon, to life as a toil because bound to inconstancy.

Sonnet: It is a beauteous evening

It is a beauteous evening, calm and free;
The holy time is quiet as a Nun
Breathless with adoration; the broad sun
Is sinking down in its tranquility;
The gentleness of heaven broods o'er the Sea: 5
Listen! the mighty Being is awake,
And doth with his eternal motion make
A sound like thunder—everlastingly.
Dear Child! dear Girl! that walkest with me here,

If thou appear untouched by solemn thought,   10
Thy nature is not therefore less divine:
Thou liest in Abraham's bosom all the year,
And worship'st at the Temple's inner shrine,
God being with thee when we know it not.

> William Wordsworth (1770–1850)

Some keep the Sabbath going to Church

Some keep the Sabbath going to Church—
I keep it, staying at Home—
With a Bobolink for a Chorister—
And an Orchard, for a Dome—

Some keep the Sabbath in Surplice—   5
I just wear my Wings—
And instead of tolling the Bell, for Church,
Our little Sexton—sings.

God preaches, a noted Clergyman—
And the sermon is never long,   10
So instead of getting to Heaven, at last—
I'm going, all along.

> Emily Dickinson (1830–1886)

Church Going

Once I am sure there's nothing going on
I step inside, letting the door thud shut.
Another church: matting, seats, and stone,
And little books; sprawlings of flowers, cut
For Sunday, brownish now; some brass and stuff   5
Up at the holy end; the small neat organ;
And a tense, musty, unignorable silence,
Brewed God knows how long. Hatless, I take off
My cycle-clips in awkward reverence,

Move forward, run my hand around the font.   10
From where I stand, the roof looks almost new—
Cleaned, or restored? Someone would know: I don't.
Mounting the lectern, I peruse a few
Hectoring large-scale verses, and pronounce
"Here endeth" much more loudly than I'd meant.   15

The echoes snigger briefly. Back at the door
I sign the book, donate an Irish sixpence,
Reflect the place was not worth stopping for.

Yet stop I did: in fact I often do,
And always end much at a loss like this,   20
Wondering what to look for; wondering, too,
When churches fall completely out of use
What we shall turn them into, if we shall keep
A few cathedrals chronically on show,
Their parchment, plate and pyx in locked cases,   25
And let the rest rent-free to rain and sheep.
Shall we avoid them as unlucky places?

Or, after dark, will dubious women come
To make their children touch a particular stone;
Pick simples for a cancer; or on some   30
Advised night see walking a dead one?
Power of some sort or other will go on
In games, in riddles, seemingly at random;
But superstition, like belief, must die,
And what remains when disbelief has gone?   35
Grass, weedy pavement, brambles, buttress, sky,

A shape less recognisable each week,
A purpose more obscure. I wonder who
Will be the last, the very last, to seek
This place for what it was; one of the crew   40
That tap and jot and know what rood-lofts were?
Some ruin-bibber, randy for antique,
Or Christmas-addict, counting on a whiff
Of gown-and-bands and organ-pipes and myrrh?
Or will he be my representative,   45

Bored, uninformed, knowing the ghostly silt
Dispersed, yet tending to this cross of ground
Through suburb scrub because it held unspilt
So long and equably what since is found

NOTES

pyx (25): a box for storing communion wafers, *simples* (30): herbs. *ruin-bibber* (42): an imbiber of ruin.

Only in separation—marriage, and birth,   50
And death, and thoughts of these—for whom was built
This special shell? For, though I've no idea
What this accoutred frowsty barn is worth,
It pleases me to stand in silence here;

A serious house on serious earth it is,   55
In whose blent air all our compulsions meet,
Are recognised, and robed as destinies.
And that much never can be obsolete,
Since someone will forever be surprising
A hunger in himself to be more serious,   60
And gravitating with it to this ground,
Which, he once heard, was proper to grow wise in,
If only that so many dead lie round.

Philip Larkin (b. 1922)

Archetypal Cycles

The Seasons

Spring

When daisies pied and violets blue
And lady-smocks of silver-white
And cuckoo-buds of yellow hue
Do paint the meadows with delight,
The cuckoo then on every tree   5
Mocks married men, for thus sings he,
Cuckoo.
Cuckoo, cuckoo: O word of fear,
Unpleasing to a married ear.

When shepherds pipe on oaten straws   10
And merry larks are ploughmen's clocks,
When turtles tread, and rooks and daws,
And maidens bleach their summer smocks,
The cuckoo then on every tree,
Mocks married men, for thus sings he,   15
Cuckoo.
Cuckoo, cuckoo: O word of fear,
Unpleasing to a married ear.

William Shakespeare (1564–1616)

NOTE

cuckoo (7): the call of the bird, which lays its eggs in the nests of others, resembles the sound of the word "cuckold."

Spring

Nothing is so beautiful as spring—
  When weeds, in wheels, shoot long and lovely and lush;
  Thrush's eggs look little low heavens, and thrush
Through the echoing timber does so rinse and wring
The ear, it strikes like lightnings to hear him sing;   5
  The glassy peartree leaves and blooms, they brush
  The descending blue; that blue is all in a rush
With richness; the racing lambs too have fair their fling.

What is all this juice and all this joy?
  A strain of the earth's sweet being in the beginning   10
In Eden garden.—Have, get, before it cloy,
  Before it cloud, Christ, lord, and sour with sinning,
Innocent mind and Mayday in girl and boy,
  Most, O maid's child, thy choice and worthy the winning.

Gerard Manley Hopkins (1844–1889)

Sumer Is Icumen In

Sumer is icumen in,
Loude sing cuccu!
Groweth sed and bloweth° med   blossoms
And springth the wude nu.
Sing cuccu!   5

Ewe bleteth after lomb,
Loweth after calve cu;
Bullock sterteth, bucke verteth,°   breaks wind
Murie sing cuccu!
Cuccu, cuccu,   10
Wel singest thu, cuccu;
Ne swik° thu naver nu.°   stop, now

Sing cuccu nu! Sing cuccu!
Sing cuccu! Sing cuccu nu!

Anonymous (early 13th century)

To Autumn

Season of mists and mellow fruitfulness,
　　Close bosom-friend of the maturing sun:
Conspiring with him how to load and bless
　　With fruit the vines that round the thatch-eves run;
To bend with apples the mossed cottage-trees,　　5
　　And fill all fruit with ripeness to the core;
　　　　To swell the gourd, and plump the hazel shells
With a sweet kernel; to set budding more,
　　And still more, later flowers for the bees,
　　Until they think warm days will never cease,　　10
　　　　For Summer has o'er-brimmed their clammy cells.

Who hath not seen thee oft amid thy store?
　　Sometimes whoever seeks abroad may find
Thee sitting careless on a granary floor,
　　Thy hair soft-lifted by the winnowing wind;　　15
Or on a half-reaped furrow sound asleep,
　　Drowsed with the fume of poppies, while thy hook
　　　　Spares the next swath and all its twinèd flowers:
And sometimes like a gleaner thou dost keep
　　Steady thy laden head across a brook;　　20
　　Or by a cider-press, with patient look,
　　　　Thou watchest the last oozings hours by hours.

Where are the songs of Spring? Ay, where are they?
　　Think not of them, thou hast thy music too,—
While barrèd clouds bloom the soft-dying day,　　25
　　And touch the stubble-plains with rosy hue;
Then in a wailful choir the small gnats mourn
　　Among the river sallows, borne aloft
　　　　Or sinking as the light wind lives or dies;
And full-grown lambs loud bleat from hilly bourn;　　30
　　Hedge-crickets sing; and now with treble soft
　　The red-breast whistles from a garden-croft;
　　　　And gathering swallows twitter in the skies.

John Keats (1795–1821)

Storm Fear

When the wind works against us in the dark,
And pelts with snow
The lower-chamber window on the east,
And whispers with a sort of stifled bark,
The beast,   5
"Come out! Come out!"—
It costs no inward struggle not to go,
Ah, no!
I count our strength,
Two and a child,   10
Those of us not asleep subdued to mark
How the cold creeps as the fire dies at length—
How drifts are piled,
Dooryard and road ungraded,
Till even the comforting barn grows far away,   15
And my heart owns a doubt
Whether 'tis in us to arise with day
And save ourselves unaided.

Robert Frost (1874–1963)

From Innocence to Experience

Subject Pair

The Lamb

Little Lamb, who made thee?
Dost thou know who made thee?
Gave thee life and bid thee feed,
By the stream and o'er the mead;
Gave thee clothing of delight,   5
Softest clothing wooly bright;
Gave thee such a tender voice,
Making all the vales rejoice?
Little Lamb, who made thee?
Dost thou know who made thee?   10

Little Lamb, I'll tell thee,
Little Lamb, I'll tell thee:
He is callèd by thy name,
For He calls Himself a Lamb:
He is meek, and He is mild;   15
He became a little child:
I a child, and thou a lamb,
We are callèd by His name.
Little Lamb, God bless thee.
Little Lamb, God bless thee.   20

William Blake (1757–1827)

The Tyger

Tyger! Tyger! burning bright
In the forests of the night,
What immortal hand or eye
Could frame thy fearful symmetry?

In what distant deeps or skies   5
Burnt the fire of thine eyes?
On what wings dare he aspire?
What the hand dare seize the fire?

And what shoulder, & what art,
Could twist the sinews of thy heart?   10
And when thy heart began to beat,
What dread hand? & what dread feet?

What the hammer? what the chain?
In what furnace was thy brain?
What the anvil? what dread grasp   15
Dare its deadly terrors clasp?

When the stars threw down their spears,
And water'd heaven with their tears,
Did he smile his work to see?
Did he who made the Lamb make thee?   20

Tyger! Tyger! burning bright
In the forests of the night,
What immortal hand or eye,
Dare frame thy fearful symmetry?

William Blake (1757–1827)

QUESTIONS

1. "The Lamb" and "The Tyger," companion poems in Blake's *Songs of Innocence and of Experience,* present contrasting images. An initial reading suggests that the images create simple symbols of good and evil and raise the commonplace question of why the god who created the lamb also created the tiger. Find evidence in "The Tyger" that suggests that it is not about "evil" but about some primal energy reflecting the power of the creator—and, perhaps, present in man.
2. The question, "Did he who made the Lamb make thee," is rhetorical. The tiger's maker is characterized by the question. Which images are particularly effective in presenting the creative process? Explain the relationship of the lamb to its creator.
3. Although presented separately, Blake saw the lamb and the tiger as inseparable symbols of God's creation and of man's experience. What phrasing in each poem suggests that something human, perhaps in the psyche, is being symbolized? Does the symbol of the tiger represent something supernatural, something in the psyche of man, or both?
4. Why does the tiger roam the forests of the "night"? How is the word "bright" used differently in the two poems? What does the image of the stars watering heaven with their tears suggest?
5. Why is "The Tyger" entirely in the form of questions?

anyone lived in a pretty how town

anyone lived in a pretty how town
(with up so floating many bells down)
spring summer autumn winter
he sang his didn't he danced his did.

Women and men(both little and small)   5
cared for anyone not at all
they sowed their isn't they reaped their same
sun moon stars rain

children guessed(but only a few
and down they forgot as up they grew   10
autumn winter spring summer)
that noone loved him more by more

when by now and tree by leaf
she laughed his joy she cried his grief
bird by snow and stir by still   15
anyone's any was all to her

someones married their everyones
laughed their cryings and did their dance
(sleep wake hope and then)they
said their nevers they slept their dream   20

stars rain sun moon
(and only the snow can begin to explain
how children are apt to forget to remember
with up so floating many bells down)

one day anyone died i guess   25
(and noone stooped to kiss his face)
busy folk buried them side by side
little by little and was by was

all by all and deep by deep
and more by more they dream their sleep   30
noone and anyone earth by april
wish by spirit and if by yes.

Women and men(both dong and ding)
summer autumn winter spring
reaped their sowing and went their came   35
sun moon stars rain

e. e. cummings (1894–1962)

Fern Hill

Now as I was young and easy under the apple boughs
About the lilting house and happy as the grass was green,
    The night above the dingle starry,
      Time let me hail and climb
    Golden in the heydays of his eyes,   5
And honoured among wagons I was prince of the apple towns
And once below a time I lordly had the trees and leaves
      Trail with daisies and barley
    Down the rivers of the windfall light.

And as I was green and carefree, famous among the barns   10
About the happy yard and singing as the farm was home,
     In the sun that is young once only,
          Time let me play and be
     Golden in the mercy of his means,
And green and golden I was huntsman and herdsman, the
               calves   15
Sang to my horn, the foxes on the hills barked clear and cold,
          And the sabbath rang slowly
     In the pebbles of the holy streams.

All the sun long it was running, it was lovely, the hay
Fields high as the house, the tunes from the chimneys, it
               was air   20
     And playing, lovely and watery
          And fire green as grass.
     And nightly under the simple stars
As I rode to sleep the owls were bearing the farm away,
All the moon long I heard, blessed among stables, the nightjars   25
     Flying with the ricks, and the horses
          Flashing into the dark.

And then to awake, and the farm, like a wanderer white
With the dew, come back, the cock on his shoulder: it was all
     Shining, it was Adam and maiden,   30
          The sky gathered again
     And the sun grew round that very day.
So it must have been after the birth of the simple light
In the first, spinning place, the spellbound horses walking warm
     Out of the whinnying green stable   35
          On to the fields of praise.

And honoured among foxes and pheasants by the gay house
Under the new made clouds and happy as the heart was long,
     In the sun born over and over,
          I ran my heedless ways,   40
     My wishes raced through the house high hay
And nothing I cared, at my sky blue trades, that time allows
In all his tuneful turning so few and such morning songs
     Before the children green and golden
          Follow him out of grace,   45

Nothing I cared, in the lamb white days, that time would take me
Up to the swallow thronged loft by the shadow of my hand,
     In the moon that is always rising,

Nor that riding to sleep
    I should hear him fly with the high fields   50
And wake to the farm forever fled from the childless land.
Oh as I was young and easy in the mercy of his means,
    Time held me green and dying
Though I sang in my chains like the sea.

                             Dylan Thomas (1914–1953)

From Youth to Age

Spring and Fall

to a young child

Márgarét, áre you gríeving
Over Goldengrove unleaving?
Leáves, líke the things of man, you
With your fresh thoughts care for, can you?
Áh! ás the heart grows older   5
It will come to such sights colder
By and by, nor spare a sigh
Though worlds of wanwood leafmeal lie;
And yet you *will* weep and know why.
Now no matter, child, the name: 10
Sórrow's spríngs áre the same.
Nor mouth had, no nor mind, expressed
What heart heard of, ghost guessed:
It ís the blight man was born for,
It is Margaret you mourn for.   15

           Gerard Manley Hopkins (1844–1889)

The Lamentation of the Old Pensioner

Although I shelter from the rain
Under a broken tree
My chair was nearest to the fire
In every company
That talked of love or politics,   5
Ere Time transfigured me.

Though lads are making pikes again
For some conspiracy,
And crazy rascals rage their fill
At human tyranny,   10
My contemplations are of Time
That has transfigured me.

There's not a woman turns her face
Upon a broken tree,
And yet the beauties that I loved   15
Are in my memory;
I spit into the face of Time
That has transfigured me.

William Butler Yeats (1865–1939)

What Are Years?

What is our innocence,
what is our guilt? All are
    naked, none is safe. And whence
is courage: the unanswered question,
the resolute doubt—   5
dumbly calling, deafly listening—that
is misfortune, even death,
        encourages others
        and in its defeat, stirs

    the soul to be strong? He   10
sees deep and is glad, who
    accedes to mortality
and in his imprisonment rises
upon himself as
the sea in a chasm, struggling to be   15
free and unable to be,
        in its surrendering
        finds its continuing.

    So he who strongly feels,
behaves. The very bird,   20
    grown taller as he sings, steels
his form straight up. Though he is captive,

his mighty singing
says, satisfaction is a lowly
thing, how pure a thing is joy.　　25
　This is mortality,
　this is eternity.

Marianne Moore (1887–1972)

The Waking

I wake to sleep, and take my waking slow.
I feel my fate in what I cannot fear.
I learn by going where I have to go.

We think by feeling. What is there to know?
I hear my being dance from ear to ear.　　5
I wake to sleep, and take my waking slow.

Of those so close beside me, which are you?
God bless the Ground! I shall walk softly there,
And learn by going where I have to go.

Light takes the Tree; but who can tell us how?　　10
The lowly worm climbs up a winding stair;
I wake to sleep, and take my waking slow.

Great Nature has another thing to do
To you and me; so take the lively air,
And, lovely, learn by going where to go.　　15

This shaking keeps me steady. I should know.
What falls away is always. And is near.
I wake to sleep, and take my waking slow.
I learn by going where I have to go.

Theodore Roethke (1908–1963)

From Death to Rebirth

Ah! Sun-Flower

Ah! Sun-flower! weary of time,
Who countest the steps of the sun;
Seeking after that sweet golden clime,
Where the traveller's journey is done;

Where the Youth pined away with desire,   5
And the pale Virgin shrouded in snow,
Arise from their graves, and aspire
Where my Sun-flower wishes to go.

William Blake (1757–1827)

There Was a Child Went Forth

There was a child went forth every day,
And the first object he look'd upon, that object he became,
And that object became part of him for the day or a certain part of
     the day,
Or for many years or stretching cycles of years.

The early lilacs became part of this child,   5
And grass and white and red morning-glories, and white and red
     clover, and the song of the phoebe-bird,
And the Third-month lambs and the sow's pink-faint litter, and the
     mare's foal and the cow's calf,
And the noisy brood of the barnyard or by the mire of the pond-side,
And the fish suspending themselves so curiously below there, and the
     beautiful curious liquid,
And the water-plants with their graceful flat heads, all became part
     of him.   10

The field-sprouts of Fourth-month and Fifth-month became part of
     him,
Winter-grain sprouts and those of the light-yellow corn, and the
     esculent roots of the garden,
And the apple-trees cover'd with blossoms and the fruit afterward,
     and wood-berries, and the commonest weeds by the road,
And the old drunkard staggering home from the outhouse of the
     tavern whence he had lately risen,
And the schoolmistress that pass'd on her way to the school,   15
And the friendly boys that pass'd, and the quarrelsome boys,
And the tidy and fresh cheek'd girls, and the barefoot Negro boy and
     girl,
And all the changes of city and country wherever he went.

His own parents, he that had father'd him and she that had conceiv'd
     him in her womb and birth'd him,
They gave this child more of themselves than that,   20
They gave him afterward every day, they became part of him.

The mother at home quietly placing the dishes on the supper-table,
The mother with mild words, clean her cap and gown, a wholesome
    odor falling off her person and clothes as she walks by,
The father, strong, self-sufficient, manly mean, anger'd, unjust,
The blow, the quick loud word, the tight bargain, the crafty
    lure,   25
The family usages, the language, the company, the furniture, the
    yearning and swelling heart,
Affection that will not be gainsay'd, the sense of what is real, the
    thought if after all it should prove unreal,
The doubts of day-time and the doubts of night-time, the curious
    whether and how,
Whether that which appears so is so, or is it all flashes and specks?
Men and women crowding fast in the streets, if they are not flashes
    and specks what are they?   30
The streets themselves and the façades of houses, and goods in the
    windows,
Vehicles, teams, the heavy-plank'd wharves, the huge crossing at the
    ferries,
The village of the highland seen from afar at sunset, the river
    between,
Shadows, aureola and mist, the light falling on roofs and gables of
    white or brown two miles off,
The schooner near by sleepily dropping down the tide, the little boat
    slack-tow'd astern,   35
The hurrying tumbling waves, quick-broken crests, slapping,
The strata of color'd clouds, the long bar of maroon-tint away solitary
    by itself, the spread of purity it lies motionless in,
The horizon's edge, the flying sea-crow, the fragrance of salt marsh
    and shore mud,
These became part of that child who went forth every day, and who
    now goes, and will always go forth every day.

Walt Whitman (1819–1892)

Journey of the Magi

"A cold coming we had of it,
Just the worst time of the year
For a journey, and such a long journey:
The ways deep and the weather sharp,

The very dead of winter."   5
And the camels galled, sore-footed, refractory,
Lying down in the melting snow.
There were times we regretted
The summer palaces on slopes, the terraces,
And the silken girls bringing sherbet.   10
Then the camel men cursing and grumbling
And running away, and wanting their liquor and women,
And the night-fires going out, and the lack of shelters,
And the cities hostile and the towns unfriendly
And the villages dirty and charging high prices: 15
A hard time we had of it.
At the end we preferred to travel all night,
Sleeping in snatches,
With the voices singing in our ears, saying
That this was all folly.   20

Then at dawn we came down to a temperate valley,
Wet, below the snow line, smelling of vegetation,
With a running stream and a water-mill beating the darkness,
And three trees on the low sky.
And an old white horse galloped away in the meadow.   25
Then we came to a tavern with vine-leaves over the lintel,
Six hands at an open door dicing for pieces of silver,
And feet kicking the empty wine-skins.
But there was no information, and so we continued
And arrived at evening, not a moment too soon   30
Finding the place; it was (you may say) satisfactory.

All this was a long time ago, I remember,
And I would do it again, but set down
This set down
This: were we led all that way for   35
Birth or Death? There was a Birth, certainly,
We had evidence and no doubt. I had seen birth and death,
But had thought they were different; this Birth was
Hard and bitter agony for us, like Death, our death.
We returned to our places, these Kingdoms,   40
But no longer at ease here, in the old dispensation,
With an alien people clutching their gods.
I should be glad of another death.

T. S. Eliot (1888–1965)

Crow's Last Stand

Burning
        burning
                burning
                        there was finally something
The sun could not burn, that it had rendered   5
Everything down to—a final obstacle
Against which it raged and charred

And rages and chars

Limpid among the glaring furnace clinkers
The pulsing blue tongues and the red and the yellow   10
The green lickings of the conflagration

Limpid and black—

Crow's eye-pupil, in the tower of its scorched fort.

                                Ted Hughes (b. 1930)

Death

Sonnet: Death be not proud

Death be not proud, though some have callèd thee
Mighty and dreadful, for, thou art not so;
For, those whom thou think'st thou dost overthrow,
Die not, poor death, nor yet canst thou kill me.
From rest and sleep, which but thy pictures be,   5
Much pleasure; then from thee, much more must flow,
And soonest our best men with thee do go,
Rest of their bones, and soul's delivery.
Thou art slave to Fate, Chance, kings, and desperate men,
And dost with poison, war, and sickness dwell,   10
And poppy, or charms can make us sleep as well,
And better than thy stroke; why swell'st thou then?
One short sleep past, we wake eternally,
And death shall be no more; death, thou shalt die.

John Donne (1572?–1631)

On the Countess Dowager of Pembroke

Underneath this sable hearse
Lies the subject of all verse:
Sidney's sister, Pembroke's mother.
Death, ere thou hast slain another
Fair and learn'd and good as she,   5
Time shall throw a dart at thee.

Marble piles let no man raise
To her name, for after-days
Some kind woman, born as she,
Reading this, like Niobe   10
Shall turn marble, and become
Both her mourner and her tomb.

William Browne of Tavistock (c. 1590–c. 1645)

Thanatopsis

To him who in the love of Nature holds
Communion with her visible forms, she speaks
A various language; for his gayer hours
She has a voice of gladness, and a smile
And eloquence of beauty, and she glides   5
Into his darker musings, with a mild
And healing sympathy, that steals away
Their sharpness, ere he is aware. When thoughts
Of the last bitter hour come like a blight
Over thy spirit, and sad images   10
Of the stern agony, and shroud, and pall,
And breathless darkness, and the narrow house,
Make thee to shudder, and grow sick at heart;—
Go forth, under the open sky, and list
To Nature's teachings, while from all around—   15
Earth and her waters, and the depths of air—
Comes a still voice—Yet a few days, and thee
The all-beholding sun shall see no more
In all his course; nor yet in the cold ground,
Where thy pale form was laid, with many tears,   20
Nor in the embrace of ocean, shall exist
Thy image. Earth, that nourished thee, shall claim
Thy growth, to be resolved to earth again,
And, lost each human trace, surrendering up
Thine individual being, shalt thou go   25
To mix for ever with the elements,
To be a brother to the insensible rock
And to the sluggish clod, which the rude swain
Turns with his share, and treads upon. The oak
Shall send his roots abroad, and pierce thy mould.   30

Yet not to thine eternal resting-place
Shalt thou retire alone, nor couldst thou wish
Couch more magnificent. Thou shalt lie down
With patriarchs of the infant world—with kings,
The powerful of the earth—the wise, the good,   35
Fair forms, and hoary seers of ages past,
All in one mighty sepulchre. The hills
Rock-ribbed and ancient as the sun,—the vales
Stretching in pensive quietness between;
The venerable woods—rivers that move   40
In majesty, and the complaining brooks
That make the meadows green; and, poured round all,
Old Ocean's gray and melancholy waste,—
Are but the solemn decorations all
Of the great tomb of man. The golden sun,   45
The planets, all the infinite host of heaven,
Are shining on the sad abodes of death,
Through the still lapse of ages. All that tread
The globe are but a handful to the tribes
That slumber in its bosom.—Take the wings   50
Of morning, pierce the Barcan wilderness,
Or lose thyself in the continuous woods
Where rolls the Oregon, and hears no sound,
Save his own dashings—yet the dead are there:
And millions in those solitudes, since first   55
The flight of years began, have laid them down
In their last sleep—the dead reign there alone.
So shalt thou rest, and what if thou withdraw
In silence from the living, and no friend
Take note of thy departure? All that breathe   60
Will share thy destiny. The gay will laugh
When thou art gone, the solemn brood of care
Plod on, and each one as before will chase
His favorite phantom; yet all these shall leave
Their mirth and their employments, and shall come   65
And make their bed with thee. As the long train
Of ages glide away, the sons of men,
The youth in life's green spring, and he who goes
In the full strength of years, matron and maid,
The speechless babe, and the gray-headed man—   70
Shall one by one be gathered to thy side,
By those, who in their turn shall follow them.

So live, that when thy summons comes to join
The innumerable caravan, which moves
To that mysterious realm, where each shall take   75
His chamber in the silent halls of death,
Thou go not, like the quarry-slave at night,
Scourged to his dungeon, but, sustained and soothed
By an unfaltering trust, approach thy grave,
Like one who wraps the drapery of his couch   80
About him, and lies down to pleasant dreams.

                          William Cullen Bryant (1794–1878)

NOTES AND QUESTIONS

1. *Thanatopsis* (title): View of death. *Barcan* (51): North African.
   Oregon (53): Bryant's way of designating the Columbia River.
2. When Bryant originally composed "Thanatopsis," at about the age
   of twenty, it was a shorter poem, beginning in the middle of line
   17 and ending in the middle of line 66. What effect have lines
   1–17 had on the identity of the speaker of the body of the poem?
   Explain why this change should be viewed with favor or disfavor.
   Do you view with favor or disfavor the addition from line 66 to
   the end? Consider particularly lines 73–81. Do you sense any
   didacticism in these closing lines? Explain.
3. Compare Donne's "Sonnet: Death be not proud"(p. 345) and Bryant's
   "Thanatopsis" (pp. 346–48) in their views of death; in the attitude
   and character of the speakers; in tone. How do they differ styl-
   istically? In what respects is one superior to the other?

Sonnet: When I have fears

When I have fears that I may cease to be
Before my pen has gleaned my teeming brain,
Before high-pilèd books, in charact'ry,
Hold like rich garners the full-ripened grain;
When I behold, upon the night's starred face,   5
Huge cloudy symbols of a high romance,
And think that I may never live to trace
Their shadows, with the magic hand of chance;

And when I feel, fair creature of an hour!
That I shall never look upon thee more,   10
Never have relish in the faery power
Of unreflecting love;—then on the shore
Of the wide world I stand alone, and think,
Till Love and Fame to nothingness do sink.

John Keats (1795–1821)

from Song of Myself, 52

The spotted hawk swoops by and accuses me, he complains of my
gab and my loitering.

I too am not a bit tamed, I too am untranslatable,
I sound my barbaric yawp over the roofs of the world.

The last scud of day holds back for me,
It flings my likeness after the rest and true as any on the shadow'd
wilds,   5
It coaxes me to the vapor and the dusk.

I depart as air, I shake my white locks at the runaway sun,
I effuse my flesh in eddies, and drift it in lacy jags.

I bequeath myself to the dirt to grow from the grass I love,
If you want me again look for me under your boot-soles.   10

You will hardly know who I am or what I mean,
But I shall be good health to you nevertheless,
And filter and fibre your blood.

Failing to fetch me at first keep encouraged,
Missing me one place search another,   15
I stop somewhere waiting for you.

Walt Whitman (1819–1892)

The last Night that She lived

The last Night that She lived
It was a Common Night
Except the Dying—this to Us
Made Nature different

We noticed smallest things—   5
Things overlooked before
By this great light upon our Minds
Italicized—as 'twere.

As We went out and in
Between Her final Room   10
And Rooms where Those to be alive
Tomorrow were, a Blame

That Others could exist
While She must finish quite
A Jealousy for Her arose   15
So nearly infinite—

We waited while She passed—
It was a narrow time—
Too jostled were Our Souls to speak
At length the notice came.   20

She mentioned, and forgot—
Then lightly as a Reed
Bent to the Water, struggled scarce—
Consented, and was dead—

And We—We placed the Hair—   25
And drew the Head erect—
And then an awful leisure was
Belief to regulate—

> Emily Dickinson (1830–1886)

Song: *When I am dead, my dearest*

When I am dead, my dearest,
   Sing no sad songs for me;
Plant thou no roses at my head,
   Nor shady cypress tree:
Be the green grass above me   5
   With showers and dewdrops wet,
And if thou wilt, remember,
   And if thou wilt, forget.

I shall not see the shadows,
   I shall not feel the rain;   10

I shall not hear the nightingale
   Sing on as if in pain;
And dreaming through the twilight
   That doth not rise nor set,
Haply I may remember,   15
   And haply may forget.

        Christina Rossetti (1830–1894)

Reuben Bright

Because he was a butcher and thereby
Did earn an honest living (and did right),
I would not have you think that Reuben Bright
Was any more a brute than you or I;
For when they told him that his wife must die,   5
He stared at them, and shook with grief and fright,
And cried like a great baby half that night,
And made the women cry to see him cry.

And after she was dead, and he had paid
The singers and the sexton and the rest,   10
He packed a lot of things that she had made
Most mournfully away in an old chest
Of hers, and put some chopped-up cedar boughs
In with them, and tore down the slaughter-house.

        Edwin Arlington Robinson (1869–1935)

The Emperor of Ice-Cream

Call the roller of big cigars,
The muscular one, and bid him whip
In kitchen cups concupiscent curds.
Let the wenches dawdle in such dress
As they are used to wear, and let the boys   5
Bring flowers in last month's newspapers.
Let be be finale of seem.
The only emperor is the emperor of ice-cream.

Take from the dresser of deal,
Lacking the three glass knobs, that sheet   10
On which she embroidered fantails once
And spread it so as to cover her face.
If her horny feet protrude, they come
To show how cold she is, and dumb.
Let the lamp affix its beam.   15
The only emperor is the emperor of ice-cream.

Wallace Stevens (1879–1955)

The Widow's Lament in Springtime

Sorrow is my own yard
where the new grass
flames as it has flamed
often before but not
with the cold fire   5
that closes round me this year.
Thirtyfive years
I lived with my husband.
The plumtree is white today
with masses of flowers.   10
Masses of flowers
load the cherry branches
and color some bushes
yellow and some red
but the grief in my heart   15
is stronger than they
for though they were my joy
formerly, today I notice them
and turned away forgetting.
Today my son told me   20
that in the meadows,
at the edge of the heavy woods
in the distance, he saw
trees of white flowers.
I feel that I would like   25
to go there
and fall into those flowers
and sink into the marsh near them.

William Carlos Williams (1883–1963)

A Refusal to Mourn the Death, by Fire, of a Child in London

Never until the mankind making
Bird beast and flower
Fathering and all humbling darkness
Tells with silence the last light breaking
And the still hour   5
Is come of the sea tumbling in harness

And I must enter again the round
Zion of the water bead
And the synagogue of the ear of corn
Shall I let pray the shadow of a sound   10
Or sow my salt seed
In the least valley of sackcloth to mourn

The majesty and burning of the child's death.
I shall not murder
The mankind of her going with a grave truth   15
Nor blaspheme down the stations of the breath
With any further
Elegy of innocence and youth.

Deep with the first dead lies London's daughter,
Robed in the long friends,   20
The grains beyond age, the dark veins of her mother,
Secret by the unmourning water
Of the riding Thames.
After the first death, there is no other.

Dylan Thomas (1914–1953)

Interrogations

How, Lord, are suicides finally left to sleep?
A crust inside the mouth, both temples emptied out,
the eye-moons whitened and enlarged,
the hands out to some unseen anchor straining?

Or, after men have left do You arrive   5
and close the lid upon the blinded eye,
arrange the viscera quietly and without pain
and cross the hands upon the chest at peace?

The rose-tree that the living tend upon the mound of bones
does it not paint its roses with the forms of wounds?   10
Is not its fragrance acrid, its beauty somber
and the small fronds with serpents all entwined?

And answer, Lord: once that the soul has fled
through the wet door of the long wounds,
can it embark upon Your zone and breast the air in calm,   15
or does one hear a thrashing as of wings gone mad?

Does a narrow, livid fence constrict about it then?
Is space a field where monsters flourish?
Do they, in their panic, not even hit upon Your name?
Or do they go on shouting at Your indifferent heart?   20

Will not one ray of sunlight reach to them someday?
Is there no water ever to clean them of their scarlet stains?
And to them, and only them, are Your heart turned cold,
Your fine ear deaf, Your eyes closed tight?

So man assures, through error or through malice;   25
but I, who like a wine have savored You, O Lord,
while others still may call You by the name of Justice,
will never call you by another name than Love!

I know that just as man was ever the rough son,
the waterfall a vertigo, the mountain range a trial,   30
You are the vessel whereat in their sweetness can expand
the nectars out of all the orchards of the Earth!

Gabriela Mistral (1889–1957)
translated by James Graham-Luján

For the Anniversary of My Death

Every year without knowing it I have passed the day
When the last fires will wave to me
And the silence will set out
Tireless traveller
Like the beam of a lightless star   5

Then I will no longer
Find myself in life as in a strange garment
Surprised at the earth
And the love of one woman
And the shamelessness of men   10
As today writing after three days of rain
Hearing the wren sing and the falling cease
And bowing not knowing to what

W. S. Merwin (b. 1927)

A Valediction Forbidding Mourning

My swirling wants. Your frozen lips.
The grammar turned and attacked me.
Themes, written under duress.
Emptiness of the notations.

They gave me a drug that slowed the healing of wounds.   5

I want you to see this before I leave:
the experience of repetition as death
the failure of criticism to locate the pain
the poster in the bus that said:
my bleeding is under control.   10

A red plant in a cemetery of plastic wreaths.

A last attempt: the language is a dialect called metaphor.
These images go unglossed: hair, glacier, flashlight.
When I think of a landscape I am thinking of a time.
When I talk of taking a trip I mean forever.   15
I could say: those mountains have a meaning
but further than that I could not say.

To do something very common, in my own way.

Adrienne Rich (b. 1929)

Picnic

Sunday in Inwood Park
     the picnic eaten
the chicken bones scattered
      for the fox we'll
        never see   5
the children playing in the caves
My death is folded in my pocket
        like a nylon
        raincoat
What kind of sunlight is it   10
     that leaves the
     rocks so cold?

    Adrienne Rich (b. 1929)

Appendix

Writing about a Poem: Two Samples

Interactions of Attitude, Image, and Sound in R. S. Thomas' "Walter Llywarch"

William Heilig

There are poems that surprise, astound us, by the patterns of their growth, as they move through a series of intuitions into revelations that no one, not even their authors, could foresee in the opening lines. And there are other poems that hold almost no surprise, but impress us rather with the sense of inevitability they convey. Reading them is like watching a prophesy fulfill itself, and when we finish we feel: Yes, it had to happen in just that way. R. S. Thomas' "Walter Llywarch" is an example of the latter kind of poem. Its germ is in the first line, that wonderfully dreary "I am, as you know, Walter Llywarch." At first we might question the "as you know." Why, after all, should we know Walter Llywarch? But we realize almost at once that the speaker is addressing us as though we were his fellow villagers, for he scarcely has the opportunity to speak to anyone else, and in this village everyone knows who Walter Llywarch is: his face is as familiar, and as unremarkable, as the label on a bottle of stout. The semi-intimate tone of voice—the tone one uses when talking to a neighbor—is the channel along which the poem moves. It allows Walter to make his story mercifully brief—he supposes we can fill in the details, as indeed we can—and to concentrate its physical and emotional atmosphere around a small number of simple, commonplace images—rain, fog, hearth, chapel—which form the background of his desolate life. The tone alters only in the last lines, where the cry of newborn infants is heard as a cry of despair, so that the parents' laughter, which is all they show of happiness, suggests also a fiendish delight in seeing their miseries perpetuated. This is wrier than anything else in the poem, but we accept it as the final disclosure of a man we have already come to know, a man who stated his name and implied his situation in the first seven words he spoke.

Read aloud in a casual tone of voice, "Walter Llywarch" may sound like a piece of highly controlled free verse. In fact, however, it is composed in a very formal measure which, once it is clearly heard, can be recognized as the source of a rough and memorable music. The measure is much like the one used by the Anglo-Saxon poets. A form of accentual (or syllable-stress) verse, its line consists of four stressed syllables, a varying number of unstressed syllables, and between the second and third stressed syllables a caesura. With stresses and caesura marked, the poem sounds like this:

> Bórn in aútumn || at the ríght tíme
>
> For héaring stóries || from the crácked líps
>
> Of óld folk || dréaming of súmmer,
>
> I píled them on to the báre heárth
>
> Of my ówn fáncy || to máke a bláze
>
> To wárm myself, || but achiéved ónly
>
> The smóke's ácid || that bríngs the smárt
>
> Of fálse teárs || into the eýes.

Strict as it is, the versification does not sound contrived, as the more brilliant accentual verse of Gerard Manley Hopkins, for example, sometimes does. Even the recurrent double-stress line endings ("right time," "cracked lips," "bare hearth"), which sound like the spondaic foot in post-Saxon verse, give the impression of being a natural speech mannerism. Insistent, blunt, monotonous, they express the man's character just as surely as his drab, monosyllabic diction does.

R. S. Thomas, of course, uses only a small part of the natural resources offered poets by the English language. He is a specialist of the severest kind, working the bedrock of our Anglo-Saxon linguistic heritage while virtually ignoring the rich and stately speech of the metrical tradition. Furthermore, his range of sympathy is almost oppressively small. It is as though "the long queue / Of life that wound through a Welsh valley," where Walter Llywarch loitered away his youth, has so troubled his spirit as to make all pleasures seem deceptive, trivial, or vain. We are all of us specialists nowadays, however; and our poets have often struck the quality ore while mining the smaller lodes. "Simply the thing I am shall make me live," says Shakespeare's rogue Parolles; and that, in effect, is what "Walter Llywarch" says of itself as a poem.

The Symbolism in Williams' "The Yachts"
James Dickey

In the daily lives of all human beings—as well as in the lives of poets— occur what might be called "instant symbols": moments when a commonplace event or object is transfigured without warning, as though by common consent of observed and observer, and becomes for the perceiver both itself and its meaning. Williams' "The Yachts" is that kind of vision, that kind of poem: a scene whose symbolic possibilities burst in upon—or out of—the observer. The poem dramatizes, rather than insists on this condition, but everywhere implicit in its matter-of-fact lines is the possibility that any of us in any situation may see not only the surface but the depth, the whole *intent* of the actions and people we live among: that at any moment anything we experience is likely to become more than what we had comfortably agreed with ourselves it is content to be, and that the world is perpetually capable of concretizing and *presenting* its most powerful, disturbing and profound symbols in an instant, and in ways known only to the private beholder.

In this case, the scene is a yacht race. The poet speaks of it matter-of-factly, in a sympathetic but curt, slightly impatient tone. Williams' voice, with its American bluntness, its imagistic concreteness, its dislike of rhetorical shows, is a convincing medium through which to feel the significance—the lightning-flash of import—that hits the poem about midway in its length. The first feeling that the reader has is one of vague unrest: it may be that the yachts are too perfect in their graceful appointments and movements, more perfect than their crews. They are like life on a greeting card, a life that no real human being has ever been able to live up to, though many have tried. Or it may be that poet and reader are troubled by the social implications that yachts usually carry: money, snobbery, privilege. Even so, none of these associations is *quite* enough to account for the feeling of unrest and dissatisfaction conveyed by the first lines of the poem. After all, why should someone so matter-of-fact as *this* poet be disturbed by an event as charming, exciting and graceful as a yacht race? And then— though no one explanation can account for it—the sea over which the yachts pass without seeming to be touched by it has suddenly changed into a sea of bodies terribly and uselessly beseeching the yachts for help, or even for notice; it has become a watery hell like something in Dante. The perfection of the yachts has something profound to do with all the loss, all the death and irrevocability in the world. It is the *cost* of this kind of perfection that makes the poet recoil in horror, as the meaning the yachts have for *him* breaks free of the first troubling but vague connotations, and "the horror of the race dawns staggering the mind." And yet it is only the poet who sees the horror, only he whose mind is staggered by what, now that he *sees* it, the race suggests.

"The Yachts" is a symbolic rather than an allegorical poem, for the vessels do not mean *just* social and economic privilege, the exploitation of the working classes who made the yachts for the enjoyment of those who race them, but rather serve as an image that catches and binds in a central figure all human situations that have to do with these things, with oppression, greed, sloth, with perfection that human creatures can create but cannot attain in themselves, but also—on the other side of the figure—with rejection, with the demise of the body, with death, with the abject yearning of the dead to possess a *significance* once more, even if only for the one instant of a watery hand grasping the prow of an inhumanly beautiful hull and making an impression on it, having some effect, mattering. As Randall Jarrell has finely said, "The Yachts" is "a paradigm of all the unjust beauty, the necessary and unnecessary injustice of the world." To that I would add that it is also a wonderful and terrible witness to the fact that the things we see every day, the things we think we know, are at any moment likely to explode in our faces with meaning, and thence to *exist* for us most obsessively and necessarily in that connection: in that system of meaning that only we have discovered, and that we must exorcise, deal with or learn from in ways equally private, equally haunting, equally difficult.

Houghton Mifflin Company. For "Ringing the Bells" from *To Bedlam and Part Way Back* by Anne Sexton. Copyright © 1960 by Anne Sexton. Reprinted by permission of Houghton Mifflin Company. For "Abortion" from *All My Pretty Ones* by Anne Sexton. Copyright © 1961, 1962 by Anne Sexton. Copyright © 1961 by Harper & Brothers. Reprinted by permission of Houghton Mifflin Company.

Indiana University Press. For "Habana" by Julian Bond from *New Negro Poets: U.S.A.* by Langston Hughes. Reprinted by permission of Indiana University Press.

Little, Brown and Company. For #341 "After great pain a formal feeling comes" from *The Complete Poems of Emily Dickinson* by Thomas H. Johnson. Copyright 1929, © 1957 by Mary L. Hampson. Reprinted by permission of Little, Brown and Company. For "Father and Son" from *Selected Poems 1928–1958* by Stanley Kunitz. Copyright © 1958 by Stanley Kunitz. Reprinted by permission of Little, Brown and Company.

Liveright Publishing Corp. For "My Grandmother's Love Letters" from *The Collected Poems and Selected Letters and Prose of Hart Crane* by Hart Crane. Permission of Liveright, Publishing, New York. Copyright © 1933, 1958, 1966 by Liveright Publishing Corp.

James Graham-Luján. For translation of "Charges" and "Interrogations" by Gabriela Mistral and for translation of "The Art of Poetry" by Pablo **Neruda, and "Sonnet: Far From Eden."**

Macmillan Publishing Co., Inc. For "Faintheart In a Railway Station," "The Ruined Maid," "The Oxen," "I Was the Midmost," "The Convergence of the Twain," "Neutral Tones," "The Darkling Thrush," "To an Unborn Pauper Child," "The Man He Killed," "I Said to Love," "During Wind and Rain," and "Sapphic Fragment" by Thomas Hardy. Reprinted with permission of Macmillan Publishing Co., Inc. from *Collected Poems* by Thomas Hardy. Copyright 1925 by Macmillan Publishing Co., Inc. For "In Distrust of Merits" and "Nevertheless" by Marianne Moore. Reprinted with permission of Macmillan Publishing Co., Inc. from *Collected Poems* by Marianne Moore. Copyright 1944 by Marianne Moore, renewed 1972 by Marianne Moore. For "To a Snail" by Marianne Moore. Reprinted with permission of Macmillan Publishing Co., Inc. from *Collected Poems* by Marianne Moore. Copyright 1935 by Marianne Moore, renewed 1963 by Marianne Moore and T. S. Eliot. For "What Are Years?" by Marianne Moore. Reprinted with permission of Macmillan Publishing Co., Inc. from *Collected Poems* by Marianne Moore. Copyright 1941 by Marianne Moore, renewed 1969 by Marianne Moore. For "When You Are Old," "The Lamentation of the Old Pensioner," and "The Song of Wandering Aengus" by William Butler Yeats. Reprinted with permission of Macmillan Publishing Co., Inc. from *Collected Poems* by William Butler Yeats. Copyright 1906 by Macmillan Publishing Co., Inc., renewed 1934 by William Butler Yeats. For "No Second Troy" by William Butler Yeats. Reprinted with permission of Macmillan Publishing Co., Inc., from *Collected Poems* by William Butler Yeats. Copyright 1912 by Macmillan Publishing Co., Inc., renewed 1940 by Bertha Georgie Yeats. For "The Magi" by William Butler Yeats. Reprinted with permission of Macmillan Publishing Co., Inc. from *Collected Poems* by William Butler Yeats. Copyright 1916 by Macmillan Publishing Co., Inc., renewed 1940 by Bertha Georgie Yeats. For "The

Index of Poets and Titles